THE TY
OPINIO

ALSO AVAILABLE FROM BLOOMSBURY

The Ethics of Climate Change, James Garvey
Personal Responsibility, Alexander Brown
Slow Philosophy, Michelle Boulous Walker
Judged, Ziyad Marar
Dying for Ideas, Costica Bradatan

THE TYRANNY OF OPINION

Conformity and the Future of Liberalism

Russell Blackford

BLOOMSBURY ACADEMIC
LONDON • NEW YORK • OXFORD • NEW DELHI • SYDNEY

BLOOMSBURY ACADEMIC
Bloomsbury Publishing Plc
50 Bedford Square, London, WC1B 3DP, UK
1385 Broadway, New York, NY 10018, USA

BLOOMSBURY, BLOOMSBURY ACADEMIC and the Diana logo are
trademarks of Bloomsbury Publishing Plc

First published in Great Britain 2019

Cover design by Irene Martinez Costa
Cover image © Getty Images

A catalogue record for this book is available from the British Library.

A catalog record for this book is available from the Library of Congress.

ISBN: HB: 978-1-3500-5599-5
PB: 978-1-3500-5600-8
ePDF: 978-1-3500-5601-5
eBook: 978-1-3500-5602-2

Series: Think Now

Typeset by Deanta Global Publishing Services, Chennai, India
Printed and bound in Great Britain

To find out more about our authors and books visit www.bloomsbury.com
and sign up for our newsletters.

To Janeen Webb, who has my back.

CONTENTS

ACKNOWLEDGEMENTS

I have talked about this book with many friends and colleagues, and they've invariably told me that I am brave writing on such a subject. But I'm not all that brave. Mostly, I'm more buffered than the many decent, socially concerned people around me who feel intimidated by the current intellectual environment. My sincere thanks to everyone who has spoken to me over the past three or four years, sharing perspectives on the sensitive topic of social and political conformity and the ways in which it is enforced. Needless to say, the particular opinions expressed herein are my own and should not be attributed to anybody else, including the people whom I'm about to name specifically.

Kenan Malik encouraged me to write a book on this topic, acted as an inspiration throughout, and kindly sent me an advance copy of his afterword to the second edition (still forthcoming at the time) of *From Fatwa to Jihad*. Thanks, too, to Laura Moriarty for providing me with an advance copy of her novel *American Heart* so I could read it for myself before its publication.

During the planning and writing phases, and beyond, Jenny Blackford encouraged and helped me in endless ways. Among other things, she put up with my distracted moods and solitary habits over the months when I worked intensely at the project for long (and usually odd) hours. I can't thank her enough. Jenny's presence in my life has kept me sane as I've wrestled with complicated issues on which I have passionate, if sometimes ambivalent, views.

Jeremy Stangroom encouraged me from the beginning and was instrumental in the book's publication by Bloomsbury. Our exchanges in person and by email have helped me hone my ideas. Jeremy is also, be it noted, a model of genuine liberalism.

Jenny and Jeremy read the first draft of the entire manuscript, and each of them provided me with astute, helpful, detailed feedback. Jenny has also helped with later drafts. I've dedicated this volume to Janeen

Webb, who has been a trusted friend and confidant throughout the process (and always). I doubt that she will agree with everything herein, but we've spoken often on related topics, and she's another person who has helped keep me going. You can blame her for that, but not for the content that follows.

Note: The text that follows discusses social and political situations that are often volatile. It is intended to be up to date as of the beginning of June 2018. One significant event that took place shortly after final corrections to the text was the settlement, announced on 18 June 2018, of litigation by Maajid Nawaz against the Southern Poverty Law Center (see pages 149–53 in Chapter 7). The settlement included a public apology to Nawaz and a sum of $3.375 million. While litigation should never have been necessary in this case, the outcome does illustrate the ongoing importance of the law for redress when individuals are harmed by unjustified attacks on their reputations.

1 INTRODUCTION AND OVERVIEW

Reasons to be fearful

I'm afraid. Like many people, I'm afraid to speak up and say exactly what I think. I'm afraid to contribute to public debate with total frankness. I'm more afraid of allies than I am of opponents, since the latter can do me less harm (though if they're so minded they can probably do enough!). I'm not afraid of my closest friends, the people who love me, who have my back and will keep my secrets, but it gets more frightening as soon as I step out into wider circles of colleagues and acquaintances.

I'm afraid, but I'm less afraid than many. I do speak out, at selected times, when I see what looks like injustice: injustice, that is, wrought by my own tribe (or some approximation of it). That takes a smidgen of courage. It takes much less to criticize opponents – which at least gets you encouragement from your own people. I'm afraid, as a matter of fact, that this very book will lose me friends (no, not my closest friends; but still …) and get me ostracized in some circles, but I've taken a deep breath and started writing. Perhaps I'm foolhardy or contrarian or pig-headed, or perhaps I have a touch of the 'Galilean personality' described by Alice Dreger in her undoubtedly brave book *Galileo's Middle Finger* (2015: 141). It's largely, I think, that I'm less vulnerable than most. I'm not as young as I'd like to be; I've accumulated some modest assets; and for now, at least, I'm semi-retired and don't need to climb a career ladder.

If I were a bit younger, a bit less physically comfortable and financially buffered, a bit more dependent on networks of contacts and others' goodwill, I'd be more afraid than I am. I wouldn't write a book like this.

Much of what follows is critical of the Left, or what popularly counts as 'the Left' in countries where socialist and communist ideas have little political clout. Much of it is critical of what currently counts as 'liberalism'. I'm especially critical of many academic and cultural manifestations of supposedly left-wing or liberal thought. But my critique does not come from the Right.

Allow me to unpack my own political views and values, insofar as I'm consciously aware of them. First, I'm not an apologist for any kind of social or religious conservatism; I'm not, for example, another Dinesh D'Souza, whom Udo Schüklenk and I somewhat excoriate throughout an earlier book (Blackford and Schüklenk 2013). I'm not keen on religion (*any* religion) or religious morality (*any* religious morality). I'm not looking backward to a better time, because there's none that I know of to be found in human history. Even since the 1970s – the optimistic, psychedelic decade when I came of age – much has improved. When it comes to economic issues, I'm a standard European-style social democrat. In the United States, I'd probably be labelled a socialist, but some Americans label people as socialists at the drop of a Stetson hat. To be blunt, not for the last time, what follows is not a taxation-is-theft sort of book. I have a libertarian streak, as will become apparent, but I'm not *that* kind of libertarian.

I do take a clear position in favour of individual liberty. This includes, for example, my support for women's reproductive rights: I see no need for the state to ban abortion at any stage of pregnancy (for a bit more, see Blackford 2002). I want the state to keep its laws off women's bodies. Likewise, I support the rights of gay men and lesbians, including the right to marry. I strongly support the option of physician-assisted suicide. I dislike the carceral state, which has expanded to an absurd and immensely destructive extent in the United States in particular, and I detest the 'war on drugs' that has dominated too much policing in Western countries.

I come from a working-class family, and I grew up in an industrial city in Australia that was dominated at the time by its steelworks. I'm the first person from my family ever to attend university. I still have those connections, and I've inherited some blue-collar, trade-union values. But my social circle is one of mainly left-wing (to varying extents) academics, authors, journalists, lawyers, and artists. Within my milieu we like fine wine, coffee (but preferably not instant coffee!), excellent cheese, and *The Guardian*. I don't want to brag, but we're sophisticated, cosmopolitan people.

This has become my tribe, or the nearest thing to one. We dislike Rupert Murdoch and President Donald Trump. We're afraid of right-wing populism: the xenophobic, nativist, isolationist brand of politics that is currently resurgent in Western nations. We deeply fear its fringes of outright fascism.

All too often, though, we're also afraid of each other.

My criticisms of the Left in what follows do not mean that I'm less critical of the Right in its various forms. On the contrary, the problems of the Right seem more obvious and more easily diagnosed, though what we can do about them is another matter. Especially in the United States, but also in other Western countries, the political Right runs an Outrage Industry (Berry and Sobieraj 2014) to intimidate opponents, produce blatant propaganda, and distort political deliberation. This is a threat to our liberties, to good governance, and perhaps even to the human future. At a time of anthropogenic global warming and heartbreaking environmental degradation, sufficiently bad policy making from right-wing populists and science-denying conservatives just might sleepwalk us to existential catastrophe. In the following chapters, I'll comment on right-wing threats to liberty and sound government, but much has been written about these in the past, including by me. On this occasion, I'm more concerned that my own tribe get its house in order.

It's disappointing when self-styled liberals narrow options, distort important debates, threaten individual freedoms, require that we walk on eggshells in our private and public speech, and generally operate in a censorious and illiberal mode. There's been too much of this, and it's not even helpful in struggles against our real political enemies. Today, we each need to guard against various large and small Outrage Machines of the political Left. Otherwise, we can be shunned, harassed, dogpiled, smeared, publicly shamed, devastatingly labelled, falsely accused of wrongdoing, or otherwise hurt and harmed for trivial, dubious, or non-existent transgressions. Our good reputations can be destroyed, our jobs can be threatened or ended, and our careers can be ruined.

The terrors of terminology

I need to say more about terminology. I've already observed that I have a libertarian streak in my temperament, but this is not based on a political philosophy that would shrink government to a bare minimum (or do away with it completely), and that generally stands in favour of the capitalist marketplace and opposed to the modern welfare state.

Libertarian thinkers in this tradition – I'll call them political libertarians where necessary – can be good companions, and sometimes they are good allies for people like me. But I'm not one of them. The best book in their tradition, at least by my lights, is Robert Nozick's *Anarchy, State, and Utopia* (1974). Do read it and consider its arguments. I enjoy it for its panache, its obvious honesty, and its penetrating criticisms of other political philosophies, but I don't agree with much of Nozick's own theory of property, freedom, and justice.

With that stated, I feel licensed to write of 'having a libertarian streak', 'taking a libertarian line', and the like, in what I trust is a transparent sense. Such phrases refer simply to an emphasis on liberty: freedom not only from the power of the state but also from other sources of restraint, whether local rules and codes of conduct, the whims of employers, or the opinions of colleagues, family, friends, local communities, and the wider public. If it helps, think of civil, social, or cultural libertarianism rather than of the theories advanced by political libertarians such as Nozick.

I wish the word *liberal* (with its cognates such as *liberalism*) were clearer and less contested. I understand liberalism as a political philosophy or tendency that emphasizes individual liberty, especially but not only freedom of speech (however *that* is to be understood; I'll come back to this at length in the chapters that follow). As I elaborated in an earlier book, *Freedom of Religion and the Secular State*, this provides the 'liberal' part of our expression *liberal democracies* – polities that are partly characterized by what I've called 'a degree of restraint [exercised] by the apparatus of the state':

> [The state] will be reluctant to impose any template, or narrow set of templates, for the good life. Instead, the assumption is made that many ways of life are at least tolerable, and perhaps even valuable. ... While the governmental apparatus of a liberal democratic society will be used for a variety of ends, including the deterrence of certain behavior, most ways of life are accommodated to the extent that social peace allows. (Blackford 2012: 4)

Several years after I first wrote this, it still seems like a useful gloss on the word *liberal*, as in the phrase *liberal democracies*. Unfortunately, the words *liberal* and *liberalism* have a rather different sense in US politics, and hence in much of the Anglophone political science and political philosophy literature. Even more unfortunately, this sense is difficult to pin down. Jonathan Haidt says that the American sense is more about 'progressive or left-wing politics' than about liberty (2012: xvi). That's intuitively right, but I've already hinted that we might worry about what *left-wing* currently means. I doubt that any of these expressions have entirely precise meanings in common parlance. Note, however, that American liberals are not necessarily all that left-wing in economic terms – they are merely more so than American conservatives.

In American usage, however, and in the popular and academic literature that is influenced by it, liberals at least favour interventions and expenditures by the state in order to address social problems. By those standards, the Democratic Party in the United States counts as liberal, though the interventions it supports fall well short of any kind of socialism or even social democracy. This is, for example, the usage of *liberal* throughout *Asymmetric Politics*, a fine study of American politics recently published by Matt Grossmann and David A. Hopkins (2016). The social problems that concern American 'liberals' are often those of historically oppressed groups of one kind or another. Mostly, however, these groups are not identified in terms of social class. Times are changing as a result of the extraordinary 2016 presidential election, but talk of social classes has long been taboo in American politics. Far more emphasis is placed on groups identified by, for example, sex, sexuality, race, religion, or cultural background.

This has implications. For instance, Grossmann and Hopkins suggest that the Democratic Party – the nominally liberal side in the effectively two-party system of the United States – tends to frame its support for abortion rights 'as a defense of the particular rights of women' and not on a more libertarian basis or one grounded in ideas from the Enlightenment. Legal abortion is, according to these authors, *not* advocated 'as an advancement of the universal principles of civil libertarianism or cultural progressivism' (Grossman and Hopkins 2016: 324). An effect of this, as Grossman and Hopkins note, is that Democrats may overstate the popularity of their position with women in the electorate.

It may also, we should add, lead Democrats and US-style liberals to overlook an implication of opinion polls over several decades: historically, much, or even most, of the heavily moralized opposition to abortion in the United States has come from socially conservative women rather than from men. Indeed, many polls in the past have found more overall opposition to abortion from American women than American men. This may finally be changing, since the latest survey figures from the Pew Research Center (2017) show American men and women to be about equally supportive of abortion rights, with women slightly more supportive. Nonetheless, 38 per cent of American women continue to believe that abortion should be illegal in all or most cases.

So-called liberalism in the American sense may, in practice, often favour individual liberty, social pluralism, and government restraint in enforcing particular conceptions of the good life. But US-style liberalism is also consistent with considerable government and non-government pressure to restrict how we speak and to control the approved forms of life. It can, in other words, operate in ways that are significantly anti-libertarian in my informal sense.

In the chapters that follow, I will try to avoid the unqualified words *liberal* and *liberalism*. I am, however, interested in the future of liberalism in all of the word's related senses. I'm especially interested in the future of liberalism in the more classical sense that emphasizes individual freedom. For this, I might have chosen the term *classical liberalism*, but it often suggests an overemphasis on property rights and freedom of contract, and so denotes a watered-down version of the political libertarianism that I've already disavowed. Instead, the term *Enlightenment liberalism* will come in handy to refer to liberalism's traditional principles, values, and emphases.

Much so-called liberalism is not very liberal at all. It's a *revisionist liberalism* increasingly grounded in identity politics and notable for its ideological purity policing. Throughout his recent book, *The Once and Future Liberal* (2017), the political scientist Mark Lilla uses the term *identity liberalism* for essentially the same phenomenon. (See also Lilla 2016, where Lilla first introduced this term to a broad audience.) Revisionist liberalism – or identity liberalism, if you prefer – shows little regard for such Enlightenment and post-Enlightenment liberal values as reason, liberty, free inquiry, individuality, originality, spontaneity, and creativity. Its proponents seldom employ this language. It does not, I suspect, capture their imaginations.

Politics involves many values and has, to say the least, more than one dimension. This is worth keeping in mind, because our political viewpoints need not take the form of package deals – integrated systems of ideas – offered to us by our supposed betters. All such packages have been shaped by history, by dominating personalities such as party leaders, and by exigencies such as the need to build electoral coalitions and alliances. No system of political ideas currently on offer need be the correct or best one. Strange to say, we can mix and match values and policies for ourselves. In fact, you can take from this book whatever you find useful, even if it doesn't all persuade you.

A roadmap

I am writing from the side of freedom. I'm writing to support nonconformists. I'm writing for the world's heretics, eccentrics, truth-tellers, artists, and jokers. You'll meet some of them in these pages – figures as diverse as Philipp Jenninger, Salman Rushdie, Napoleon Chagnon, J. Michael Bailey, Wendy Doniger, Alice Dreger, Justine Sacco, Tim Hunt, Erika Christakis, and Rebecca Tuvel. I am writing against anyone who'd crush them, even with good intentions. In what follows, I'll defend the freedom to express our thoughts – though not an absolute freedom to attack each other verbally. As a complication, I'll support (though I won't exactly stand with) individuals far less sympathetic, at least as I see them, than those whom I've just named.

Like John Stuart Mill in his classic text *On Liberty* (originally published 1859), I am not concerned only about governmental threats to liberty and related values. Those threats are, of course, serious. The organized power of the modern state is vast and conspicuous. It merits vigilance for its grave potential to restrict our liberties. History shows, however, that it's possible to devise institutions and principles to restrain the power of the state. Even more dangerous, perhaps, and certainly more difficult to understand or restrain, is a less overt, more insidious kind of tyranny: what Mill called 'the tyranny of the prevailing opinion and feeling' ([1859] 1974: 63).

As Mill knew and explained, this can be more intrusive, pervasive, and effective than state power, even though the punishments it exacts are usually less devastating than those available to the state. In the upshot, I'm less absolutist than some about our negative rights, as individuals, against the state. But I'm more alert than most to the tyranny of opinion, whether that of the public as a whole or that of any powerful individual, institution, or group that demands conformity.

In Chapter 2, I explain and, in the main, adopt Mill's approach of restricting individual liberty only where this is required to prevent secular, substantial, direct, and wrongful harms to others. Importantly, Mill applied this reasoning not only to actions by the state, such as passing legislation, but also to less formal exertions of social pressure. Mill's discussion needs updating in the light of subsequent history. Nonetheless, his approach of fearing the tyranny of opinion, and not just that of despotic governments, remains valuable.

Chapter 3 focuses on issues relating to freedom of speech – or, in Mill's formulation, liberty of thought and discussion. I offer a rationale for this liberty, based partly on Mill's but with some thoughts borrowed from the distinguished legal theorist Frederick Schauer. We need free speech to participate meaningfully in democratic deliberation, to pursue knowledge and understanding boldly, for our self-development or self-actualization, and to challenge various claims of authority over our lives (and thereby, to protect all our other freedoms).

In Chapter 4, I examine some possible limits to our liberty of discussion. When, for example, can speech be used to inhibit the freedoms of others? In responding to such questions, we should bear in mind the reasons we need freedom to speak our minds in the first place. In large part, these relate to our ability to discuss ideas on important general topics, whether those of religion, science, morality and politics, philosophy, culture, or otherwise. This reminder can help give structure to an analysis of defamation, invasive speech, and hate speech.

In Chapter 5, I introduce some of the literature on social and political conformity, and particularly the pressure to remain silent or to lie about what we really think (and what we know, believe, feel, desire, and prefer as policy outcomes). When participants in public discussion misrepresent what they really think, this creates a gap between the local or wider public opinion (in the sense of opinion actually being expressed in the public sphere) and private opinion (the distribution in the population of opinions held privately by individuals).

Chapter 6 examines ideology, propaganda, and the phenomenon of politically weaponized outrage. Propaganda appears at all social levels, from a nation's widest political debates to contests of individuals and ideas within smaller 'publics' such as the participants in a cultural movement, the members of a club or a local community, or perhaps a college's student body or a church's congregation. I especially consider the politicized Outrage Industry as it manifests on the Right and Left of contemporary politics.

Restrictions on our liberty to act and speak as we please are traditionally associated with the Right: with despots, dictators, and religious organizations that claim a monopoly on truth. But the Left and/or (so-called) liberals can be illiberal. This applies well beyond communist regimes and the like. Supposed liberals often have their own ideas about what action and speech should be restricted by state power, or otherwise hindered and punished. All of this arises for discussion in Chapter 7. I examine a range of examples, among them the furore over Salman Rushdie's novel *The Satanic Verses*, published in 1988. I include some current examples, noting that more come to public attention almost daily.

In recent decades, advances in electronic communications have been liberating in many ways, opening up unprecedented possibilities for discussion and cooperation. In Chapter 8, however, I consider the internet's dark side. Some sites on the internet are, to varying extents, aptly described as cyber-cesspools (Leiter 2010). Moreover, the rise of social media has provided new opportunities for all kinds of smearing, abuse, and cruelty. This includes new ways to pressure employers, and others with private power, to bring nonconformists into line.

In Chapter 9, I ask, very generally and I hope not too rhetorically, 'What can you do?', and I intend this in two senses. First, the question underlines concerns about how much liberty *we now retain* in a world of ideology, propaganda, and outrage, a world of surveillance and control. But second, I am really asking about *what we can do to push back* against pressures to conform. Finally, I reflect on a practical question. In an era of aggressive right-wing populism (and worse), how can we best continue the struggle for liberty?

In Chapter 10, I sum up and offer readers a positive message – the most positive that I reasonably can. I also discuss some deep issues arising from Angela Nagle's recent book, *Kill All Normies* (2017), which covers some of the same territory as this one.

On complications and implications

One especially helpful discussion of free speech and related issues is Schauer's 1982 volume, *Free Speech: A Philosophical Inquiry*. There is much to question in this book, but also much to heed and learn from.

Schauer provides a comprehensive investigation of the arguments for free speech, as well as their limitations.

Schauer's conception of free speech is strongly influenced by the constitutional protection of 'the freedom of speech' referred to in the US Constitution's First Amendment. Thus, Schauer is particularly concerned in a way that I am not – and Mill was not – with freedom from *governmental* abridgments of what we can say. His book justifies this focus with arguments to the effect that governments are incompetent, or only dubiously competent, regulators of speech. As I'll explain in Chapter 3, this is important but too narrow in its focus. All the same, I'm attracted by Schauer's insistence on the nuances, layers, and complexities that arise with difficult issues. Do look at his book for yourself.

For Schauer, a right against the government to freedom of speech does not mean that the government can never interfere with our speech at all. It means, rather, that there are very strong general considerations against governmental interference, and so something unusually significant must be adduced to justify it. There must be important interests at stake. On Schauer's account, however, there is no simple technique for assessing and weighing interests against each other. It's impossible, therefore, to devise a master plan for balancing interests when it comes to which government restrictions on speech are legitimate. 'Balancing interests', Schauer says, 'cannot be reduced to simple formulae, much as we might wish this could be so' (1982: 144).

In general, I agree with this – and I note that similar problems arise outside the domain of government censorship. They arise with governmental restrictions on conduct that does not fall under the concept of speech; they also arise with *non*-government efforts to restrict action and speech. In all these domains, there are powerful considerations that favour liberty and individuality. And yet, my goal is not to defend any kind of absolutism, as if I could identify simply stated moral and political laws that must, at all costs, never be broken. Even in elaborating considerations adduced by Mill and others – considerations that appear suitably powerful – I acknowledge that different considerations might prevail in particular cases. One such case is the problem of dehumanizing hate speech.

This creates a risk for my whole project. I could introduce so many layers, complexities, nuances, and exceptions that the arguments herein would have no clear practical implications. But at the same time, I have a fear that is almost the opposite. Under current social conditions, even the most layered and qualified opinions can be distorted, misrepresented, over-simplified, exaggerated, and generally treated as those of enemies whose voices must be shut down. As a result, it can be foolhardy to explain whatever complexities we honestly perceive, rather than to express a simplistic view tailored to please an audience. Complexity seldom pleases others, yet it's indispensable for serious understanding.

There's little I can do about this. I can only write honestly and as clearly as the complexities permit; and I ask, in turn, for honest attention to what is being said. I'll express myself with a minimum of jargon even when explaining difficult ideas, and I'll state my actual positions as correctly as I can. What I can't promise is to write something simple or to have all the answers to thorny contemporary problems. Nonetheless, I think this book has implications. If it's taken to heart, some behaviour will change. Perhaps even mine, dear reader. Perhaps even yours.

2 MILL ON LIBERTY: MORALITY, PATERNALISM, AND HARM

Mill's approach – a prelude

John Stuart Mill argued for restricting individual liberty only where required to prevent certain kinds of harms. His approach rules out moralistic and paternalistic approaches to law-making, but its implications go further. Mill applied his reasoning not only to state action but also to wider social pressures. His approach depends on a view of humans as progressive beings. For beings like us, originality, individuality, and spontaneity are crucial for moving forward – for a synergy of intellectual and social progress.

In this chapter, I'll sketch Mill's approach and offer a qualified defence. It is not my goal, however, to uphold everything that Mill says in *On Liberty*. For instance, several of the examples in his final chapter – 'Applications' – involve proposals that would seem very radical if put forward seriously in contemporary political deliberation. Some appear highly intrusive by our current standards, such as Mill's preparedness, in principle, to impose population controls. Again, I don't share his distrust of state education, which he saw as a 'contrivance for moulding people to be exactly like each other' (Mill [1859] 1974: 177), and thus a tool for the government of the day to control its citizens by shaping their thinking. (Mill was not opposed to all state education, but he thought that it should be, at most, a relatively minor component within a mix of varied and competing systems.)

We now have far more experience than Mill and his contemporaries with the outcomes of state education systems. Perhaps we have enough experience to obviate fears that were reasonable in the 1850s, though there are still radical scholars who claim that education functions to produce a compliant population. Important issues remain regarding the content of state school curricula, including how far they should attempt to mould moral character in specific ways and how far they can, or should, encourage originality of thought. At the same time, many private providers of education – established along religious or ideological lines – might be more inclined than state-run teaching services to try to mould students' characters. I can't deal here with these important educational controversies, but the debate has moved on since 1859.

Mill also gives some support to industrial capitalism and to a wide range of private initiatives, partly from fear that wholesale government control of a nation's major enterprises would itself produce uniformity and despotism. It is easy to imagine a bureaucracy, however talented, capable, and benevolent, imposing its values and ethos – and protecting its own interests – with no effective resistance. Again, this debate has moved on, and a greater or equal fear nowadays might be the imposition of consensus values from the domain of large trading and financial corporations.

As with state education, Mill did not adamantly oppose all government enterprises. His view, rather, was that the freedom to live in original, individual ways would come under threat if an all-powerful public bureaucracy were allowed to emerge. As far as it goes, this is a reasonable warning against ubiquitous government power, but not a case for an unregulated capitalist economy. Supporters of free market capitalism can endorse the main arguments set out in *On Liberty*, but so can people who support extensive intervention in capitalist markets (or even economic arrangements along more socialist lines). Mill's arguments for individual liberty, and against conformity, are largely independent of debates over economic arrangements.

The spectre of tyranny

Mill places his arguments in historical perspective by pointing to ancient societies where liberty was understood as a limitation on the powers of potentially tyrannical governments. On Mill's account, a certain sphere of individual action was regarded as immune to state interference. In some cases (generally later in European history), state power was also restrained by constitutional arrangements according to which some governmental actions required the community's consent or the consent of a body representing the community's interests.

However, as Mill continues the story, a time came 'when men ceased to think it a necessity of nature that their governors should be an independent power opposed in interests to themselves' ([1859] 1974: 60). With the introduction of democratic elections, and thus the ability of electorates to remove governments through peaceful means, limits on the scope of political power came to appear less important – at least to some European political thinkers. Limits on government power had seemed necessary when the rulers' interests seemed largely opposed to those of the people; this perception changed once rulers became accountable to the people and expected to act in their interests:

> The nation did not need to be protected against its own will. There was no fear of its tyrannizing over itself. Let the rulers be effectually responsible to it, promptly removable by it, and it could afford to trust them with power of which it could itself dictate the use to be made. (Mill [1859] 1974: 61)

As he develops the themes of *On Liberty*, Mill rejects this perception as too complacent. Though democratic governments might be accountable to their electorates, he says, this does not amount to the people ruling themselves. The people who exercise power are not necessarily the same as those over whom it is exercised. For Mill, individuals do not rule themselves in a democracy: they are ruled by the rest, and majorities (or whoever can get themselves accepted as the majority) may seek to oppress minorities. In short, the mere establishment of democratic elections does not remove the need for limits on governmental power.

Borrowing from Alexis de Tocqueville, Mill warns that in modern circumstances we must still guard against 'the tyranny of the majority' ([1859] 1974: 62–3). Furthermore, the majority's means of tyrannizing over minorities and individuals are not confined to the acts of state officials. Indeed, majority opinion tyrannizes more extensively, intrusively, and pervasively than the apparatus of the state ever could:

> Protection, therefore, against the tyranny of the magistrate is not enough; there needs protection also against the tyranny of the prevailing opinion and feeling, against the tendency of society to impose, by

means other than civil penalties, its own ideas and practices as rules of conduct on those who dissent from them; to fetter the development and, if possible, prevent the formation of any individuality not in harmony with its ways, and compel all characters to fashion themselves upon the model of its own. (Mill [1859] 1974: 63)

To summarize this point, Mill seeks to protect individuals, and their individuality, against tyranny, whether exercised by state officials or by the prevailing opinion of society. Thus, he says: 'Precisely because the tyranny of opinion is such as to make eccentricity a reproach, it is desirable, in order to break through that tyranny, that people should be eccentric' (Mill [1859] 1974: 132). Mill does not deny the benefits of social living – or even that we are inherently social animals – but he strongly emphasizes the value of individuality. The question then arises: When can we reasonably hold individuality in check?

The harm principle

For Mill, the obvious answer is a principle of 'self-protection'. Put simply, we don't, of course, have to defer to the liberty of others when they would use it to harm us. More specifically, he claims, 'the only purpose for which power can be rightfully exercised over any member of a civilized community, against his will, is to prevent harm to others' (Mill [1859] 1974: 68). Thus, he introduces what is now known as the harm principle, intended to apply to all social control over individuals, 'whether the means used be physical force in the form of legal penalties or the moral coercion of public opinion' ([1859] 1974: 68). This principle rules out punishing someone because her action is imprudent or viewed as morally wrong. In what Mill regards as standard situations in societies such as his own – situations involving ordinary, competent adults – we are not accountable to society as a whole for our self-regarding actions. We're accountable only for actions that harm others.

Mill justifies all this in consequentialist terms, but in a specific way. He expresses willingness to forego arguments based on abstract rights and to appeal ultimately to general utility. But he quickly adds that 'it must be utility in the largest sense, grounded on the permanent interests of man as a progressive being' (Mill [1859] 1974: 70). The view here is that 'individual spontaneity' ([1859] 1974: 70) is not merely of value to the individual – something that it would be tyrannical to suppress without a compelling reason – but also of long-term value to society in generating new ideas and ways of living. Likewise, Mill defends liberty of thought and discussion as a requirement 'that human beings should be free to form opinions and to express opinions without reserve' justified by 'the baneful consequences to the intellectual, and through that to the moral nature of man' if this liberty is not asserted ([1859] 1974: 119). Later, he writes:

> There is always need of persons not only to discover new truths and point out when what were once truths are true no longer, but also to commence new practices and set the example of more enlightened conduct and better taste and sense in human life. ([1879] 1974: 129)

Throughout *On Liberty*, Mill elaborates and qualifies this position, considering many abstract and historical examples. He postulates a sphere of action in which society has at most an indirect interest when the agent's conduct 'affects only himself or, if it also affects others, only with their free, voluntary, and undeceived consent and participation'. He immediately clarifies that he is not thinking of indirect harms to others: 'When I say only himself, I mean directly and in the first instance; for whatever affects himself may affect others through himself; and the objection which may be grounded on this contingency will receive consideration in the sequel' (Mill [1859] 1974: 71). Mill also acknowledges that many actions which are widely considered legitimate are nonetheless harmful to others. Thus, 'in pursuing a legitimate object' an individual might necessarily cause others pain or loss, or might intercept a good that someone else 'had a reasonable hope of obtaining' (Mill [1859] 1974: 163). As an example, consider rivalry in competitive careers:

> Whoever succeeds in an overcrowded profession or in a competitive examination, whoever is preferred to another in any contest for an object which both desire, reaps benefit from the loss of others, from their wasted exertion and their disappointment. But it is, by common admission, better for the general interest of mankind that persons should pursue their objects undeterred by this sort of consequences. In other words, society admits no right, either legal or moral, in the disappointed competitors to immunity from this kind of suffering, and feels called on to interfere only when means of success have been

employed which it is contrary to the general interest to permit – namely, fraud or treachery, and force. (Mill [1859] 1974: 164)

We could extend this further, beyond the narrow situation of applying for jobs. We often encounter each other as rivals for economic gains, social status, romantic partners, and so on. In pursuing these goals we find ourselves in competition with others – not only from time to time, but very frequently. On an approach such as Mill's, it is not society's business to prevent these kinds of competition. Economic rivalry, in particular, might be seen as socially beneficial up to a point. When it comes to competition for desired offices and positions in society, competition can help match talent to society's needs, even though some people lose out in the process. Doubtless, the process of matching positions to talents is not as efficient as we might hope, and perhaps it merits scrutiny for failures and biases, but the harms it brings to people who miss out are not the sort that our political and social arrangements seem aimed at preventing.

For Mill, therefore, harm to others is a *necessary* condition before conduct should be suppressed by legal or social power. It is not a *sufficient* condition, however, since many actions that might cause harm to others are for one reason or another socially acceptable in the pursuit of legitimate objectives. In these cases, we don't view the harm as infringing on the rights of whoever is harmed. At the same time, Mill is quick to acknowledge that there are cases where we have positive duties to others – in which cases inaction and non-fulfilment count as harm. He sees individuals as owing a debt to society, and to each other, in return for the protection that society provides. While otherwise living in our own preferred ways, we should each bear our individual shares 'of the labours and sacrifices incurred for defending the society or its members from injury and molestation' (Mill [1859] 1974: 141).

Mill holds that we must not act so as to be nuisances to others, but if we merely act in accordance with our inclinations and judgement with things that concern our own lives, we should be allowed to do so unmolested. More than that, our individuality of action will prove beneficial to society as a whole and to humanity's overall advancement. Mill states, in particular, that there should be free scope for 'uncustomary things', partly 'in order that it may in time appear which of these are fit to be converted into customs' ([1859] 1974: 132). But it is also simply desirable that individuals be permitted to live in a variety of ways that suit their individual tastes and temperaments.

For Mill, then, we are entitled to punish others only for behaviour that illegitimately and directly harms others. If we find others' conduct merely distasteful in some way, we should at most leave them to themselves. Thus, the only 'punishment' allowable is whatever follows naturally from how we decide to live our own individual lives – perhaps choosing not to associate with someone whom we dislike. We are entitled to express our distaste for their behaviour and to stand aloof from them, as individuals, as we do from other things that displease us. 'But', says Mill, when someone acts in a manner that we have no right to control, 'we shall not therefore feel called on to make his life uncomfortable' (Mill [1859] 1974: 146). We won't go out of our way to harm those we dislike.

There's a lesson here. I can't, of course, share my individual life with *everyone*, and it's reasonable to choose my friends, lovers, and other close associates on the basis of whom I find congenial or otherwise. But a point quickly arrives where shunning, engaged in deliberately and collectively, is a weapon to harm others. It is going out of our way to make the victim's life 'uncomfortable', in Mill's phrasing, and can easily be a mechanism to enforce conformity.

Problems of defining harm

An obvious problem for Mill's overall account is the difficulty of defining an area of activity that affects only our own interests. Still, this problem can be exaggerated. Mill's concepts of harms that are only indirect or seem socially legitimate doubtless accorded with the common sense of his own place and time – and with much current common sense. *On Liberty* does not purport to be a scientifically precise analysis. It offers, instead, an attractive vision of individual and social flourishing (and improvement) over time. It mainly uses commonsensical ideas and concepts to provide adequate detail.

It's true that precise boundaries of what counts as harm are difficult to draw, and to some extent there may be cultural differences in perceptions. At the same time, much of what human beings think of as harm (or, conversely, as benefit) is cross-culturally uncontroversial. An Australian philosopher, Neil Levy, has examined how this provides something of a shared set of concepts for communication across cultures about moral and political choices – even if we make some moderately cultural relativist assumptions. Psychological pressures operate on the participants in cross-cultural conversations to justify practices with reasons that relate to benefits and harms of widely recognized kinds (Levy 2002: 191–2). These involve ordinary kinds of pleasure and pain, which, as Levy shows, arise for consideration in debates about practices that subordinate girls and women.

The issue may, however, go deeper if we take into account spiritual and psychological harms. In his important critique of the Enlightenment liberal project, *The Poverty of Liberalism*, Robert Paul Wolff questions whether the view developed in *On Liberty* is adequate to protect religious heresies and blasphemies and various morally despised practices. Can it rule out punishing these?

> But Mill also seems to think it obvious that when Smith practices the Roman faith, or reads philosophy, or eats meat, or engages in homosexual practices, he is *not* affecting Jones' interests. Now suppose that Jones is a devout Calvinist or a principled vegetarian. The very presence in his community of a Catholic or a meat-eater may cause him fully as much pain as a blow in the face or the theft of his purse. Indeed, to a truly devout Christian a physical blow counts for much less than the blasphemy of a heretic. (Wolff 1968: 24)

We might think that these are exactly the beliefs and practices that Enlightenment liberals such as Mill would hope to protect from legal bans and the tyranny of opinion. Thus, Wolff's point goes very deep. If Mill cannot locate eating meat, reading philosophy, and engaging in homosexual acts in a protected zone, his entire analysis is in trouble. As far as I can see, unfortunately, he does not have an available defence that could satisfy everybody. If my starting point were a highly religious one that included commitment to a specific view of ultimate truth and the good life for human beings, I might well be unwilling to accept the pluralism of belief and practice at the heart of Mill's philosophy. In Chapter I of *On Liberty*, Mill outlines the development in Europe of religious freedom and 'the separation between spiritual and temporal authority' ([1859] 1974: 74), but he offers no new arguments that are likely to convince a theocrat.

It's fair to say, I think, that Mill assumes theocracy to be a non-starter for his sophisticated audience. But if I began with a theocratic viewpoint, I might be unimpressed by the arguments actually developed in *On Liberty*. Mill relies on values of secular progress and individual development that might have no appeal *for me*. To talk me around, he might first need to talk me out of my larger world view, and that might prove to be impossible even if I were offered cogent arguments. Religious world views, in particular, have impressive resources for evading rational critique. Their adherents are often more committed to their substantive understandings of the world than to any premises and standards of reasoning that could ever be used to argue against them (see Blackford 2012: 11–12).

The result might be a standoff. In practice, a viewpoint such as that expressed in *On Liberty* might be difficult, or impossible, to defend in a society that is highly, and somewhat uniformly, religious. The kinds of hurt that Wolff mentions might be considered inevitable and legitimate in a society that is already characterized by a degree of religious toleration. But that would not get us far if we were arguing for individual liberty in, say, Saudi Arabia.

Nonetheless, large historical events and processes have brought about a situation in the West where it is frequently assumed that the state should confine itself to serving its citizens' civil interests – what John Locke called our interests in 'things belonging to this Life' ([1689] 1983: 26). Those events and processes included the religious warfare that wracked Europe in the sixteenth and seventeenth centuries, sparked by the Protestant Reformation (see Mill's own comments; [1859] 1974: 66). This led to new conceptions of the state such as Locke's, in which human beings are not accountable to the secular authorities for their religious beliefs. By Mill's time, such ideas had largely prevailed, though as Mill observes ruefully the resulting forms of religious tolerance were in practice varied, incomplete, and of little force in places where 'the [religious] sentiment of the majority is still genuine and intense' ([1859] 1974: 67).

Although Mill disclaims any idea, such as Locke's, of a social contract, he assumes a secular role for the state, inherited from 'great writers' ([1859] 1974: 66), and at least some diversity of religious views. If we grant Mill that much, as I think we should (see Blackford 2012: 35–46), the spiritual and psychological hurts that Wolff describes are fairly much inevitable. They must be tolerated by the state, and they are inflicted legitimately in at least a restricted sense: they cannot rightly be prohibited by the secular law, and indeed they might be regarded as part of the price of living under a secular government.

It does *not* follow merely from this that theologians and religious moralists can no longer offer moral condemnations of whatever they might regard as sinful beliefs and practices. I could consistently accept a role for *the state* in protecting only a limited range of secular interests without thinking that *morality itself* must be so constrained. I could, for example, acknowledge that it lies beyond the proper role of the state to punish homosexual acts (if they don't harm anyone's civil interests) while also thinking that they are contrary to God's will.

In practice religious sentiment tends to soften when persecutions are withdrawn and government becomes more secular. Most people are not religious zealots and will accept the state's toleration of heresies, blasphemies, and sinful acts, provided that it offers security for our lives and earthly goods (see Owen 2001: 151–72). Once heresies are tolerated by the state, most of us might be willing to tolerate them more generally. Indeed, part of the point of the secular state's toleration of heresies is that they will continue for as long as they can attract adherents, and that it is better to go along with this than to engage in persecutions. If they pain us in the way that Wolff describes, we might learn to be more thick-skinned. In an era of secular government, possession of a thin spiritual skin can be seen – at least by many people – as more a vice than a virtue.

Thus, Wolff's point would be more compelling if we began the discussion with neutrality between the ideas of secular government and something more like theocracy. Historically, however, that has changed, and the change was already well advanced when Mill published *On Liberty*. There are, nonetheless, still many people even in Western liberal democracies who reject purely secular understandings of the role of the state. Depending on their exact starting points, there might not be much that we can say to them, or that Mill could have said to the zealots of his time, unless they first changed their underlying world views. This is a problem for any form of liberalism, and I'll return to it.

Offensive conduct

Although Mill does not countenance the prohibition of heresies, he does proscribe some kinds of public conduct on the basis (essentially) that they are offensive. He deals with this by stating that many acts, although not directly injurious to others, are violations of good manners – and are hence offences against others – when done in public. Thus, their public performance 'may rightly be prohibited' (Mill [1859] 1974: 168). Mill mentions offences against decency as an example, but he refrains from any elaboration – seemingly out of a sense of discretion. We might, unkindly, wonder whether he senses that he's on shaky ground here, though in fairness he claims to see the issue as peripheral to his larger project.

One problem is that many kinds of conduct – including a wide variety of speech and expression – can be perceived as at least breaches of good manners, and this might cause understandable offence to others. But if all this conduct could be restrained consistently with the harm principle, we might wonder whether the harm principle had any teeth. Even when it comes to the narrow issue of public decency (in the relevant sense of that chameleon-like word), what might seem indecent in one place and era, such as a London street in the 1850s, might seem perfectly acceptable in another, such as a topless beach on the Mediterranean coast in 2018.

More recent thinkers in the Enlightenment liberal tradition accept offence to others as a basis for legal prohibitions, but only in a narrow range of cases. In *Freedom of Religion and the Secular State*, I suggested that the law should 'lean against the prohibition of mere offense', focusing, instead, 'on more clear-cut harms than "harms" to particular sensibilities' (Blackford 2012: 75). But we must at least acknowledge that some high-impact assaults on our senses that we call 'offensive' – nauseating smells, such as that of faeces or vomit; images of deep, raw wounds – have an unavoidable psychic impact that shades into outright harm with no clear way to draw a line (see Feinberg 1985). I don't doubt that exposure to heresy, blasphemy, and explicit sexual images can also have a high (negative) impact for many people. For other people, however, all of these might have intellectual or emotional value.

The emotional susceptibilities of some citizens can more readily justify restriction of expression in spaces where the public is more or less a captive audience. Government policy and sensible private decisions need to work around this, taking into account such factors as how intense the impact is likely to be for most people, how easily it can be avoided (or shut off from consciousness if we happen to stumble on it), and how much utility is lost if the offending conduct or expression is restricted from certain spaces or confined to others.

This might provide a justification for such regulatory responses as classification codes (though perhaps not actual censorship) for television, cinema, and certain other entertainment media. It might also justify restrictions on the content of billboards, and strict approval processes for images displayed within buses, trams, and train carriages. That much conceded, there is a serious risk that the state will use this rationale to interfere unnecessarily with individual self-expression. Many things that initially seem shocking become less so over time. The wisest response leans in favour of liberty, accompanied, we might hope, by a Zeitgeist of increasing toleration.

Paternalism

Mill was well aware that a wide range of actions can have indirect effects on the welfare of others – and in particular, that actions which harm our own capacities, or our own property, can diminish our power to benefit fellow citizens. Self-harming 'vices or follies' (Mill [1859] 1974: 147) can also set a bad example to others – who might thereby come to imitate us and so harm themselves. With all that acknowledged, Mill opposed punishments for harms to others caused indirectly via self-harming conduct.

In *On Liberty*, he is especially critical of temperance campaigners of his day who argued for the prohibition of alcohol on the basis of what amounted to its indirect harms: not harms to the person drinking but to others who might be affected by concrete dangers and disorder, or by a general weakening of society. On such an approach, Mill argues, anyone could demand as a 'social right' that nobody act in any way falling short of her own standards of perfection. He sees this as a 'monstrous' principle with the potential to justify virtually any interference with individual liberty – ultimately leaving us no zone of freedom beyond, perhaps, 'that of holding opinions in secret, without ever disclosing them' (Mill [1859] 1974: 158).

From a viewpoint similar to Mill's, we should not draw the boundary of what is tolerable in a place that allows sanctions for remote harms to others resulting indirectly from harms we caused to ourselves. Drawing the line here, rather than at direct harm to others, would allow endless scope to encroach on what Mill values most: liberty of action, and the originality, individuality, and spontaneity that it enables. Even if we share these values, however, we might wonder whether the boundary of tolerance could nonetheless be drawn safely in a way that involved at least a degree of paternalism.

We now live in highly complex societies where we could often benefit from guidance, especially when it comes to choices that have little to do with our fundamental sense of ourselves as individuals, yet have great impact on our health and well-being. Even if we think of the state as existing primarily to protect us from each other, its agencies recruit expertise that could be used to protect us from some of our own naive, untrained, or irrational choices. In our current circumstances, then, persuasive arguments can be developed for some legal constraints grounded in paternalistic considerations. In practice, many such laws are imposed, though this is seldom given much in the way of philosophical defence. American philosopher Sarah Conly has, however, published just such a defence of strongly paternalistic policies in some areas. In *Against Autonomy: Justifying Coercive Paternalism*, she bluntly proposes that some things should be banned even as individual choices: 'We should, for example, ban cigarettes; ban trans-fats; require restaurants to reduce portion sizes to less elephantine dimensions; increase required savings; and control how much debt individuals can run up' (Conly 2013: 1). She uses the example of prescription medicine as one where it is widely accepted that restrictions are appropriate:

> we seem to think that medicine is complicated and that most people don't have the expertise to decide on their own medication, even if, indeed, they read lots on the Internet about their own symptoms and the medicine they think may cure it. (Conly 2013: 4)

Conly has a point. Public policy would be far simpler if we were all reliable, rational choosers. But, as she makes clear, that is not a realistic assumption. In a large class of cases, people may not know what is best for them even by their own lights. Conservative political philosopher John Kekes shows more realism than Mill in this respect. Kekes sees individual liberty as an important value, but not the *overriding* political value (2008: 94–7). This is partly because so many people – he thinks half the population – are unable to use liberty to their benefit. For example, it has little value for people suffering from serious mental disorders, suicidal tendencies, total or functional illiteracy, or dementia. Likewise, it is of limited to use to children below a certain age (Kekes refers to fourteen as a rough cut-off point). If it comes to that, the rest of us, as Conly rightly insists, are beset by numerous cognitive biases and limitations.

But even Conly acknowledges the dangers if paternalism is not reined in. Paternalistic policies can become too intrusive or too ubiquitous, they can be enforced too harshly, or they can be based on what Conly sees as the wrong kind of paternalist theory (such as a theory that there are objectively 'correct' goals for us to adopt, knowable by the government and overriding whatever goals we actually have). Thus, much of her detailed analysis can be read against the grain of her main argument. Although her book is provocatively entitled *Against Autonomy*, it seems that she is not really against individual autonomy. Rather, she attempts to show – perhaps successfully – that there is no single knock-down argument against all forms of coercive paternalism. At the same time, she identifies numerous dangers if paternalism is not employed in a severely defined, restricted, and discriminating way.

For his part, Mill emphasizes that public opinion is unreliable – he sees this as grounding the strongest argument against paternalistic interventions. The majority is likely to impose its own preferences and forbid behaviour that offends its feelings. Paternalism can then grow to cover a vast range:

> And it is not difficult to show, by abundant instances, that to extend the bounds of what may be called moral police until it encroaches on the most unquestionably legitimate liberty of the individual is one of the most universal of all human propensities. (Mill [1859] 1974: 152)

Mill is surely correct about this. I suggest – and I think Conly might agree – that we be *very* careful in what we assume about other people and what is good for them. In his classic defence of legal moralism, *The Enforcement of Morals*, Patrick Devlin asserts at one point: 'There must be some homosexuals who believe theirs to be a good way of life but many more who would like to get free of it if only they could' (Devlin 1965: 107). Compare this wording with some of Conly's remarks on smoking:

> Even though it's a good bet that the majority of those who smoke wish they didn't, incentivizing good actions, and discouraging bad ones, just isn't enough. Smokers typically wish they hadn't started, but the only way to have stopped them would be something we don't now embrace – coercive paternalism, where people are forced to do the right thing, or, in this case, prevented from doing the wrong one. (Conly 2013: 4)

I'm not suggesting that the two cases are exactly analogous: that Devlin was wrong, and so Conly must also be wrong. Surely the situation is more subtle. For a start, there may have been an element of truth in Devlin's words, written in different social circumstances from ours more than half a century ago. That is, many gay men (the whole debate of the time seems to have had little to do with lesbians) might, indeed, have believed they were living a bad way of life – but that would largely be explained by socialization into thinking that their deepest desires were wicked. Furthermore, their lives were blighted by social intolerance and the prospect of legal prosecution, requiring of them constant caution and deception. Social intolerance of homosexuality is still a serious problem, but at least it has somewhat lessened since the early 1960s.

By contrast, the main problem with smoking is simply its risks to physical health. It does, therefore, seem safer and wiser to make Conly's pronouncement about smoking than Devlin's about homosexuality. My point, then, is not that Conly is incorrect in supposing that the majority of people who smoke wish they could give it up. In many countries, including the United States, the UK, and Australia, that may now be true, as we've all become highly conscious of smoking's detrimental effects on health. In drawing attention to Devlin's claim, I wish only to make the modest point that we can be too quick to assume that a practice or a way of life that *we* find unattractive is oppressive for those who have actually taken it up. Moreover, if they do find it oppressive that might be more because of social disapproval and persecution than its inherent effects. Conly may, therefore, be right about the particular practice of smoking, but Mill is also right that our paternalistic assumptions can be shaped by our personal tastes and moral views.

Sometimes we – or at least well-trained government officials, after specialist investigations and appropriate deliberation and debate – really do know better than individuals who are set on a self-destructive course. In those cases, not much might be lost if the law interfered in specific ways. The trick, then, is not to adopt a policy of absolute non-interference in individual choices. But we should interfere only with great caution and in a spirit of self-doubt, knowing that interference might be based on very contestable ideas and might prove counterproductive.

Other things being equal, paternalistic laws might be more acceptable when they impose only trivial burdens, or merely 'nudge' us. Here their effects are not oppressive, though there might be an issue about emotional manipulation and subversion of our rational wills. This creates its own dangers, and I don't propose on this occasion to examine the large emerging questions on the moral acceptability of nudging. Still, well-crafted nudges might leave us with the final decision, while pointing us in a safe direction (for more on these issues, see Thaler and Sunstein 2009; but compare Berg 2016: 140–2). At least this seems more acceptable than outright removal of options.

Likewise, legal paternalism seems more acceptable in areas where something more than ordinary adult understanding is required to make a sound decision. To revert to one of Conly's examples, the scientific study of medical drugs is highly complex and few people can plausibly claim the expertise to diagnose and treat themselves. Hence, it is not an insult to our competence – and we may even welcome it – when governments enact laws and establish agencies to regulate the availability and prescription of medical drugs.

Likewise, paternalism is more acceptable where those who are protected from themselves fall within the categories sketched by Kekes: that is, they are for one reason or another identifiably impaired in making their own decisions. By contrast, adults at the height of their deliberative powers have good reason to trust their own decisions about how to live their own lives. Yes, cognitive biases and limitations do affect us all, but there's also a danger in exaggerating this or overly relying on it in our political deliberations. That way lies the madness of interfering in others' highly personal choices. Self-doubt is crucial, lest our paternalistic impulses do more harm than good.

Conformity in modern societies

In *The Enforcement of Morals*, Devlin claimed that ideas of separating the law from morality had had no effect on the development of the English law. For example, incest and homosexual crimes were added to the statute books with no inquiry as to whether their private practice was socially harmful. The relevant passage is worth reading and considering, if only because it exemplifies a certain way of thinking about society and the law. Devlin suggests that sex crimes relating to incest and homosexuality were added to English law simply because they were (viewed as) morally wrong. There was, at the relevant time, no deep division of opinion in the UK over issues of sexual morality. However, he grants that this had changed by the time he was writing around 1960:

There are now in England men who secretly see nothing wrong with the homosexual relationship. There are others, to be found mainly among the educated classes, who, while not themselves practising homosexuality, are not repelled by it, think it a permissible way of life for those so constituted as to enjoy it, and deplore the misery the law inflicts on the comparatively few victims it detects. (Devlin 1965: 87)

Later he states: 'I do not think that there is anyone who asserts vocally that homosexuality is a good way of life but there may be those who believe it to be so' (1965: 116).

Devlin also says, of legislators, 'Naturally he will assume that the morals of his society are good and true; if he does not, he should not be playing an active part in government' (1965: 90). Let's note, then, that it seemed natural to someone like Devlin – not writing all that long ago, and not an especially conservative figure in his day – to assume that dissent from the prevailing morality of the time is a disqualification for political office. When that view is widely held, even if seldom articulated so explicitly, it inevitably chills debate on moral issues.

Over the past six decades we have seen enormous social changes, not least the sexual revolution of the 1960s and early 1970s, the contemporaneous rise of 'second-wave' feminism (often promoted during the early 1970s as the Women's Liberation Movement), feminism's own various changes and internal conflicts beginning in the later 1970s, the social and political reactions of the 1980s, the fall of communism in Europe and its repercussions in Western thinking, globalization in all its forms, the challenge of political Islam, and the recent shift towards an online society. In 2017, after all this and much more, plenty of people in the UK will assert, as vocally as we might wish, 'that homosexuality is a good way of life' (though the 'way of life' formulation might now seem tone deaf and trivializing). Yet this might provide little consolation to a gay couple who are regarded with distaste in their local community, perhaps having to hide their relationship if they want to get along with their neighbours. More generally, the pressure of conformity does not need consensus across an entire society to achieve its effect. All that's needed to generate pressures to conform is the opinion of whoever impinges on the lives of potential nonconformists. This might be individuals in the local community, or it might be powerful institutions or groups.

Joshua Greene emphasizes throughout his 2013 book, *Moral Tribes*, that contemporary Western liberal democracies are not culturally closed or monolithic in their values. They include different groups with their own traditions and histories. On the issues of the day, opinion can be sharply polarized, with many people urgently seeking that their own moral views – or those of their particular group or tradition – prevail over those of others. This situation is rather different from that in Mill's time, when a common morality could usually be assumed in the UK and other countries that had emerged from medieval and early modern European Christendom.

Some demands for conformity still seem to come from society as a whole; after all, few people in the UK, for example, would countenance incest among close family members, no matter the circumstances. That has not changed since Mill's time. But many other moral demands come from particular groups – moral and political tribes – that exert their power in particular contexts. These rival tribes strive for domination in a way not altogether unlike the warring religious denominations of the sixteenth and seventeenth centuries.

Other demands for conformity come from more specific sources. Employers possess great power because almost all of us need to work to make a living. At the same time, we're forced to accept employer controls over our behaviour; in some ways, employer encroachment on individual liberty and spontaneity, and more generally on how we live our private lives, is becoming more severe. During the later decades of the twentieth century, new social and technological developments created a trend towards task-performance (rather than time-service) contracts of employment. Employees on task-performance contracts are required to complete certain tasks or play a certain role within the employer's operations, as opposed to turning up, week by week, to provide allocated hours of service. Together with this development, employers increasingly offer written contracts that include extensive codes of conduct aimed at protecting their brand or corporate image (see generally McCallum 2000).

If employers use their power to impose their own opinions and attitudes on employees, or to impose whichever opinions and attitudes prevail in the wider society or a large section of it, this produces a strong pressure to conform. In an economic system – such as exists in the United States – where most employers have an almost unfettered prerogative to hire and fire, this can lead to frightening situations where zealous bosses try to control even their workers' out-of-hours expression of religious, social, and political opinions (for more, expressed trenchantly and with examples, see Barry 2007). Even in countries where employment and labour relations law imposes more restrictions on the right to hire and fire, there is still much scope for employers to usurp control over their employees' private lives.

As they protect their corporate images, employers may monitor the lives of their employees intrusively. With the advent of social media such as blogs, Facebook, and Twitter, employers are increasingly taking an interest in the online footprints of job applicants. Complaints to employers provide a mechanism to retaliate against individuals for behaviour or speech that offended somebody but may have little to do with the workplace. Indeed, the online shaming campaigns that I discuss in Chapter 8 often have the effect that victims lose their jobs or even have their careers ruined.

Apart from their relations with employers, individuals form many private associations, and it might seem reasonable to abide by their rules. However, it is not always so simple. Individuals often have little freedom to leave and no prospect of changing the rules from within. In the case of religious affiliations and associated communities of believers, membership seldom comes about voluntarily. More typically, children find themselves involved via their parents. In consequence, many adults may belong to a religious community of some kind for no better reason than that they grew up within it.

In particular, women who do not accept the demands of a religious community can come under irresistible pressures to conform: pressures from family members, authority figures, and peers. In some cases, the pressure is backed by implicit or explicit threats. One way or another, there can be considerable costs to defying or leaving a community. Consider, for example, a woman for whom it entails being ostracized by her family, forcibly kept from her children, and left with neither financial support nor skills that are valued in the wider labour market. In cases such as this, there is an obvious potential for non-government power to be exercised tyrannically and experienced as oppressive.

Media organizations can also function as enforcers of social convention. We might hope that the large media organizations that regard themselves as 'the press' would act as defenders of individual liberty, celebrating individuality and eccentricity, and opposing various social pressures to conform. But it seldom turns out like that. Indeed, the so-called free press often takes on the role of moral police that Mill decried. Media organizations sell newspapers, magazines, or online clicks to shame individuals for breaches of (conventional) morality, respectable opinion, or whatever standards of taste are currently fashionable.

In all, the state and its agencies wield frightening powers, including the power to imprison and sometimes even to kill, and this should make us especially anxious to keep governmental power under control. But at the same time, a great range of institutions, associations, and relationships exists in modern societies. Numerous pressures to conform are exerted by individuals, institutions, and groups, not necessarily by anything as vast and inchoate as society as a whole. More local or tribal opinion can be as effective and tyrannical as the universal opinion of society.

The harm principle and the spirit of *On Liberty*

In the spirit of *On Liberty*, we can embrace such values as originality, individuality, and spontaneity. We should, then, be reluctant to use punishments – whether legal or social – to force others to speak, behave, and generally live their lives, as *we* might wish. With some qualifications, we can adopt the Millian harm principle. We should not inflict punishment, through the power of the state or by other means, except in response to serious harms relating to others' civil interests: interests in worldly things, such as life, health, liberty, and property, rather than spiritual interests in salvation, holiness, rightness with God, or purity from sin. The harms should also be direct, although directness is a matter of a degree. Perhaps what really matter are such things as the urgency of a situation, the likelihood of harm eventuating, and the futility of attempts to avert the risk by relatively non-coercive means.

As I've explained, the harm principle justifies punishments only for wrongful harms, not those that are somehow deserved, consented to, or otherwise considered socially legitimate: harms that are tolerated in societies like our own as being the inevitable outcomes of acceptable objectives pursued in accepted ways.

In *On Liberty*, Mill introduces the harm principle as a simple, clear, and absolute method for drawing the boundary between actions that are and are not proper targets for interference by state power and social opinion. As it turns out, the principle is not so simple, the boundaries of its application are rather blurred, and it seems that we need to make exceptions. For all that, Mill's discussion is immensely useful. Once we understand that Mill is trying to protect our spontaneity, our individual conceptions of what might be good lives for ourselves, and our ability to experiment with ways of life that don't match old templates, his analysis is precise enough for the purpose. He may be relying on values that can't ultimately be justified to all possible opponents. But for many of us, the considerations that he introduces seem powerfully relevant.

The harm principle could not be applied in a mechanical way. By itself, it would not be clear enough to use as a constitutional standard restricting government power (Blackford 2012: 84). But it is clear enough to be used in public discussions of many issues that appear on political agendas. Whenever needed, all the more specific distinctions made by Mill are available to enrich those same discussions. *On Liberty* is a valuable part of our cultural heritage and still an invaluable political resource.

3 FREEDOM OF THOUGHT AND FREEDOM OF SPEECH

Free speech: Origins

In his important 1982 book, *Free Speech: A Philosophical Inquiry*, legal theorist Frederick Schauer traces the origin of our modern concept of free speech to two sources in early European modernity. One of these is the theory of religious toleration developed by such thinkers as John Locke, Pierre Bayle, and Anne Robert Jacques Turgot. While this was a crucial development, since theocratic governments are strongly motivated to suppress heretical speech, Schauer pays more attention to the historical debates over freedom of the press. As he puts it, 'religious toleration provides the fallibilistic and individualistic roots for modern free speech doctrine' while the historical doctrine of freedom of the press relates free speech 'to the operation of government, and to the demarcation between citizen and government' (Schauer 1982: 106).

In its seventeenth- and eighteenth-century usage, talk of *the press* did not refer to an institutionalized set of media reporting and discussing news and current affairs. The reference, rather, was to all printed (as opposed to spoken or handwritten) material, and especially to the work of lone pamphleteers writing on contentious political issues (Schauer 1982: 106–7; Lewis 2007: 97). From debates about the freedom of the press – originally in this broad sense – has emerged our modern emphasis on freedom for distinctly political speech, particularly for speech that addresses a large audience and includes criticism of government officials and their policies.

These developments have been hugely consequential over the long haul. They have eroded two major taboos: a taboo against blasphemy and heresy, and a taboo against criticizing the government. The situation in Western Christendom at the beginning of European modernity has been reversed in contemporary liberal democracies. Far from being taboo, speech that criticizes governments and their policies is now seen as especially valuable. It is considered essential that voters receive, express, hear, and debate whatever ideas and information are relevant to the exercise of their democratic choices. Likewise, we now place a high value on investigations, debates, and public discussions that may affect our overall views of the world and, in the process, undermine traditional religious orthodoxies.

All of this is crucial for democratic deliberation, intellectual progress, and our own development and self-actualization as individuals. One eminent contemporary philosopher, John R. Searle, defends freedom of speech on the basis that we are inherently 'speech-act performing animals' and that we understand speech as something especially central and valuable to our flourishing (Searle 2010: 190). On this account, demands for freedom of speech follow from our nature as a species and from a rational, widely shared conception of what is valuable about human existence itself. Searle makes this point within his defence of a more general account of social institutions and norms, politics, and rights. It is, however, independently compelling whether or not we accept his wider theory. It serves to explain why we so often crave freedom to express our views, whether our freedom is restricted by state action or by others' private efforts. It also explains why any account of free speech grounded solely in ideas of democratic deliberation seems inadequate. History and everyday experience suggest that guarantees of free speech are meant to reassure us that we can have our say on all topics without punishment.

John Stuart Mill's defence of the liberty of thought and discussion is the most famous ever published, but it is often seen as merely a defence of academic or intellectual speech. Indeed, it's true that Mill mainly wanted to ensure that no ideas or opinions should be regarded as heretical (and so suppressed by governmental or social power). But there's more to his thinking than that. In *On Liberty*, he places value on political speech and also on individual development. For Mill, all of this is synergistic; it all fits within his wider defence of liberty. In this chapter, I follow Mill (and Schauer) in not relegating our freedom to speak our minds to a single, isolated purpose.

Liberty of thought and discussion – Mill's argument

Mill begins Chapter II of *On Liberty*, entitled 'Of the Liberty of Thought and Discussion', with the hope that it is not necessary to defend 'liberty of the press' as a security 'against corrupt or tyrannical government' ([1859] 1974: 75). He deals with this quickly, however, because he thinks that it goes almost without saying. Even in 1859, this aspect of freedom of the press seemed uncontroversial.

Nor was Mill unaware of the value for individuals in speaking their minds and hearing the thoughts of others. Chapter II of *On Liberty* is, after all, embedded within a larger argument about the importance of individual liberty and freedom in general. Throughout the book, Mill offers a coherent, integrated view about the liberty to think, speak, act, and live our lives, all of which is said to contribute to our own development and to the development of human knowledge, understanding, and taste. Still, the emphasis of Chapter II is undoubtedly on ideas and opinions, and not just those directly concerned with politics. Mill, recall, conceives of humanity as a progressive species. He understands liberty as needed for individuality of thought and character that leads, in turn, to intellectual, cultural, and moral improvement. Thus, he argues for social – and not just legal – toleration to encourage individuality. He regards it as crucial for that purpose that we be able to *hear* all views, and so he emphasizes the availability of speech to the hearer more than the self-actualization of the speaker.

On Liberty moves swiftly to its main line of argument – that diverse opinions, whether true or false, are of value to current generations and to posterity. Something is always lost when an opinion is suppressed:

> If the opinion is right, they are deprived of the opportunity of exchanging error for truth; if wrong, they lose, what is almost as great a benefit, the clearer perception and livelier impression of truth produced by its collision with error. (Mill [1859] 1974: 76)

There is, of course, another possibility – that the disputants on both or all sides of an argument hold views with an element of truth – and Mill soon discusses this. First, however, he emphasizes human fallibility and the wisdom of constantly testing our own opinions against alternatives and counterarguments. Throughout the chapter, he is focused on the evils of censoring opinions, and his examples are often opinions on religious issues such as the existence of God and an afterlife, and the correct view to take of Christian morality. Mill finds little to criticize in the sayings of Jesus of Nazareth, as recorded in the canonical gospels, but he has much to say against the one-sided, ascetic, often servile moral teachings developed and preached by the succeeding generations of churchmen. For Mill, this version of Christian morality must not be allowed to predominate unchallenged:

> I believe that other ethics than any which can be evolved from exclusively Christian sources must exist side by side with Christian ethics to produce the moral regeneration of mankind; and that the Christian system is no exception to the rule that in an imperfect state of the human mind the interests of truth require a diversity of opinions. (Mill [1859] 1974: 114)

(We might wonder how far Mill exaggerates his fondness for Jesus' supposed words, perhaps as a form of protective colouring. Be that as it may, his critique of Christian morality is worth considering, both for its own sake and as a model for the rest of us when we dare to challenge popular ideas.)

Mill worries that public silence about heretical ideas discourages those who adhere to them from arguing on the basis of their actual assumptions, while preventing the heretical views from being given 'fair and thorough discussion' ([1859] 1974: 95). Silence prevents unmeritorious ideas disappearing under the weight of criticism, while at the same time discouraging many intellectually promising, but relatively timid, people from following their thinking where it leads them. This discourages the appearance of great thinkers, and it also discourages the development of ordinary people's minds in an intellectually active environment. Mill also considers it essential to hear the side of an argument contrary to one's own, in order to hold one's own view with proper understanding and confidence:

> So essential is this discipline to a real understanding of moral and human subjects that, if opponents of all-important truths do not exist, it is indispensable to imagine them and supply them with the strongest arguments which the most skilful devil's advocate can conjure up. ([1859] 1974: 99)

This might seem exaggerated, but let's give it further thought. We often encounter people who won't even entertain arguments against their views – merely dismissing opponents as morally bad (or at best duped) individuals. These dismissers often seem to think they know the answers to all objections, but that may be because they've learned potted answers to crude or silly versions.

Mill predicts that there will be a gradual increase in the number of claims that are not seriously disputed, which he sees as 'salutary' when they are actually true and 'noxious' when they are false ([1859] 1974: 106). But even when they're true, Mill sees a downside: he fears the loss, to some extent, of an 'intelligent and living apprehension of the truth' when it no longer needs to be explained and defended to doubters ([1859] 1974: 106). Lack of contestation leads to truth claims being understood lazily and unclearly, so much so that we should be grateful to anyone who looks for weaknesses in received truths or mistakes in their application.

This is worth reflection. It's another of Mill's points that might seem exaggerated – but I think he is basically right. Widely accepted truths are often understood in ways that are simplified, distorted, and applied thoughtlessly. As an idea becomes popular, its meaning may be 'lost or enfeebled' (Mill [1859] 1974: 116), and its expression then becomes a formality rather than something heartfelt and properly understood. The idea of free speech is itself an example of this. While almost everyone in contemporary liberal democracies gives lip service to *some* conception of free speech, the rival conceptions on offer tend to be simplistic, and they often bear little relationship to the values and considerations that make liberty of thought and discussion so important.

Mill turns to the possibility – the most common, as he sees it – that rival disputants may possess elements of the truth relating to a particular issue. Popular opinions will often be true, but seldom the entire truth even when planted on strong ground. Rather, 'They are a part of the truth, sometimes a greater, sometimes a smaller part, but exaggerated, distorted, and disjointed from the truths by which they ought to be accompanied and limited' (Mill [1859] 1974: 108).

While all this detail provides an argument against suppressing disliked *opinions*, Mill also insists that we not suppress speech merely because of its *intemperate tone*. As he says, opponents will always view us as intemperate merely for expressing ourselves in a strong, forthright way – someone passionately committed to a rival view will likely feel this as an attack. There are, Mill acknowledges, ways to express an opinion that are open to criticism, but they consist not so much in an intemperate tone as in suppressing facts and arguments and misrepresenting opponents. Even these faults are difficult to stamp as morally culpable, according to Mill, because they are so often 'done in good faith by persons who are not considered, and in many other respects may not deserve to be considered, ignorant or incompetent' ([1859] 1974: 117). This observation is worth taking to heart in two ways.

First, we should beware of our own temptation to treat opponents unfairly, even if we're acting in good faith. Second, perhaps we should cut (some!) slack for opponents who are arguing unfairly. It can seem deliberate and infuriating, but it's a common human weakness. (Still, it's a weakness worth keeping in mind and drawing attention to when it happens, since it can derail discussion even among well-meaning people.)

With regard to general incivility – sarcasm, personal insults, and the like – Mill notes that denunciation of these 'would deserve more sympathy' if directed at both sides of an argument, when in practice it is reserved for advocates of unpopular views. He states that 'The worst offence of this kind which can be committed by a polemic is to stigmatize those who hold the contrary opinion as bad and immoral men' (Mill [1859] 1974: 117). Once again, however, he thinks this tactic is employed mainly against speakers with unpopular views. As a result, those speakers are forced to employ 'studied moderation of language and the most cautious avoidance of unnecessary offence' while those defending the received opinions employ an 'unmeasured vituperation' that 'really does deter people from professing contrary opinions and from listening to those who profess them' ([Mill 1859] 1974: 117).

It's worth noting that there is a tension here. Mill acknowledges that vituperation can, indeed, rise to a level where it chills discussion by deterring some expressions of opinion and, in any event, forcing speakers to express their thoughts with extreme care. Mill sees this as mainly a problem for speakers with unpopular views, but in our own current circumstances the situation may be less clear cut. In a society of warring moral and political tribes, a range of views can attract highly vituperative and intimidating responses, depending on the circumstances. In some settings, even views that are popular in the wider community might not be safe to express within the tribe.

Mill suggests that the law should not restrain vituperative language on any side of an argument. In many or most circumstances, this may well be wise (e.g. where exactly should we draw a line as to what is forbidden?). Nonetheless, he urges what he calls 'the real morality of public discussion'. While the law should stay aloof, opinion should condemn advocacy on any side of an argument that shows 'want of candour, or malignity, bigotry, or intolerance of feeling' – without, however, inferring these vices from anyone's substantive view on the topic at hand. Conversely, we should honour anyone, irrespective of their substantive view, 'who has the calmness to see and honesty to state what his opponents and their opinions really are, exaggerating nothing to their discredit, keeping nothing back which tells, or can be supposed to tell, in their favour' ([1859] 1974: 118). This is good advice for today's world of Manichaean politics and ferocious online disputation.

Wolff on knowledge and liberty

In *The Poverty of Liberalism*, Robert Paul Wolff critiques Mill's approach to free speech, which he understands as merely a defence of free discussion to advance the growth of knowledge. Wolff's critique is deep, but ultimately it does little to undermine the arguments of *On Liberty*. At one point, Wolff suggests that we make distinctions between different kinds of knowledge in order to throw light on the relationship between knowledge and liberty:

> Among the species of actual or supposed knowledge which can be distinguished, Mill pays particular attention to at least three, namely religious knowledge, scientific knowledge, and what might be called moral or normative knowledge. I think a closer look will reveal that the usefulness of free discussion to the advance of each of these species is quite different. (Wolff 1968: 12)

This is useful to highlight Mill's primary interest in discussion of general topics – such as religion, science, morality and politics, philosophy, history, and culture – rather than, for example, in what individual people have done in their private lives. Of the three categories identified by Wolff, I'll deal last with religious knowledge, as it raises special problems similar to those that I dealt with (also in response to Wolff) in the previous chapter.

Wolff does not doubt that, as a rule, and leaving aside such frightening technological developments as weapons of mass destruction, the ongoing advance of science is socially beneficial. But it's not so clear, he says, 'that scientific research demands an absolute freedom of speech and debate' (Wolff 1968: 15). In particular, nothing seems to be lost by suppressing discarded bodies of theory such as phrenology, astrology, and the phlogiston theory of combustion. On Wolff's account, physical scientists don't need to study these or even how current theories came to be established. Therefore, 'Orthodox science is "established" in our society in just the way that particular religious creeds have been established in earlier times' (Wolff 1968: 16).

For example, mainstream science is taught in educational institutions that have the imprimatur of the state, official positions are available to mainstream scientists, and there are strong social pressures directed against discarded theories. Although belief in such phenomena as astral influences is not legally prohibited in Western liberal democracies, there are many circumstances in which a person who believes in astrology would be severely discredited. In some cases – Wolff singles out the practice of medicine – there are legal constraints on how far dissenters from mainstream science can act on pseudoscientific theories.

Wolff is correct, of course, that working scientists don't need to understand debunked ideas such as phlogiston theory. That said, it does no harm when universities teach the history of science, including the means by which old theories were refuted. While this knowledge is not critical for the day-to-day work of scientists, it sheds light on how science progresses, and such an understanding might be important for defending science from its numerous detractors. To that extent, studying the history of science might have value even for scientists who are focused closely on their own research. Indeed, I think we can go much further. More widespread knowledge of how science advanced through evidence and reasoning could have considerable social benefit. It might be helpful, for example, if it were more generally known how Galileo convinced his contemporaries that his telescopic observations provided genuine images of astronomical objects and revealed such new phenomena as the moons of Jupiter (e.g. Kitcher 1993: 227–33). Nobody can hope to understand the complete story, in all its details, of how the current edifice of science was built. But I see only advantages from more widespread acquaintance with the basics.

Perhaps Wolff could accept this point. Nonetheless, he might insist, the essential criticism remains. If we teach, say, the phlogiston theory of chemical combustion, it should be solely as an example of a *false* theory.

That seems fair, but even here we should be careful. There is much dispute about what distinguishes science from pseudoscience, and there's a lively academic debate among scientists and philosophers about the nature of scientific methodology. This includes whether any single approach can meaningfully be designated *the scientific method*. For example, much scientific inquiry is probably *not* best understood in terms of testing hypotheses, framing and refuting conjectures, and so on, despite the importance of such approaches to studying the natural world. Some scientific inquiry might be better described as systematic observation of natural phenomena, or as drawing conclusions based on converging lines of observation. At a minimum, however, it's clear that some scientific hypotheses and theories have been utterly discredited and abandoned.

That being so, geocentric theory, phlogiston theory, phrenology, astrology, and the like should play no role in deliberation over public policy, and they should clearly not be taught as if they were true. It's not so clear, though, that defending them should be punished by the state in ways that go beyond, say, firing crackpot professors from public universities. That's partly because of more general concerns about entrusting such power to the state, partly because this sort of suppression would be a waste of public resources, and partly because even false theories might contain – if not exactly a grain of truth – at least enough elegance and ingenuity to be worth preserving. I'm not thinking only of their aesthetic value, although some may possess that, but also the possibility that some might provide analogies or inspiration for later thinkers.

We may need to be more aggressive in some cases than others about addressing bad science and pseudoscience. We can tolerate astrology, as long as it's not taught in schools and universities as legitimate science. But more aggressive steps seem needed to keep anti-vaccination propaganda out of public policy. I'm not suggesting that the state should go as far as punishing anti-vaccination activists via the criminal law. However, some of their efforts at least render them unfit to be licensed as medical practitioners. To the extent that it gains a public following, anti-vaccination activism might also justify forceful government information campaigns in response.

All of this suggests that Wolff is correct only up to a point. The situation with strictly scientific knowledge is, indeed, complex, perhaps more complex than Mill describes in *On Liberty*. At the same time, Wolff's own account misses some important nuances. In any event, as

Wolff acknowledges, the advance of science cannot accept hindrances at the frontiers of knowledge. Scientific dogmas – theories that are treated as immutable and unrevisable – can impede scientific creativity, so none should be exempt from criticism. That, I think, is a recognizably Millian view.

When it comes to moral and political issues, Wolff thinks that Mill was essentially right: all views should be permitted, although not necessarily for the reasons offered in *On Liberty*. In fact, Wolff's appeal to historical experience is expressed in a way that is reminiscent of some arguments for *religious* toleration:

> But in matters of collective social action concerning moral and political issues, the freest possible expression of competing views does seem called for. Even before we have reasoned out the principles underlying the right ordering of the political community, our instincts tell us that society is diminished by the arbitrary stifling of dissenting parties. Experience suggests that a vigorous competition of opposed policies, however disruptive of social tranquility, is to be preferred to the enforced quiet of political repression. (Wolff 1968: 17)

While such an approach is persuasive, it will seem viable only in a society that already favours considerable religious toleration. That is, religious toleration seems, in practice, to be a necessary condition, if not strictly a *sufficient* condition, for a wide toleration of moral and political ideas. The reason, of course, is that religious organizations have their own views on moral questions – and they often have views on more strictly political ones. If a particular religious organization gained control of the government, the likely result is that many moral and political ideas would soon be officially heretical. Accordingly, liberty of moral and political thought is not independent of liberty of religious thought (which I'll come to in the next section). Once the latter is accepted, on the other hand, increasing liberty of moral and political thought is almost – if not strictly – inevitable.

Wolff suggests that we need free debate on political and moral issues for reasons that don't relate to the advance of knowledge. Rather, we need a guarantee that all citizens will have a say in political deliberation and that no grievances will be left unredressed because they are silenced. Thus, 'Justice, not truth, is the ideal served by liberty of speech' (Wolff 1968: 18).

All of this has a good rhetorical ring and much intellectual merit, but a few caveats are in order. First, it's not as if Mill denies the importance of such considerations. As I've already noted, he begins Chapter II of *On Liberty* by reaffirming the need for liberty of the press as a security 'against corrupt or tyrannical government' ([1859] 1974: 75). He does not develop the point at length, but he would likely agree that government censorship of moral and political viewpoints should be set aside partly so that all grievances and legitimate concerns can be heard. For Mill, this is more or less obvious and uncontroversial. He leaves the point underdeveloped because he proposes to introduce more far-reaching ideas. Thus Wolff makes a worthwhile positive point, but it is not in itself an effective criticism of Mill. Furthermore, the point could be developed to emphasize that the government is not the only social institution that can exercise tyrannical power over individuals, creating concerns that need redress. Freedom of speech is invaluable for resisting tyranny from *all* sources.

Wolff also makes the point that we have no real knowledge in the realm of goals and norms, whereas if ethics were mathematics there would be genuine expertise and progress, and we could identify a path along which knowledge has advanced, with 'a hinterland of discarded doctrines that it would be neither fruitful nor desirable to keep alive' (Wolff 1968: 18). Leaving aside a point that I've already made – that it might be prudent to avoid suppressing even the most discredited scientific theories – there's a certain amount here that seems correct. Mill would agree that moral and political issues are perennially contested, so these are issues where there is always more than one side to a discussion. He would not, however, agree that there is no real moral knowledge.

It is controversial to claim that we make no progress in obtaining moral and political knowledge. Even moral relativists can account for moral progress of a non-trivial sort (Blackford 2016: 70–3). Furthermore, we can learn much about the world and ourselves that is at least *relevant* to moral and political reasoning. Even if there is no objective fact as to whether, say, lying to save others from harm is morally required, permitted, or forbidden, it might still be true that some moral and political ideas are socially useful. Mill, in fact, makes exactly the point that arguments about moral ideas include arguments about whether or not they are useful. Presumably there can be knowledge about *that*. And these arguments about the usefulness of moral ideas will inevitably raise arguments about their truth, even if the latter cannot be resolved, because we might doubt the usefulness of a false claim (see Mill [1859] 1974: 82). This set of issues could take us far afield, but suffice to say that Mill has subtle things to say that are pertinent to the points raised by Wolff.

Finally, the wider claim in *On Liberty* is that individuals should be free not only to form and discuss opinions, but also, more generally, to live as they wish so long as they don't harm others. Ways of life, like opinions, may make contributions to social progress. Whether or not he deals adequately with the point, Mill's overall approach would support the development of potentially valuable ideas about morality and politics even if they were not strictly true or false.

Religious knowledge

With regard to religious knowledge, Wolff makes the point that traditional Christianity 'promises eternal bliss, and threatens eternal torment' (1968: 13). If, therefore, I think that a particular creed such as this has any chance of being correct, I should hold to it unquestioningly and dogmatically, rejecting secular alternatives and competing faiths, and becoming intolerant and persecutory – or so Wolff claims. This, of course, relates to a more general claim by Wolff that I discussed in the previous chapter: someone with strong, perhaps theocratic, religious commitments might well reject Mill's overall views entirely.

There's a great deal that could be said at this juncture, and I don't want to repeat the points made about religion and religious morality in the previous chapter. Although I could quibble with Wolff at length (e.g. what if I'm choosing between two or more rival religions that offer salvation to adherents and damnation to everyone else?), it's plain enough that there's a tension between Enlightenment liberalism and a religion such as Christianity. Since traditional Christianity claims to be the only path to salvation, it looks aghast at anything that facilitates, or even permits, belief in rival religions (or, of course, outright rejection of religious belief). Not surprisingly, therefore, when Christian organizations gained access to state power during the late Roman Empire they became highly persecutorial of heretics and unbelievers. With eternal salvation and damnation at stake, all other values are overridden.

Following the pressures of history, however, many religious people can now be persuaded that it is not the role of the state – and possibly not the role of private power – to coerce others in matters of religion. If we can agree that the state does not legitimately possess, and/or cannot be trusted with, a role of settling religious issues, one of the great barriers to liberty of discussion thereupon falls.

In Mill's time, this was not a concluded argument in Europe. Mill received much criticism for his temerity in scrutinizing aspects of Christian morality and in viewing such (supposedly certain) doctrines as the existence of God as open to doubt and discussion. Some critics considered it a powerful answer to *On Liberty* to point to divine revelation as an infallible source of knowledge without which there would be no adequate foundation for government and law. Mill discussed religion, and especially Protestant forms of Christianity, with evident respect; but he undoubtedly intended to free up debate on just such topics as the grand claims of religion. Though freedom of religion had made great advances by 1859, Mill's call for complete liberty to discuss such topics still had a radical edge.

A much wider point arises from this. The higher the stakes (as we perceive them), the less likely we'll be to permit our opponents to speak freely. This applies starkly if we believe that immortal souls are at stake or that we are warriors in a cosmic war of good versus evil. But it also applies in more secular contexts: if we believe that our ideas must prevail to address a situation of social and political emergency, we will probably care little for whatever grains of truth can be found in the speech of our opponents.

Artistic freedom

Speech that has little to do with ideas and opinions is relatively peripheral to Mill's thinking in *On Liberty*. Though it is not his entire focus, Mill is primarily concerned with rational inquiry and with intellectual, discursive speech. In large part, *On Liberty* stands as a rebuke to the propensity of governments, others with social power, and of course social opinion at large, to suppress heresy and punish heretics. This remains important today. Mill's emphasis does, however, entail that *On Liberty* is unhelpful – or, rather, less helpful than it might have been – for modern debates over the censorship of novels, plays, films, songs, paintings and photographs, games, and other cultural products.

Mill was familiar with Europe's long history of heresy trials and wars of religion, but he wrote before the twentieth-century disputes about major literary works such as those of James Joyce, D.H. Lawrence, and Henry Miller. We don't know how he'd react to a detailed indictment of literary censorship, such as Edward de Grazia's monumental *Girls Lean Back Everywhere* (1992). In *On Liberty*, Mill does not specifically address the role of art and narrative in expanding human understanding and sympathies. He contemplates that opinions will be expressed fiercely in the heat of public debate, but not how they might be expressed in forms that seek to open our minds by appeals to the imagination.

Any liberal thinker writing in the traditions of the Enlightenment will naturally tend to support artistic freedom. Such a person might readily conclude that interference with art and literature – at least beyond a certain point – is tyrannical. We should, however, acknowledge in passing that Mill was not a defender of erotic expression. According to O'Rourke (2001: 139), he endorsed English obscenity law as it existed in his day (and well into the twentieth century), including the power of the Lord Chamberlain to prohibit plays that jeopardize good manners, decorum, or public peace. This makes sense in the context of *On Liberty*, since these performances do not, at least straightforwardly, amount to expressions of ideas and opinions, and from Mill's perspective they might cause some degree of harm.

Still, this was possibly a personal or cultural blind spot of Mill's. To take up a theme from the previous chapter, unwilling exposure to certain high-impact sights might produce offended feelings of a sufficiently strong kind to count as a form of harm. That being so, it might provide a reason to restrict, for example, sexual acts performed in public. But what about willing exposure to high-impact sights in a theatre that people attend voluntarily? Perhaps there should be some warning of, for example, explicit sexual scenes, but their presence in a theatrical performance will usually be notorious and known to patrons well in advance. In any event, when we attend a play marketed to an adult audience, we should expect to be exposed to emotionally powerful action and dialogue even if we don't know exactly what form they will take.

Mill was not confronted by relentless, philistine censorship of the greatest literature of his age (the story told movingly by de Grazia). In any event, more modern defences of free speech go beyond ideas of free inquiry and discussion. They emphasize the particular importance of language, symbolism, and representation for our lives, and our self-presentation and self-development. This includes the great personal importance of communicating deeply held religious and similar beliefs, but it can also include the importance of self-expression through literature and art.

If we value literature and art as important components of individuality we are likely to take a hostile attitude to their censorship. It is not good enough to allow, say, D.H. Lawrence to express his opinions in discursive form, while censoring his novels and other creative writings. Admittedly, creative literature seldom expresses a straightforward opinion, as opposed to exploring the complexities of issues and provoking thought. But even if Lawrence's novels were straightforwardly didactic, it's not clear that he could have done justice to his viewpoint by writing only discursive prose – nor would his readers have had the same experience if he'd so confined himself. We should resist censorship of literature and art, not only in a spirit of allowing all opinions but also in a spirit of not suppressing individual development through the creation of art and engagement with it.

Finally, Mill himself was not concerned solely with the advance of knowledge, even though that is the main focus of Chapter II of *On Liberty*. He was interested in individual development, intellectual advance, and social progress in a more general sense, and these are values that deeply pervade the traditional liberal project. At one point Mill encourages liberty to live as we please, without harming others, in order to spur progress in 'better taste and sense in human life' ([1859] 1974: 129), and it's a natural step to see the development of literature and art as part of that kind of progress. It's not surprising, then, that successors to Mill's tradition of liberalism have strongly defended artistic freedom.

The foundations of free speech – gathering the reasons

The analysis to this point suggests a number of conclusions. First, there are powerful overlapping arguments for free speech as a basic political principle in any liberal democracy. Mill himself explained the liberty of thought and discussion as contributing to individual and social development mainly through its contribution to a quest for truth and understanding. However, he also saw it as part of a larger freedom to act and speak as we judge fit, provided we don't harm others. He acknowledged the importance of political speech as a bulwark against tyranny, and he valued the freedom to express ourselves as part of our individuality, not to be encroached upon lightly by the tyranny of governments or social opinion. Thus, Mill identified most of the values relied upon in more recent defences of free speech – while certainly emphasizing some more than others.

Second, we should note that freedom of speech is not a simple, absolute, and opaque concept. It is justified by even deeper values. Third, however, these are not wholly independent but overlap to some extent. For example, there is an overlap between freedom for self-actualization's sake and the freedom to discuss deep questions of how we understand the world. The values underlying free speech are closely integrated within an account, such as Mill's, where intellectual and social progress are linked, as are progress at the individual and social levels.

In his careful analysis of the nature of freedom of speech and its possible justifications, Schauer concludes that there is no single argument that carries the day. Rather, there are various acceptable and overlapping arguments that each have a certain amount of force. Schauer is slightly suspicious of Mill's emphasis on a search for truth, but he ultimately gives this argument a degree of support. In doing so, however, he adds a characteristic twist that we can't entrust governments with the role of arbiter of truth: 'The reason for preferring the marketplace of ideas to the selection of truth by the government may be less the proven ability of the former than it is the often evidenced inability of the latter' (Schauer 1982: 34).

On Schauer's approach, then, we should view the suppression of opinions by governments as especially dangerous. While we should be properly sceptical about our own ability 'always to distinguish truth from falsity' we should, as a rule, be even more sceptical about the ability of the government to do so on our behalf (Schauer 1982: 34). Schauer refers to historical experience to suggest that governments are simply bad at censorship: 'They are less capable of regulating speech than they are of regulating other forms of conduct.' Indeed, history shows governments making 'what we now see to be fairly plain errors' including 'the condemnation of Galileo, religious persecution in the sixteenth and seventeenth centuries', persecutions of patriots for allegedly seditious views, and 'the banning of numerous admittedly great works of art because someone thought them obscene' (Schauer 1982: 81).

Many arguments based on ideas of a slippery slope fail (as a starting point, see Blackford 2007), but on Schauer's approach the idea of a slippery slope is more compelling when it comes to freedom of speech. We can see difficulties in drawing clear lines and drafting simple, intelligible rules, and there are psychological pressures to push lawmakers down the slope towards enforced conformity of opinion. As Schauer develops the arguments, people in general feel a desire for unanimity. This may reveal itself especially strongly when it comes to unanimity of actual and communicated opinions. It's likely, for many people, that 'the values of disagreement and challenge are especially counterintuitive' (Schauer 1982: 85). As a result, even democratically elected governments can overreach, attempting to impose an orthodoxy. For Schauer, arguments in support of free speech are to some extent overlapping but also to some extent distinct. Though there is no single decisive argument, the best arguments emphasize a distinction between the individual and the government. They involve a suspicion or distrust of governmental power when it comes to regulating speech:

> Freedom of speech is based in large part on a distrust of the ability of government to make the necessary distinctions, a distrust of governmental determinations of truth and falsity, an appreciation of the fallibility of political leaders, and a somewhat deeper distrust of governmental power in a more general sense. (Schauer 1982: 86)

From this analysis, it follows that the most persuasive argument for a political principle of free speech 'is what may be characterized as the argument from governmental incompetence' (Schauer 1982: 86). We should be distrustful of any government body that is granted 'the authority to decide what is true and what is false, what is right and what is wrong, or what is sound and what is foolish' (Schauer 1982: 34).

Though Schauer makes various specific criticisms of Mill's arguments, his overall approach is consistent with Mill's. Furthermore, both are consistent with the general idea that we need freedom to speak our minds in order to participate meaningfully in democratic deliberation, to pursue knowledge and understanding freely and boldly, to further our own self-development or self-actualization, and to challenge various claims of authority over our lives (and thus protect all our other freedoms). Schauer's key point in addition to all this is his heavy stress on *governmental incompetence* when it comes to regulating what we say and how we express it. Overall, he makes a strong case for resisting government power to censor any kind of speech or expression, perhaps including speech or expression rather remote from Mill's main concerns.

What, however, of non-government efforts and pressures to produce conformity in how we speak and otherwise express ourselves? Here, Schauer's approach diverges clearly from Mill's. We should, I think, side with Mill.

Non-government pressures on speech

Schauer notes that 'To Mill, freedom of speech meant not only freedom from any form of governmental control, but also freedom from private social pressures that could also inhibit thought and opinion' (1982: 113). Mill refers to liberty of thought and discussion or simply 'free discussion' ([1859] 1974: 99), not to 'freedom of speech', but in substance Schauer is correct. Mill was concerned not only with the potential tyranny of governments in controlling how we live and what we say but (even more so) with the tyranny of social opinion.

It's true, of course, that an entrenched protection such as the First Amendment to the US Constitution is useful to hold government power in check, whereas it has no application to the pressures for conformity of thought from employers, religious communities, the mass media, and other non-government sources. Nonetheless, most of our reasons to value candid speech and protect it from governmental censorship remain in play when the desire to express ourselves meets non-government pressures to conform. Likewise, the widespread desire for unanimity – along with the fact that valuing disagreement and challenge so often seems counterintuitive – gives us a reason to distrust non-government as well governmental efforts to restrict speech. The desire for unanimity affects employers, religious communities, the mass media, and many others with views about what expression is acceptable. None of these is necessarily much – or at all – more competent than the government as an arbiter of what we can say and how we can say it.

Schauer correctly points out that not all cases where some kind of speech is locally restricted are, in a pejorative sense, censorship. For example, I might have a political right – a right held against the government – to express my support for astrology or flat-earth theory 'to anyone foolish enough to listen' without having a similar right against my employer. As Schauer points out, 'If I am Professor of Physics at a major university, it is silly to gainsay that such public utterances might validly cause my superiors to wonder if perhaps I am in the wrong line of employment and to take action accordingly' (1982: 119).

But what if I am *not* a physics professor? Imagine that I'm a professor of anthropology, and that I'm not advocating anything as discredited as astrology or flat-earth theory. Rather, I hold certain views about human nature, or about universal tendencies in human societies, that are currently out of fashion in my discipline but remain live options. These views are about as compatible with the evidence as more fashionable ones, and they have never been decisively refuted or definitively rejected within the discipline as a whole. Their current unpopularity is more for political reasons than because of any particular empirical findings that cast doubt on them. What if, in *these* circumstances, my superiors start to wonder whether I am in the wrong line of employment, and they begin to take action accordingly? This looks far less like a routine, socially acceptable personnel decision than does Schauer's example of the professor of physics. Other things being equal – assume that I am a competent teacher, and so on – this is, indeed, looking like censorship in a pejorative sense.

As a further variation, what if I'm booked to speak at a conference on a topic well within my expertise and within the remit of the conference itself? Subsequently, my opponents conduct a campaign seeking that my invitation to speak be rescinded. Under pressure, the conference organizers give in: they do, in fact 'no-platform' me. They tell me that I am no longer invited to speak (I may not even be welcome to attend). Other things being equal – I have not committed some perfidious act in the interim, I have not expressed an intention to speak off the agreed topic, and so on – this exercise in no-platforming does look like a case of censorship in a pejorative sense.

Schauer describes many other circumstances in which people make what seem like legitimate decisions affecting others' speech. They may decline to publish certain items submitted to them for consideration, decide not to permit certain speech on their private or commercial premises, or choose not to associate personally with individuals who have certain views. Intuitively, none of this seems untoward in any way. After all, we are always making choices of this kind, and, as Schauer remarks:

'I cannot invite everyone to my house, I cannot listen to everything, and as editor [of, say, *The Times*] I cannot publish everything' (Schauer 1982: 121). Evidently enough, Schauer is correct. Each of these choices, taken individually, seems intuitively legitimate. But even with the example of *The Times*, we might start to wonder if we changed some details.

What if the mainstream media as a whole, or at least the most revered outlets that play a key role in the political life of a nation, begin systematically excluding certain kinds of views? Imagine that these views are unpopular with proprietors and editors for political reasons rather than because they are empirically untenable and scientifically discredited. Perhaps there's nothing to be done about this situation, if it arises (except, perhaps, to look for other venues to publish the unpopular views in question). And yet, *something* seems not quite right if we ever reach this point.

With other possibilities, the problems are more blatant. For example, it's fine for me to invite like-minded people to my house for dinner, wine, and conversation – and surely it would be oppressive for the government to prevent my acting like this. But what if a powerful lobby group pickets my house in protest at my choice of dinner guests – angry at their views on some controversial issue? What if, as a punishment, it launches a campaign that misrepresents and vilifies me? Alternatively, what if numerous individuals – some with large mainstream media or social media platforms – collaborate to launch such a campaign? This campaign might come complete with false and devastating accusations. Or what if my employer fires me over my choice of whom I associate with outside of working hours? *These* choices don't appear intuitively legitimate. None is a case of government censorship, but I still have grounds to resent what is being done to me. My dinner guests have similar grounds for resentment, especially if this treatment is meted out to *everyone* who invites them into his house.

Thus, contrary to Schauer's line of argument, it is not a straightforward contrast to say that 'private choice is [to some extent] inevitable and government choice often superfluous' (Schauer 1982: 122). It is equally true to state that government choice is, to a large extent, inevitable and private choice is often superfluous. For example, the government and its agencies are often involved in awarding prizes, honours, and grants, based on the ideas and expression of those receiving them. Here, it's inevitable that some will be chosen while others miss out. While the latter might be disappointed, they cannot (unless there's some special circumstance) claim that they are being punished or victimized or that their speech is being suppressed.

Likewise, private choice is very often *not* inevitable. In Schauer's terminology, it is often 'superfluous'. It's inevitable that I invite only some people to my dinner parties, and it's reasonable enough if I prefer to invite like-minded individuals with whom I can easily 'be myself' (with relatively little filtering of what I say or how I act). It is *not*, however, inevitable that I take part in cybermobs, smear campaigns, no-platforming decisions, and the like, punishing individuals for their expression and deterring others from expressing similar viewpoints. It's not a matter of which individuals I choose to treat in these ways. I needn't act like this at all, or I could do so in only the most extreme circumstances involving overriding values.

Many non-government efforts to control the acceptable boundaries of ideas and opinions – and of speech more generally – are perfectly lawful and could not be prohibited without creating more problems than solutions. This makes it impossible to create something like a First Amendment protection against *non*-government abridgments of free discussion and expression. I'm not calling for any such thing. However, some efforts to silence us are, indeed, unlawful: some might, for example, involve crimes, such as acts of violent intimidation; while others might involve contractual breaches. Even where attempts to suppress disliked speech are lawful and cannot safely be made otherwise, we can ask people to undertake voluntarily to resist the urge to suppress opinions and other speech they dislike.

Final thoughts: On terminology and substance

Even if we decided to reserve the expression *freedom of speech* for a constitutionally entrenched freedom from state censorship, we should acknowledge that there are many questionable ways in which non-government power can be used to hinder free inquiry and free discussion of our thoughts, opinions, and ideas. Likewise, non-government power can hinder creative writers and artists, and it can generally hinder the way we present and express ourselves. If, therefore, Jones laments that her employer violated her freedom of speech when he fired her for her political opinions, it's of little help to tell her (perhaps pedantically or perhaps just incorrectly) to use a different phrase instead of *freedom of speech*. Whatever terminology we use, and other things being equal – for example, Jones is a competent employee and her job still has to be performed by *someone* – she has been mistreated.

By all means, then, let's control governmental efforts to suppress speech and punish speakers. But Schauer is not entirely correct when he writes, 'Private intolerance was a worthy object of Mill's attention, but it is a wholly distinct problem from those questions of political philosophy that generate a political principle of freedom of speech' (1982: 122). To say the least, it is not *wholly* distinct.

The government is an especially frightening censor. But non-government methods of suppression and punishment are frightening enough, and they are personally and socially damaging. If we care about the ability of people to live and speak in accordance with their own values, temperaments, opinions, and ideas, and to offer and hear opinions in an environment of free, open discussion, we will not fetishize governmental power – seeing the state as a unique adversary. In his 2014 book *Freedom from Speech*, high-profile free speech activist Greg Lukianoff makes the point well. He distinguishes between First Amendment jurisprudence and what he intends by the phrase *freedom of speech*: a broader idea incorporating a cluster of cultural values. These are all recognizable as themes in Enlightenment liberalism:

> giving the other side a fair hearing, reserving judgment, tolerating opinions that anger or offend us, believing that everyone is entitled to his or her own opinion, and recognizing that even people whose points of view we find repugnant might be (at least partially) right. (Lukianoff 2014: 5–6)

My main concern is with freedom of speech in this cultural sense, which is not to dispute the importance of constitutional provisions and public sentiments restricting strictly governmental censorship. Lukianoff rightly emphasizes that epistemic humility (or epistemic modesty) lies at the heart of free speech. As he puts it, talk of epistemic humility is 'a fancy way of saying that we must always keep in mind that we could be wrong, or at least that we can always learn something by listening to the other side' (2014: 6). In the end, a bit of epistemic humility all round is one of the best defences for free inquiry and discussion of ideas.

None of the analysis in this chapter is meant to deny that some ideas have been shown by experience to be very bad. There may be no merit in trying to protect the worst ideas, such as the racial theories of the Nazis, for posterity – except as cautionary examples. Contrary to Mill, then, perhaps some moral and political opinions are so discredited and dangerous as to be worth hindering in one way or another. But even this has its dangers. If we're going to think this way, that some specific ideas are so exceptionally bad as to merit suppression, we'd better confine the exceptions as narrowly as possible. Once we countenance the possibility that some ideas lie beyond the pale of democratic legitimacy or liberal toleration, there's a natural temptation to enlarge the category and consign the ideas of more and more of our enemies and opponents to it.

In Chapter 4, I'll look more closely at the legitimate limits of speech and the legitimate limits of its suppression. Do we need defamation law? Should we reveal very private information about each other? Should we try to stop hate speech, or at least the worst such speech, such as dehumanizing propaganda? All of this merits further thought.

4 THE LIMITS TO SPEAKING OUR MINDS

Horizons of tolerance

As we've seen, John Stuart Mill's conception of a liberty of thought and discussion is both broader and narrower than many current conceptions of free speech. It is broader than the idea of free speech as a liberty from governmental censorship, since Mill opposes the suppression of ideas and opinions by either government action or social condemnation. At the same time, it's clear enough that Mill is thinking mainly of opinions on rather general issues of, for example, religion, science, morality and politics, philosophy, history, and culture.

Although *On Liberty* does not include any detailed analysis of the abuse of non-government power, it is clear that Mill would oppose private efforts to suppress ideas and opinions or to punish those who advocate them. He proposes an ethic of public discussion in which, in particular, we refrain from condemning individuals with opposed ideas as bad and immoral people. On this approach, we should engage in discussion in a spirit of charity to opponents and their ideas, not overlooking whatever might seem compelling or attractive in their arguments. We should give our praise to honest, fair, charitable discussants, while condemning those with the opposite approach.

Because Chapter II of *On Liberty* is focused mainly on ideas and opinions, and on the freedom to discuss them, its central arguments do not apply to the full range of speech. For example, they have no obvious application to purely commercial advertising aimed at publicizing a product and extolling its quality and value for money (and, under current conditions, probably trying to associate it with sexual pleasure, good clean fun, or happy families). Perhaps there's something to be said for a light hand in censorship even of commercial advertising. But an appreciation of Mill's approach – and especially of what the arguments in Chapter II do *not* cover – illuminates why unregulated commercial advertising does not, intuitively, seem to be central to freedom of speech.

Again, even if we supplement Mill's specific arguments with others that provide more protection for literature and art, this might not take us far in justifying the legality of most pornography – which is surely unoriginal and adds nothing to public discussion of ideas and opinions on general topics. The broader harm principle might nonetheless protect the commercial production and distribution of pornographic material (depending on what harms it can be shown to cause). More generally, arguments based on governmental incompetence might favour protecting even the most meretricious forms of expression from legal prohibition.

My aim, therefore, is not to suggest aggressive censorship of pornography or commercial advertising. The case for either form of censorship would need to be made on its merits, and it might well fail. Commercial advertising has a useful role in the operation of capitalist markets (and some of it has aesthetic value). Pornography has value to those who use it, and most kinds of pornography may be wholly or relatively harmless: I say 'most kinds' because revenge porn and child pornography immediately come to mind as exceptions. Outside those exceptional categories, it might be dangerous to start censoring porn more actively. That way might lie a slope that would lead us back to censorship of James Joyce, D.H. Lawrence, and Henry Miller. But a more modest point remains: protecting pornography and commercial advertising is at least not *central* to free speech concerns.

This distinction is relevant for various forms of speech that arguably should not be protected. They may lie beyond the pale of liberal toleration. In this chapter, I'm concerned with harmful, or potentially harmful, kinds of speech: especially speech that incites, encourages, or lays a foundation for violence, and speech that by its nature harms individuals. I'll especially focus on defamation, invasion of privacy, and material that amounts to hate propaganda.

The scope and strength of protection

As Frederick Schauer points out, the social and personal importance of communication is crucial to our understanding of free speech and the scope of any right that protects it. The use of language is significant, but communication can include expressive noises, visual symbols, various kinds of images, and anything else that is even remotely likely to communicate a message. On this account, then, all communicative elements of conduct are protected by a right to freedom of speech, but non-communicative elements may not be (see Schauer 1982: 99–101). I cannot, for example, convey my dislike of an idea by murdering one of its proponents. I was within my rights to *oppose the idea*, but not by means that directly caused someone harm.

In one sense, freedom of speech is broad in what it covers: communication by a wide range of means. But a right to freedom of speech – perhaps enshrined in a country's constitution – need not be absolute. It might be understood to yield to other considerations if they are very strong in a particular case. For example, the Canadian Charter of Rights and Freedoms contains, among other provisions, constitutional protections from government action against 'freedom of conscience and religion' and 'freedom of thought, belief, opinion and expression, including freedom of the press and other media of communication'. However, all of the Charter's protections are said, in Section 1, to be 'subject only to such reasonable limits prescribed by law as can be demonstrably justified in a free and democratic society'. This places a heavy, but not impossible, burden on the government (whether federal, provincial, or municipal) to justify infringements on the relevant freedoms. It must demonstrate some compelling, overriding interest to the satisfaction of the Canadian courts.

In practice, the courts have struck down some legislation that restricts speech, while saving some legislation by reading it narrowly: treating it as aimed at only the most extreme, and arguably socially dangerous, kinds of speech that could fall within its words. The phrasing of the Charter gives the courts – and ultimately the Supreme Court of Canada – a relatively broad discretion to decide when a restriction on freedom of conscience, religion, thought, belief, opinion, and so on, 'can be demonstrably justified', but the courts appear to have exercised the discretion fairly cautiously. (In any cases where the Canadian courts have been too lenient in allowing exercises of governmental power to abridge speech, they are, of course, open to criticism.)

While I'm somewhat sympathetic to the Canadian model, there's a more general point to be made. We can support freedom of speech on strong grounds – such as those discussed in the previous chapter – without thinking that those grounds override all other considerations whatsoever. The relevance of 'free speech values' will vary with circumstances. In some cases, even our justified suspicion of governmental claims to competence will not be sufficient to rule out legal restrictions on speech.

Paradox explained – defamation and privacy law

At this point, one thing is clear: Mill's arguments provide very limited resources to defend defamatory speech and invasions of personal privacy. Indeed, defamatory and personally invasive speech can themselves be used to punish people for their opinions, so support for Millian free discussion can sometimes give additional justification to restrictions. This might sound paradoxical, but it is easily explained.

If I reply to your opinion on a topic, not with my arguments against it but with a campaign to punish you and deter others from expressing similar opinions, I am not assisting a social environment where it is easier to formulate and discuss our thoughts. The effect might be completely the opposite. Recall that Mill's main goal, or at least the one that he gives most attention in Chapter II of *On Liberty*, was to ensure that ideas and opinions on general topics are not treated as heretical by the law or by society as a whole. This goal is quite different in character from permitting defamatory or invasive attacks on individuals.

At various times during his career as a philosopher, public intellectual, and parliamentarian, Mill turned to the issue of defamatory speech and speech that exposes private conduct to the public gaze. His usual approach was to permit true claims about others, although with reservations about matters not of public interest. In 1834, he even argued against a legislative proposal that would have made truth a defence against libel claims, since he believed that accusations about immoralities performed out of public sight violated the privacy of the person accused (O'Rourke 2001: 35).

For Mill, public discussion in the press (what we would now call trial by media) was not an appropriate procedure to judge such accusations. This was best left to individuals familiar with all aspects of a person's character. At the same time, he viewed privacy as something needed for individual liberty. He foresaw two possible results from a press empowered to pry into our private lives and then rely on a defence of truth. Either most lives would become 'thoroughly artificialized' – as Mill expressed it in a letter to William John Fox – in an attempt to avoid scandalous appearances, or a proliferation of scandal and calumny would undermine the credibility of the press until 'nobody believes anything which appears in print' (see O'Rourke 2001: 35). This was prescient: we've surely reached a point where a mixture of these results is the current reality. We see careful maintenance of their image by almost anybody who is likely to come under the slightest public scrutiny, but at the same time there's widespread, and largely justified, cynicism about the accuracy and fairness of press reports.

In all, the law of defamation (libel and slander) has a legitimate role in our legal system. Most fundamentally, this depends on the fact that we are social animals. Without the good opinion of others in the society where we live, and on which we depend economically and psychologically, whatever freedom we retain is of little value to us. In his groundbreaking book *The Future of Reputation*, Daniel J. Solove points out that our reputations affect our conceptions of ourselves and our ability to engage in even the most basic social activities:

> We depend upon others to engage in transactions with us, to befriend us, and to listen to us. Without the cooperation of others in society, we often are unable to do what we want to do. Without the respect of others, our actions and accomplishments can lose their purpose and meaning. Without the appropriate reputation, our speech, though free, may fall on deaf ears. Our freedom, in short, depends in part upon how others in society judge us. (2007: 31)

Solove accepts that we would not wish people to have complete control of their own reputations. To some extent, we need to gossip about each other and share information on who can be trusted. But nor should we want false negatives about each other's reputations.

In his book *Making the Social World*, John Searle discusses cases where the individual who is the actual target of the speech is harmed by its effects *on other speakers* over which she has no control. This is the case with defamatory speech:

> If you say something hostile *to* me it is in an important sense up to me how much I am hurt by this. But if you say something *about* me, which is entirely false and deliberately and maliciously false, to other

people, this can do great damage to me in a way that is totally out of my control. … It seems to me that the laws of libel and slander, if anything, should be stronger in the United States than they are. (Searle 2010: 191)

Nonetheless, laws relating to defamation must be framed carefully (as narrowly and clearly as practicable) so as not to chill public debate. In the UK, this point was underlined within recent memory by a libel case mounted against popular science writer Simon Singh. This followed an article by Singh in *The Guardian*, published in April 2008. Entitled 'Beware the Spinal Trap', the article criticized the practice and marketing of chiropractic, and, in particular, the attitude of the British Chiropractic Association (BCA):

> The British Chiropractic Association claims that their members can help treat children with colic, sleeping and feeding problems, frequent ear infections, asthma and prolonged crying, even though there is not a jot of evidence. This organisation is the respectable face of the chiropractic profession and yet it happily promotes bogus treatments. (Singh 2008)

In response, the BCA sued Singh for libel and gained a favourable outcome from a preliminary hearing. In a ruling issued in May 2009, the presiding judge held that Singh's phrasing meant that (as an assertion of fact, not a matter of opinion) the BCA, through its officials, knowingly promoted treatments for which there was no supporting evidence (see *British Chiropractic Association v. Simon Singh* [2009] EWHC 1101 QB). In elaborating, the judge held that the imputation was of plain, knowing dishonesty about what were merely quack remedies. Since the truth of such imputations would be almost impossible to prove in further proceedings, Singh, as defendant in the case, was placed in an untenable position.

In the end, however, he prevailed. In April 2010, he won an appeal heard by the England and Wales Court of Appeal (*British Chiropractic Association v. Dr Singh* [2011] 1 WLR 133). This gave him the right to defend his words as fair comment or honest opinion. The BCA withdrew its claim, and in response to these events English libel law was amended by Parliament to make it more difficult to sue over such disputes. Among the reforms enacted by the Defamation Act 2013, plaintiffs were henceforth required to demonstrate serious harm from the alleged defamation. Nonetheless, Singh's life was turned upside down and his case highlighted the dangerous power of defamation law.

We should be suspicious about *any* government restrictions on what we can say – recall, once again, Schauer's important point about governmental incompetence. As the philosopher and legal scholar Brian Leiter notes in a related context, 'Government actors have too many obvious incentives to overreach in placing restrictions on speech' (2010: 155). In principle, nonetheless, the law of defamation has an important role. What, for example, if a sceptic of chiropractic treatments had falsely accused certain BCA officials of paedophilia – perhaps as a way of discrediting them in public debate? In such circumstances, a lawsuit for defamation would be entirely justified. The point is not to abolish defamation law entirely, but to keep it in its place.

In the United States, the Supreme Court once viewed defamation as lying outside the protection of the First Amendment because it was not essential to the exposition of ideas. This has a certain logic – at least superficially, it sits well with the arguments in *On Liberty*. However, the legal position changed in 1964, with the landmark case of *New York Times v. Sullivan* (376 U.S. 254 (1964)). This constrained the legal ability of public figures to sue for defamation: in the United States they must now prove *actual malice* in the sense of proving the defendant's knowledge that an imputation is untrue, or at least proving the defendant's reckless disregard for its truth or falsity.

The operative policy here is to provide a margin of safety for harsh criticism of public officials and others who wield political power. Rather than chill such criticism by letting it be easy to sue, the American courts will allow publication of inaccurate criticisms that were made without knowing or reckless falsehood. Thus, some damaging untruths are given legal protection as a price for the press's historical role in resisting tyrannical government. This is all salutary. As Anthony Lewis, the great legal journalist, points out in *Freedom for the Thought That We Hate*, the result in *New York Times v. Sullivan* emboldened American reporters to challenge official truth – leading to the 'penetrating coverage of the Vietnam war and Watergate' (2007: 56).

But Lewis questions subsequent developments in American law, whereby celebrities – such as movie stars – and ordinary people who have thrust themselves into public controversy (perhaps over merely local issues) must also prove actual malice. As a result, they have lost much of the protection of defamation law. Lewis asks why, if the press publishes 'a sensational story about a movie actress', she should meet the same test as a powerful politician. He adds: 'What does she have to do with what the *Sullivan* decision called "the central meaning of the First Amendment," the right to criticize government officials?' (Lewis 2007: 57). This development in American law seems far less salutary. It should be reconsidered by the courts, and I hope it will not be followed in non-US jurisdictions.

Invasion of privacy

There is a more direct clash between free speech and privacy law than between free speech and defamation law, since with the former the information may be true (Solove 2007: 126–7). If so, the law can operate to censor the truth. However, Solove argues that privacy – and with it a properly framed public disclosure tort – serves many of the same interests as the idea of free speech. For example, invasions of our privacy, with subsequent publicity given to our private behaviour, can harm our autonomy (or self-actualization, to use my language from the previous chapter) by intimidating us into avoiding socially taboo activities and keeping quiet, even in private, about our grievances and unpopular ideas. Invasions of privacy and subsequent public disclosures can inhibit our formation of views on topics that arise for democratic deliberation. And of course, much information about people's private lives is of no worth to any quest for truth or understanding related to general issues.

Solove examines how the disclosure of private information about other individuals might not necessarily enable more accurate judgements about them. Indeed, it can lead to misunderstandings of their circumstances and misjudgements about their characters. In response to a view (attributed to American jurist Richard Posner) that concealing information about ourselves is like concealing product defects, Solove insists, 'People are far more complex than products. Knowing certain information, especially out of the context of deeper familiarity with the person, can distort judgment of another person rather than increase its accuracy' (Solove 2007: 66).

All this seems correct. For example, if I were a gay man living within a milieu where homosexual conduct is regarded as sinful, others' knowledge of my sexuality might be highly prejudicial when they decide whether they can trust me in, say, joint business ventures. In many settings, the same might apply to almost any unconventional sexual interests. Even if they are not regarded as forms of wickedness, they might at least be seen as indications of someone who shouldn't be taken seriously. Even our tastes in books, movies, or television programmes might sometimes place us in a false light. As Solove states, some facts can be especially stigmatizing, for example facts about 'addiction, alcoholism, suicide attempts, mental disorders, unemployment, and illiteracy' (2007: 70). Likewise, he adds, for certain diseases such as AIDS, and, in a different way, cancer.

Privacy is not a straightforward concept. It is 'a complicated set of norms, expectations, and desires that goes far beyond the simplistic notion that if you're in public you have no privacy' (Solove 2007: 166). We all have complex and multifaceted personalities, and the self that we present in any particular setting will be 'shaped by the roles we play'; and thus, because much of this is widely (if not explicitly) understood, 'society recognizes and accepts that the public self is a partly fictional construct' (Solove 2007: 69).

Solove discusses cases of video voyeurism, such as surreptitious upskirt photographs, photos of naked athletes in locker rooms, and photos of nude festival goers in settings such as the Burning Man Festival. In all these cases, the setting might not be strictly private – if we used a binary conception of private and public – but there are legitimate, if nuanced, social expectations of being accorded a degree of privacy. Inevitably, this raises difficult questions for the law. It is difficult to develop a flexible and fine-grained conception of privacy, but there is a 'wide swath of middle ground between the realms of absolutely private and absolutely public' (Solove 2007: 170).

The precise drafting of the law is difficult in an area like this, but there is theoretical room, recognized even in American law with its broad interpretation of the First Amendment, for a public disclosure tort. That is, we need a closely defined right to sue for non-newsworthy speech that discloses private facts of a kind that most people would experience as deeply violating. The law might employ an expression such as 'highly offensive to a reasonable person', but the high-level offence involved would not be merely intense annoyance. Rather, it is the experience of having the curtain torn away from deeply private matters, exposing them to the public gaze.

Hulkster versus Gawker

Large media organizations provide forums for discussion of important topics, and they should enjoy broad freedom from government interference. But media organizations can themselves be enforcers of conformity. They can hurt nonconforming individuals by telling lies about them, by exposing small foibles (previously known to just a few people or to a limited group), or by intruding deeply into private lives.

Let's consider a controversial example. In March 2016, a Florida jury awarded $140 million to the professional wrestler Hulk Hogan (real name Terry Bollea) in court proceedings against Gawker Media and several related defendants. This extraordinary sum was eventually negotiated down in November of the same year to the lesser (but still huge) figure of 'only' $31 million. The settlement involved the defendants' abandoning their right to appeal, and the case can now be regarded as closed.

There is a separate issue – beyond the scope of the present discussion – relating to awards of crushing sums as legal damages. This applies to any court case where the damages are out of proportion to whatever harm can be identified. But with that caveat, the outcome in favour of Hogan was, I submit, correct in principle. The court awarded him compensatory and punitive damages for online publication, by the gossip blog Gawker, of a tape showing him having sex with his one-time friend Heather Clem. The effect was to bankrupt Gawker Media and to destroy Gawker itself, all of which produced much hand-wringing in the wider press and on social media platforms. Many commentators treated the case as a threat to freedom of speech or freedom of the press, but we ought to be sceptical about this. If what we primarily care about is liberty of thought and discussion, where is the problem? Perhaps the award should have been smaller, which might have allowed Gawker to survive and publish whatever material it wanted that actually had social value. But its invasive treatment of Hogan's life added nothing to political deliberation or to public discussion of topics of general importance.

This provides an example of how expressions such as *freedom of speech* and *freedom of the press* can become little more than slogans. Rather than seeing the Hogan–Gawker conflict simply as state censorship of Gawker, via the courts, we'd do better to ask whether we really want wealthy media organizations deciding on the guilt or innocence of individuals accused of crimes, or even of non-criminal but deeply stigmatized behaviour.

When the news media, including online gutter-press outlets such as Gawker, set themselves up as investigators, prosecutors, and judges of real or imagined wrongdoings, that can be unfair and socially dangerous. Unfortunately, many well-meaning people took the stance of announcing 'I Stand With Gawker'. In May 2016, those words were used for the title of a *New York Times* op-ed by Stephen Marche, a novelist and contributing editor to *Esquire*. They even became a Twitter hashtag.

Part of the sympathy for Gawker arose from the fact that Peter Thiel, a controversial Silicon Valley billionaire, was revealed to be funding Hogan's litigation. Thiel had, himself, been treated harshly by Gawker, creating an appearance that he was supporting litigation against it as a means of revenge – and he probably was. An obvious fear when immensely wealthy individuals such as Thiel underwrite lawsuits is that this will itself send a silencing message: that they can exact revenge on media outlets even when they don't have plausible legal claims themselves. There is a need to be vigilant about how individuals such as Thiel employ their wealth, possibly to silence debate on important topics.

In this instance, however, Thiel did nothing so unscrupulous. In funding Hogan's claim against a cashed-up and determined defendant, he made the legal system more accessible to someone with a strong case that he'd been legally wronged. If anything, the problem here is that even someone like Hogan – himself a successful and wealthy man – needed help from someone like Thiel to pursue his claim.

Incitements and dehumanization

Setting aside defamatory or invasive attacks on individuals, one possible limit to the general liberty of thought and discussion appears in Mill's famous example of the corn dealer and the 'excited mob' assembled in front of his house (Mill [1859] 1974: 119). According to Mill, the opinion that corn dealers are starvers of the poor should be permitted expression in the regular press. If, however, it's delivered to the excited mob it might instigate immediate violence – and that can merit social condemnation or a legal remedy. Thus, Mill is allowing as much liberty as he believes safe. He sets the boundary for socially and legally tolerable speech at a point where speech is merging into action: there is, at this point, an immediate danger of violence with little to be done about it. It is too late for persuasion or reflection, since an attack on the corn dealer or his property might be imminent.

While this seems reasonable, it might not always provide a straightforward solution to current social problems. There are now many circumstances that fall within a grey area between vituperative remarks in the mass media and outright demagoguery that might incite a potentially violent mob. What if a newspaper prints, instead of a merely vituperative remark about corn dealers in general, a call to assassinate a specific person? What if there's a public campaign to exterminate corn dealers, or some other hated group, as a class of wrongdoers, public enemies, or worse? What if that call is from a political demagogue or – perhaps even worse, because he is even more likely to have fanatical acolytes – a revered religious authority? Think of the notorious death sentence pronounced on Salman Rushdie in 1989 by the Ayatollah Khomeini (see Chapter 7 for more). What if the call for murder and extermination is not printed in a newspaper but goes viral on the internet? Or what if it is not a single article, but instead a hate campaign conducted day after day via radio broadcasts and other media?

Before we lose perspective, we should *not* adopt an idea that the state may ban any and all speech that might tend, through whatever direct or indirect processes, to cause hostility or violence. This could affect a vast range of intuitively legitimate speech including many holy books. If promulgating certain ideas encourages hostility by a relatively indirect and uncertain process, we might need to combat the tendency with better speech and other more subtle means than prohibitions. But in some cases, we really might have reason to act more assertively. It should be clear that calls to violence don't have to be physically proximate to a potential violent event before they meet the spirit of Mill's corn dealer example. Communications from afar involving Grand Ayatollahs in foreign countries can create imminent and specific dangers for individuals such as Rushdie and his associates. Public policy should reflect this current reality.

We might also consider the effects of the worst racial hate speech, and one good place to start is David Livingstone Smith's challenging volume *Less than Human*. Smith describes how hate speech can exploit a human propensity to view people from other places and cultures as something ersatz human and so (inevitably) subhuman. Once we're in the grip of this way of thinking and speaking, we can readily come to see others as demons or predators, as quarry to be hunted, as interchangeable cattle, or (worst of all) as vermin: often as snakes, rats, spiders, or cockroaches. Applied to a whole group of people, dehumanization is often 'a prelude and accompaniment to extreme violence' (Smith 2011: 13). The dehumanized group is usually understood in racial terms and identified by facial features (the shape of the eyes, lips, and nose) and skin colour. But its markers can also include clothing, customs, beliefs, and other cultural features. Dehumanization can even be applied to hated professions and social classes, as with the Soviet extermination of the Kulaks – independent farmers or relatively affluent peasants (Smith 2011: 147–8).

Dehumanization goes much further than seeing a group of people as opponents or enemies. Opponents and enemies can sometimes attract our charity and gain our admiration even as we criticize them, oppose them, or fight with them. Once effectively dehumanized, people are viewed as not really human at all, despite appearances, and hence they deserve no better treatment than we'd give dangerous predators to be hunted down or vermin to be exterminated: 'To the Nazis, Jews weren't just nonhumans; they were rats in human form. And to the *genocidaires* of Rwanda, Tutsis were cockroaches' (Smith 2011: 223). When hated groups are perceived as fake human beings, this makes them seem all the more dangerous and sinister.

There's much that's rhetorically attractive in the claim that no ideas should be seen as heretical or beyond the pale of toleration. But we might wonder how literally to take this when we think of the idea that certain groups of people in our midst are fake humans and vermin. This seems like it might be an exceptional case.

In the seventeenth century, John Locke suggested that some beliefs are especially subversive of the social order and can rightly be suppressed by the state (not on any theological grounds, but because these beliefs seemed, to Locke, incompatible with the functioning of society itself). On this approach, the state could legitimately suppress denial of the existence of God and an afterlife, as well as such doctrines as that citizens need not keep promises, that princes can be dethroned if they differ from the 'correct' religion, that the speaker has a claim to dominion of all things, that faith should not be kept with heretics, and that joining the speaker's – and hence the 'correct' – religion requires accepting subjection to a foreign power (Locke [1689] 1983: 49–51).

Locke's examples might not be good ones, and Mill deals rather robustly with the first two that I've mentioned ([1859] 1974: 90–3).

But perhaps Locke was correct that we can't tolerate simply *all* views, no matter how extreme and potentially subversive. Viewpoints based upon – and advocating – racial enmity might be good candidates for what lies outside the limits of legitimate speech in a contemporary liberal democracy. Historical experience suggests that people might be especially, and irrationally, inclined towards these sorts of views (compare Schauer 1982: 28), and we know the horror that can result. A society in which some people are widely regarded as vermin is already endangered. If it is nonetheless stable, this might be at the expense of a class of people who are atrociously oppressed.

It's an explosive mix when extreme racial viewpoints are expressed with viscerally powerful dehumanizing language and images. Even when this is not aimed at inciting specific acts of violence, it is likely, as Smith puts it, to be the prelude and accompaniment to violence. All of this gives us reason to take dehumanizing hate propaganda very seriously, and to condemn it with the utmost severity. Whether we should go further, and try to prohibit it by law, is another question.

Responding to hate

In his fascinating memoir *Defending My Enemy* (1979), Aryeh Neier, a distinguished civil liberties activist of Jewish heritage, explains why he was prepared to defend the right of Nazis to march in Skokie, Illinois, in 1977. Skokie is a largely Jewish suburb of Chicago, and at the time many of its residents were either survivors of the Nazi Holocaust or closely related to Holocaust survivors. Neier writes movingly of the Holocaust and its impact on Jewish people in the United States and elsewhere, including the widespread sentiment expressed by many Jews and others that such a thing must never happen again. One completely understandable Jewish viewpoint was that all signs of a Nazi resurgence must be stopped at the very earliest stage, including by stopping the Nazis' marches and propaganda efforts.

Neier's own view, as expressed in *Defending My Enemy*, is rather different: that anything short of absolute freedom of speech, or at least of political speech and protest, is not in the best interests of Jews as a unique and uniquely vulnerable group. Otherwise, on this view, the likelihood is that any restrictions will be used against persecuted Jews just when they are needed.

Neier includes a brief chapter on the history and fall of the Weimar Republic, often seen as an example of the destructive power of racial hate propaganda if it is allowed to flourish. However, it was also a society torn apart by the bitter experience of defeat in the First World War, and by ongoing political violence on an extraordinary scale, with many assassinations carried out by right-wing paramilitary organizations and a somewhat smaller number by left-wing groups such as the Spartacists. The former, at least, went largely unpunished or derisorily punished. Adolf Hitler himself was punished only leniently after his failed beer hall putsch in Munich in 1923. The Weimar Republic enforced its laws against offensive speech with some aggression, but this did nothing to halt the ascension of the Nazis to power (even as it harmed great artists and literary figures such as George Grosz and Bertolt Brecht).

The lesson that Neier draws is not that laws are needed against hate propaganda. Rather: 'The lesson of Germany in the 1920s is that a free society cannot be established and maintained if it will not act vigorously and forcefully to punish political violence' (Neier 1979: 167).

There is much that can be said for and against the idea that narrowly drafted and prudently enforced laws against dehumanizing propaganda, in particular, could play a useful role in combating racial division and violence. In the end, I am willing to support laws that prohibit the worst kinds of racial hate propaganda, but only with doubts and reservations. These laws bring their own risks, and they should at least be used sparingly. An obvious danger, as suggested by accounts such as Neier's (and see also Borovoy 1988: 40–53), is that putting Nazis and other hatemongers on trial may prove ineffectual or worse. It can even amplify their speech and turn them into martyrs. It might be more effective if their language were met with social disdain, cautionary analysis as part of children's education, and perhaps a panoply of relatively unobtrusive legal and social norms, such as broadcasting standards (whether imposed by governments or adopted by broadcasters as voluntary codes).

I'm not sure that there is a single correct answer as to where we should draw the line on hate speech, or how we should word any prohibitions if we decide, after due reflection, that they are wise. The best answers might vary from one jurisdiction to another, and they might depend on the current, local circumstances. Reasonable minds will probably differ in weighing the considerations and deciding exactly what ought to be done.

Whatever laws are drafted must, however, be as clear as possible and as narrowly focused as the circumstances permit. In principle, speech that incites or prepares the way for violence is a fair target for legal prohibitions; however, administration and enforcement of the law will need to be discerning. Any prosecutions would need to be aimed at truly serious dehumanization of vulnerable groups, both to reflect the policy behind the law and to avoid bringing the law into disrepute. Notice, for example, that not all animal metaphors, when we're speaking of opponents, enemies, or simply people with whom we're currently angry, are seriously dehumanizing in the sense under discussion. There's an enormous gulf between describing a stubborn person as pig-headed (or even describing a random obnoxious person as a pig) and churning out the incessant anti-Tutsi propaganda that was broadcast in Rwanda in 1994. The latter portrayed the Tutsis as snakes and cockroaches to be exterminated, and it played a crucial role in the genocidal massacres in which 800,000 Tutsis were killed.

There is always a danger in regarding opinions as, in themselves, beyond the pale of toleration. Once we identify even one class of formally proscribed views, rival ideologues engaged in culture warring can be expected to expand that class or to identify other classes that they argue are 'just as bad' or, by a particular ideologue's lights, 'really even worse'. The more we attempt to expand the range of what are regarded as intolerable views, the more illiberal we become: the more we look like petty authoritarians, rather than genuine liberals and successors to the Enlightenment and John Stuart Mill. Hence, understandable pressures to establish seriously dehumanizing speech as beyond the pale of toleration must be accompanied by a counterpressure to define the categories of proscribed speech as narrowly and precisely as is practical for the needs of society.

The dangers of proscribing speech

Unfortunately, it can be tempting to seek legal bans and social intolerance for viewpoints that we merely dislike (this is a theme of Lukianoff's *Freedom from Speech*, 2014). In twenty-first-century circumstances, the temptation applies especially to viewpoints on community relations, gender issues (broadly understood), immigration, cultural practices, and religious beliefs. Though these are complex and sensitive topics, even heated debate over them is, in itself, perfectly legitimate.

For example, some cultures may be more resistant than others to liberal principles such as individual liberty and (in its various senses) freedom of speech. Some may be more racist, harshly patriarchal, sexually puritanical, homophobic, militaristic, inclined to glorify interpersonal violence, or otherwise unpleasant than others. Some may favour harmful practices such as feuds, vendettas, seclusion of women, or female genital mutilation. These are all legitimate issues to think about and discuss with others. Likewise, some religions may be greater threats to individual liberty than others, whether because they have harsher moral codes, because they're more inclined to impose their sectarian views through state power, or more generally because they have been less 'tamed' by historical events. Many religions have socially dangerous or regressive tendencies, and it can be quite rational to worry about these and to discuss them.

It would help, no doubt, if all such discussions were conducted with grace and civility. But such topics arouse strong emotions, and feelings may run high on more than one side of an argument. In any case, even the calmest speech on such topics is likely to bruise feelings and provoke suspicions. That is simply part of robust public debate; it should not be used as a test of whether or not certain speech is beyond the pale of toleration.

Overly protective laws, attempting to suppress merely offensive, upsetting, or disliked speech, lend themselves to abuse. Important conversations, and important contributions to them, can be shut down, at least locally, and disliked ideas can be driven out of the local public square. One prominent example in recent years was the unhappy saga relating to *The Hindus: An Alternative History*, a book by American scholar Wendy Doniger. It was first published by Viking Penguin in 2008, and an edition was later released by Penguin India. This met with criticism that rose to the level of outrage.

Doniger was at the time – and still is – a major international contributor to the field of Indology. She is the Mircea Eliade Distinguished Service Professor of History of Religions at the University of Chicago. In short, she is a highly respected academic with a long and impressive record of teaching and publication. Although it is innovative, and perhaps iconoclastic in some respects, *The Hindus* is a serious, deeply researched scholarly tome. When I read it for myself, I found it fascinating, and I can testify that it does not deal with its topic in a mocking or derogatory way. (There's a certain amount of gentle humour enlivening its prose, but that's all. It is not obvious, in any event, why religions should be protected from mockery, satire, or severe criticism by authors less sympathetic to them than Doniger.)

The Hindus aroused the anger of right-wing (Hindu nationalist) groups in India, and in early 2010 the activist Dinanath Batra served a legal notice on Penguin India and the US-based Penguin Group. In 2011, Batra and other petitioners commenced a lawsuit invoking section 295A of the Indian Penal Code, which relevantly provides for criminal punishment of anyone deliberately and maliciously outraging religious feelings:

> Whoever, with deliberate and malicious intention of outraging the religious feelings of any class of citizens of India, by words, either spoken or written, or by signs or by visible representations or otherwise, insults or attempts to insult the religion or the religious beliefs of that class, shall be punished with imprisonment of either description for a term which may extend to three years, or with fine, or with both.

We might expect that the high-level mental element in this legal offence (the high level of *mens rea* or guilty mind) would make it difficult to obtain convictions for breach of section 295A. It is difficult to prove something as strong as 'deliberate and malicious intention'. This wording even goes beyond the concept of actual malice, which is so difficult to prove in American defamation cases brought by public figures. In practice, however, even with this *mens rea* component, s. 295A creates a chilling effect on speech and expression in India. The chill extends as far as scholarly speech. Penguin ultimately settled the case in early 2014 by withdrawing the book from the Indian market and pulping all remaining copies within the jurisdiction. In late 2015, *The Hindus* was republished in India by Speaking Tiger, an independent press.

As so often in such cases, the author concerned may have ended up selling more copies of her book than she'd have done otherwise. Speaking for myself, I bought and read a copy partly out of a sense of supporting Doniger and partly to see at first hand what the fuss was about. Whether or not the legal proceedings and their outcome produced overall economic loss to the author and her publisher is unclear, but that is not the most important point. Even if Doniger and Penguin came out ahead as a result of the book's notoriety, cases such as this can intimidate other authors and publishers that might not be so well resourced (as Penguin), daring (as Speaking Tiger), or renowned and well established (as Doniger).

Whether a book such as *The Hindus* could be stopped in its tracks in other countries depends not only on the local legislation but also the attitudes of local judges, government officials, and the general population. I can't imagine the book meeting such a fate in the United Kingdom or Australia (and it certainly could not in the United States), but it should again be emphasized that the Indian legal provision invoked against Doniger was not especially adverse to the tactical position of defendants. Despite this, Penguin elected to settle on seemingly unfavourable terms. In many other cases, in a wide range of jurisdictions, legitimate speech on topics of political or general interest has been punished or hindered by one or another form of legal action.

The moral of this story is not that the state must totally keep out of regulating speech that involves religious, racial, cultural, and similar sensitivities. There is no knock-down argument for that, and some of this speech is grounded in forms of hostility that can rise in intensity to the worst kinds of racism. Hostility to foreigners and foreign cultures, and to other people's religions, can reveal ignorance, irrational fear, unthinking tribalism, and callous attitudes to anyone who is seen as Other. All of this merits critique, but there must be some margin for it to happen or much legitimate speech will be chilled or unfairly punished. The moral of the story, then, is that any restrictions on offensive speech or speech on sensitive topics must be scrutinized constantly. This includes the way laws are drafted and the way they're interpreted and applied in practice. If we're going to have these laws at all, we need to keep them focused on the worst hate propaganda.

A need for vigilance

As must be said again and again, governments are dangerous when they start to restrict our speech, but they are not uniquely incompetent censors. Indeed, the government may have a valuable role in deterring the worst forms of defamation, invasive speech, and dehumanizing speech that incites or lays the groundwork for violence. There may be other categories where government involvement is, all things considered, needed or desirable, but the dangers should prompt us to suspicion of any laws that restrict what we can think and say. It's imperative that we continually scrutinize, challenge, and rein in government censorship.

At the same time – and this should also be said again and again – we have reasons to scrutinize and challenge *non*-government constraints on our speech. We should worry about any overly broad or zealous social responses to speech that some dislike or find upsetting. Non-government attacks on people, ideas, and cultural products can chill opinion and creativity. Many social forces and participants in society enforce one or another kind of conformity through subtle or not-so-subtle means. We should keep these under scrutiny, expose them to wider discussion, and, as and when needed, object to them strongly.

If we take this approach, we might disappoint absolutists about freedom from government intervention in speech, though in practice – at least in jurisdictions outside the United States, with its unique approach among liberal democracies – we'll usually be seeking to narrow, rather than to extend, current speech restrictions. We might also disappoint those who support a plethora of government and non-government constraints on offensive speech.

It seems that more and more people, especially in younger generations, now support substantial legal and other formal restrictions on speech that they dislike. They can be very aggressive about this view, and some regard free speech advocacy as itself politically suspect. In this environment, free speech advocates, no matter how conscientious, well informed, cogent, and sympathetic to others they may be, can expect accusations of bigotry or secret agendas. At best, they'll be accused of insensitivity and cluelessness. These suspicions and accusations may, unfortunately, be the price we have to pay. Often, the only alternative is remaining silent about unfair treatment of individuals, illiberal social developments, and an anti-liberal trend that's apparent in much left-wing or (revisionist) liberal thought.

5 CONFORMITY AND ITS LIMITS

Conformity, pro and con

In *Making the Social World*, John Searle observes that there seems to be a 'human urge to conform, to be like other people and to be accepted by them as a member of the group' – and this provides our motivation to accept the institutions and conventions that constitute our social reality (2010: 108). In large part, the urge is benign, and human societies could not function without it. In many situations some convention must be agreed on, whether it's the values assigned to coins and notes in the local currency or an authoritative rule about the correct side of the road to drive on.

Conformity does, however, have a downside. It lends itself to tribalism, to punishment of harmless (or even socially helpful) nonconformists, and to demands for unnecessarily uniform speech and action. In most cases, alas, conformity does not involve reservations and discernment. That is, it does not combine general acceptance of the group's attitudes, beliefs, and ways of acting and speaking with selective areas of doubt or dissent. Individual conformity to a group's values and practices tends to be all or nothing. Individuals within a group tend to develop a tacit consensus on what it looks like to be a prototypical group member. Each member will be more accepted, trusted, and rewarded to the extent that she resembles the prototype. More marginal or peripheral group members – those who diverge from the prototype for whatever reason – are highly vulnerable:

> They will be viewed as deviants and outcasts rather than people who simply have different opinions and behave in different ways within the group. Diversity is translated into deviance and pathology. (Hogg 2005: 251)

There are penalties for thinking independently, whereas there are social rewards for becoming as much as possible like the prototype – and particularly for imitating the views and behaviours of the group's leaders. Strangely or not, marginal members are sometimes the most zealous in enforcing the group's norms, 'the most fiercely intolerant of normative diversity' (Hogg 2005: 253), although some do eventually disaffiliate from the group. Pressures to conformity in ideas and opinions, including the exclusion of some individuals, produce harmful outcomes for the group itself – most obviously when potentially valuable ideas are rejected or useful knowledge is kept hidden. Rejection of individuals by the group harms those rejected, of course, and the consequences may ripple out if (as is likely) rejected members become hostile:

> The experience of social exclusion makes people hostile and aggressive. Rejection intensifies the typical aggressive responses following provocation, but it also instigates aggressive responses in the absence of any provocation. When people are alienated and excluded from the social community the results are harmful, not only to those individuals but to the community at large. (Catanese and Tice 2005: 305)

Roy F. Baumeister and Mark R. Leary are the authors of an important article that examines what they see as a fundamental human need to participate in groups and to seek close relationships. Their main emphasis is on the value of frequent close contact, but they also stress the devastating psychological impact of exclusion and loneliness:

> A general pattern may well be that cultures use social inclusion to reward, and exclusion to punish, their members as a way of enforcing their values. As is well known, many early civilizations equated exile with death, which seems to suggest that life is desirable only within the network of close relationships to which the person belongs. (Baumeister and Leary 1995: 521)

Conformity is driven by a variety of factors, and research continues in the social sciences to establish precisely how these interact and in what circumstances. Conformity is obtained, in part, through all of the following:

1 Socialization of children to accept local values and beliefs;
2 Patterns of emotional manipulation and propaganda;

3 The genuine superiority of certain methods over others;

4 The social need to solve coordination problems (and stick with solutions);

5 A seemingly innate human tendency to conform; and, of course,

6 The use of inducements and punishments (whether formal or otherwise).

In most cases, punishments need be no more than expressions of disapproval, but these can escalate to denigration, shaming, ostracism, and formal legal sanctions.

As usual with topics such as this, John Stuart Mill had something important to say. In *On Liberty*, he complains that even social reformers seek conformity and dislike individual spontaneity:

> spontaneity forms no part of the ideal of the majority of moral and social reformers, but is rather looked on with jealousy as a troublesome and perhaps rebellious obstruction to the general acceptance of what these reformers, in their own judgement, think would be best for mankind. ([1859] 1974: 120–1)

Conformity and cascades

In an influential article on the mechanisms of conformity, Sushil Bikhchandani and his collaborators acknowledge the factors usually identified in the academic literature. However, they invoke 'informational cascades' as an additional and powerful mechanism to explain the phenomenon of localized conformity (the tendency towards uniform social behaviour in any particular place and time) and what they call 'the fragility of mass behaviors'. They observe that most factors postulated as mechanisms for conformity suggest that it would take a rigid form, yet in practice 'mass behavior is often fragile in the sense that small shocks can frequently lead to large shifts in behavior' (Bikhchandani, Hirshleifer and Welch 1992: 993).

As defined by Bikhchandani, Hirshleifer, and Welch, an informational cascade takes place 'when it is optimal for an individual, having observed the actions of those ahead of him, to follow the behavior of the preceding individual without regard to his own information' (1992: 994). If, for example, I am asked to review a paper for possible publication in an academic journal I might have regard (if I somehow find out) to the fact that it was rejected by a previous journal. If a reviewer at the next journal (somehow) discovers that the paper has been rejected twice, that can look like strong evidence of its low quality, and so we are into a cascade of decisions, as successive decision makers rely on their knowledge of what was decided by earlier decision makers.

If teenagers are deciding whether or not to experiment with drugs, 'A strong motive for experimenting ... is the fact that friends are doing so. Conversely, seeing friends reject drugs could persuade a youth to stay clean' (Bikhchandani, Hirshleifer and Welch 1992: 994). And so, a sequence of decisions can take on a life of its own, irrespective of the merits (viewed from outside the sequence as a whole) of the earliest decisions. Later decision makers in the sequence are not acting irrationally in using earlier decisions as evidence – this is cogent evidence of a sort – but their decisions will not necessarily be the best for the purpose at hand, or for meeting independent criteria of merit. Cascades can, in other words, 'often be mistaken' (Bikhchandani, Hirshleifer and Welch 1992: 995).

In the upshot, confident, well-informed opinion leaders wield enormous influence. If, as is likely in practice, they make decisions early in a sequence, they will be followed by less confident individuals. In the (perhaps unusual) circumstances that they are late entering the sequence, they may rely more than others on their own information and be able to shatter a cascade. Cascades can also be shattered by other means, such as when new information is disclosed to the public.

To the extent that informational cascades operate through individuals – 'especially those [individuals] with little information or experience' – looking for guidance from the decisions of others, the mechanism is not coercive (Bikhchandani, Hirshleifer and Welch 1992: 1013). However, individuals who are judged negatively at some stage in a sequence of judgements may be unfairly stigmatized. An example is a job applicant who is turned down by employers based partly on the information that she was turned down by earlier employers; she may thus become unemployable even though she is well qualified and competent. Conversely, 'a job applicant who receives early job offers' might receive 'star' status without necessarily possessing any extraordinary merit (Bikhchandani, Hirshleifer and Welch 1992: 1014). And so, cascades provide one mechanism that tends towards conformity.

Loury on political conformity

In a much-discussed 1994 article ('Self-Censorship in Public Discourse: A Theory of "Political Correctness" and Related Phenomena'), American economist Glenn C. Loury examines the mechanisms of political conformity: in particular, conformity to political ideas and language. He explains a pernicious logic whereby a policy or way of speaking can take on symbolic significance. Any opposition to policies that are currently favoured by the group will be interpreted as dissent from the group's values – revealing the dissenter as an apostate and as likely sharing the despised values of an out-group. This creates a pressure to self-censor any doubts, with the further effect that only those who really do reject the value system of the in-group are likely to express whatever doubts they have. The rest of us keep our silence or speak insincerely.

Even factual claims can become fetishes or shibboleths, whether or not they are actually true. An example mentioned by economist and political scientist Timur Kuran, in his book *Private Truths, Public Lies*, relates to the incidence of male homosexuality. Writing in the mid-1990s, Kuran pointed out that the number of exclusively homosexual men in the United States was frequently cited as 10 per cent of the general male population, even though a rigorous study released in 1993 found a figure of only 1.1 per cent, plus another 1.2 per cent who had had homosexual sex in the previous decade (Kuran 1995: 11).

Over two decades later, we still don't know the precise proportion of exclusively gay men in current Western populations, with inherent methodological problems in obtaining data and a variety of figures cited in the relevant social science literature (Gates 2011: 3–5). However, the figure of 10 per cent is still frequently used, even though it is undoubtedly much too high. Based on the research of Gates (2011), this figure would be about right, and even slightly on the low side, only if it were used for all individuals of either sex who acknowledge at least some same-sex attraction. That is a very different concept. As an informal social experiment, try quibbling about this next time you hear someone mention the figure of 10 per cent, and see how the conversation unfolds. Let's not even start on the complex factual issues relating to different patterns of sexual attraction, activity, and identification in the male and female populations.

But why should it matter? Our support for the rights of gay men, lesbians, and bisexual people should have little – if anything – to do with estimates of their numbers, or their presence as percentages, within the overall population. They do no harm by being attracted to, and enjoying sexual intimacy and pleasure with, other people of the same sex. It's oppressive to them, and clearly unjustifiable, when they're regarded by the law as second-class citizens or when they are treated with social hostility. That should be enough for them to gain the support of well-meaning people of all sexualities. All of this follows from very familiar liberal principles.

Pressures towards conformity, self-censorship, and political solidarity within our various in-groups have almost inevitable consequences. We end up with impoverished debate and possibly the implementation of flawed policies. This applies to the classic political witch hunt of the McCarthy trials. During the McCarthy era, many Americans sympathized with the ideals of a powerful global adversary, the Union of Soviet Socialist Republics (USSR) under Stalin, leading to governmental efforts to identify, and somehow neutralize, local communists. In the circumstances of the time, any qualms about civil rights or due process of law could easily be portrayed as evidence of disloyalty:

> After all, there were real communists amongst us, committed to advancing the agenda of the Soviet Union. Besides, who exactly were these people, voicing such vehement procedural objections to the employment of reasonable safeguards against possibly damaging breaches of security? Just what kind of person would, under the circumstances, quibble about the civil liberties of a few communists and their fellow travelers? (Loury 1994: 443–4)

Loury continues with a forceful description of the USSR's expansion across Europe and other aspects of the supposed communist menace. He then presents a couple of devastating questions:

> Could we not infer something about their [i.e. civil libertarians and quibblers] values from their refusal to 'name names' or their willingness to speak openly on behalf of the accused? Perhaps those objecting to our methods of inquiry should themselves be sanctioned? (Loury 1994: 444)

In an endnote, he adds, for caution, 'I hereby declare, for what it may be worth, that this account does not express my personal views, but describes the hypothetical views of a "typical American" in the early Cold War period' (1994: 457). As he implies, even this disclaimer might not necessarily be enough to avoid harsh interpretations. After all, suspicious minds might think, a traitor to progressive values *would* say something like that, wouldn't he?

Under the social circumstances of early-Cold-War America, even genuinely anti-communist civil libertarians were often silent about what was happening. For a time, during this dark period in US history, Joseph McCarthy and other witch hunters were left free to say whatever they wanted about others, however lurid, vicious, unfounded, and even outright false it might have been, without being called to account. This phenomenon of smearing reputations – and thereby destroying lives – extends, as Loury demonstrates, to many situations that seem remote from Cold War scares about communists. In many circumstances, it is easy to represent opponents on some specific issue, or one aspect of a specific issue, as not just wrong but morally unsound. (Mill warned us against this, of course, in *On Liberty*, [1859] 1974: 117.)

Complaining when such smears are used to suppress debate will be taken as an especially strong sign of morally bad character and loyalty to hateful values. Thus, the logic of smearing creates a Catch-22 situation: the smearing itself cannot be challenged without heavy personal cost. As Loury expresses it, 'Under a convention of restrained public expression, prudent people do not protest for the right to say imprudent things' (1994: 446). Strategically minded speakers might try to make some room for their views with weakly worded and imprecise statements, but even if this sometimes works to protect reputations it undermines useful discussion.

Loury defines political correctness, or PC, as a form of social constraint: 'I treat the PC phenomenon as *an implicit social convention of restraint on public expression, operating within a given community*' (1994: 430; Loury's italics in all relevant quotations). Complaints about political correctness are themselves widely seen as marks of moral unsoundness. There is also an issue, for me personally, that such complaints are often from individuals with substantive views quite remote from my own (see Chapter 1). In some contexts, I might be accused of political correctness merely for supporting abortion rights or same-sex marriage. Hence, I have misgivings about the actual term *political correctness*. Even Loury warns that complaints about political correctness sometimes appear to be no more than complaints that the particular views of the person complaining are locally unpopular. If so, the term is not helpful.

But even with all those caveats, Loury is analysing a real problem. It might be better to call it the problem of political conformity than to use such a weaponized and contested term as *political correctness*, but whatever we call it the problem is there for us to see. The unceasing pressure to conform distorts consideration of important issues. As Loury explains with care, the larger problem is not the latest excesses of language policing on university and college campuses, troubling though these are for academic freedom and for other reasons (for which see Lukianoff 2014), so much as more universal pressures to conform. Conventions of restraint on public expression can arise, Loury says, because:

> (a) a community may need to assess whether the beliefs of its members are consistent with its collective and formally avowed purposes, and (b) scrutiny of their public statements is often an efficient way to determine if members' beliefs cohere with communal norms. (1994: 430)

The policing that results leads to self-censorship when individuals whose beliefs generally match the group's, 'but differ from some aspect of communal wisdom', keep quiet from fear of ostracism (Loury 1994: 430). This leads Loury to an insightful discussion of strategic behaviour in the way we communicate our thoughts. Most speakers soon learn enough sophistication to edit and censor what they say, although some clearly have less knack for this (or less patience with it) than others. These correspond to the 'Galilean personalities' identified by Alice Dreger in *Galileo's Middle Finger* (2015: 141). We'll meet some in later chapters.

Acting strategically and going to extremes – conformity on steroids

The result of pressures to conform can be an arms race in which the ideals of epistemic humility, sincere conversation, and openness to other viewpoints are lost. Speakers want to persuade, and they certainly do not want to be dismissed, even demonized, without consideration of what they are actually trying to say. Their listeners want to distil useful information, but don't want to be deceived or manipulated. As Loury puts it, 'both parties need to behave *strategically*' (1994: 431). He continues in the same vein:

Naive communication – where a speaker states literally all that he thinks, and/or an audience accepts his representations at face value – is rare, and foolish, in politics. A political speaker's *expression* is more often a calculated effort to achieve some chosen end, and an audience's *impression* of the speaker is usually arrived at, recognizing that this is so. (Loury 1994: 431)

Thus, with political discourse, we are always reading between the lines. We ask whether the people addressing us share our values, and whether we could trust them with power. We must, as Loury puts it, 'wonder, "What type of person is it who would speak to me this way?"' (1994: 432). Thus, the search to construe meaning involves judgements about the speaker's character, while speakers who sense this adjust their messages as protection against whatever judgements the listeners are likely to make, employing some arguments and expressions while avoiding others – not for the purposes of logical cogency but for successful performance. All this adjustment, camouflage, insincerity, and obfuscation can extend beyond politics into academic discussion. We can also see it at work in much religious, cultural, and moral – rather than narrowly political – debate in the public sphere. It can infiltrate private conversation, stopping, if at all, only at confidential exchanges among loved ones and intimate friends. Thus, Loury comments ruefully on the likely reception of his own article:

Take this essay as a case in point. It is public and political, despite the academic veneer. To address the subject of 'political correctness,' when power and authority within the academic community is being contested by parties on either side of that issue, is to invite scrutiny of one's arguments by would-be 'friends' and 'enemies.' (1994: 434)

The same, of course, applies to writing this book! In each case, the author will be scrutinized for tribal allegiances and hidden motivations. This will, consistent with Loury's account, involve assessments of character based on whatever clues are available. As authors, he and I are aware of this, and whatever else we do we can't simply ignore it. Whether to a greater or a lesser extent, we inevitably 'write between the lines' (Loury 1994: 435), knowing that readers will read between the lines. My own intent is to be as transparent as possible about my assumptions, beliefs, values, and motives, but even so I find myself (frustratingly) making just the kinds of fine adjustments that Loury refers to.

Within a milieu of political conformity, anyone who speaks out on a particular topic in a particular manner will be judged personally. Meaning will be read into her manner of expression, and her arguments may never be examined on their merits. Questions about her data and her reasoning may well be set aside, and instead she will be assessed as someone who was willing to speak in that way, at that time, on that topic. This may reveal her as an apostate from her group, especially if its true believers are hiding whatever misgivings *they* have about the local orthodoxy. A likely consequence is that a group's moderates and internal dissenters will be driven out of conversations, or at least be forced to keep silent about their moderate and dissenting opinions (Loury 1994: 43–6).

A further result is that the process contributes to group polarization, a phenomenon studied by psychologists since the early 1960s. As the distinguished legal scholar Cass Sunstein expresses the idea in his book on the subject, *Going to Extremes*, 'members of a deliberating group usually end up at a more extreme position in the same general direction as their inclinations before the deliberation began' (2009a: 3). As a result, a roughly like-minded group will veer towards the most extreme or (when viewed from the outside) implausible opinion to be found within the group before discussion and deliberation commenced. In fact, the result may be a more extreme opinion than anyone in the group began with.

Group polarization amplifies differences between groups, but it lessens diversity of views within groups. The dynamics of interaction among group members encourage extreme variations on what views are considered acceptable. The result is, as it were, conformity on steroids. Members of the group will likely frame their positions to impress other members, often taking more radical postures than they could honestly justify. They may withhold any information they possess that might moderate the views of the group or cast doubt on those of its high-status members. If this behaviour is rewarded with status, praise, and other benefits – while advocacy of moderation is punished – the outcome may be a group viewpoint far removed from any evidential support.

Group polarization is not always bad. It can sometimes have socially useful effects if group members push each other to respond decisively to clear injustices. It is, however, a danger to accurate, well-evidenced opinions – and the exotic viewpoints that it generates may be enforced by purity police to quash internal dissent. This blocks the development of more moderate and better-evidenced ideas.

A further result of conformity is that the only views that are frequently expressed in the public square will be those already acceptable to one or another politicized group:

> For every act of 'aberrant speech' seen to be punished by 'thought police,' there are countless other critical arguments, dissents from received truth, unpleasant factual reports, or nonconformist deviations of thought that go unexpressed, or whose expression is distorted, because potential speakers rightly fear the consequences of a candid exposition of their views. (Loury 1994: 438)

The process of adjustment and distortion can lead to the use of code words that reassure certain audiences and to avoid certain (perhaps previously useful) expressions that have become code words used by opponents. Some topics even become off-limits except to individuals with 'natural cover'. Unless you can claim a relevant group identity, bad faith may be assumed. Thus, thoughtful individuals may be cowed into silence, at least if they have something to say beyond the most banal agreement with the view of the tribe. (A further implication discussed by Loury is that insiders who have a semblance of cover may be treated very harshly if they break ranks publicly with their political allies: these insiders may have *all too much credibility* with the wider public. As a high-profile African American public intellectual, Loury is acutely aware of such issues.)

Politicization of discussion and debate affects even the practice of academic research, with scientists and scholars coming under pressure not to pursue certain lines of inquiry. In this environment, the academy becomes a minefield to negotiate in safety. Pressures towards self-censorship can distort what gets published and what counts as knowledge. Moreover, compromises with the truth as we understand it accumulate over time and among the many agents involved. We yield to a system in which the overall truth is clouded, though at some level we're all aware of this and complicit in it.

Preference falsification

In *Private Truths, Public Lies*, Timur Kuran discusses the classic conformity experiments conducted by Solomon Asch in the 1950s (and variants carried out since). These experiments reveal the powerful effect on isolated individuals of others' expressed perceptions. The experimental subjects were given a set of simple tasks. They were instructed to match a 'standard line' on a large white card with one of three 'comparison lines' (for a description of the basic experimental setup and instructions, see Asch 1952: 451-7). Two of the comparison lines were clearly and substantially different in length from the standard line, leaving no room for doubt as to which answer was correct. However, experimental subjects were placed with confederates of the experimenters, who acted on instructions to provide glaringly wrong answers on pre-arranged occasions. Each subject was in a minority of one within the group on the occasions when the rest of the group called an incorrect comparison line.

Despite the overpowering visual evidence, the experimental subjects frequently conformed to the incorrect judgements of confederates. As Asch puts it (1952: 457), 'There occurred ... a pronounced movement toward the majority; their erroneous announcements contaminated one-third of the estimates of the critical subjects.' Nonetheless, there were also 'extreme individual differences in response to majority pressure, ranging from complete independence to complete yielding' (Asch 1952: 459). 'Very simply', Kuran says, 'the experiment ... demonstrates the considerable power of group pressure on individual choice' (1995: 27; see, more generally, the full account in Asch 1952: 450-501 and the brief account in Sunstein 2009b: 29-30).

When such experiments are conducted, and the experimental subjects are debriefed, subjects often explain that they thought their judgements must have been wrong, or even (in a minority of cases) that they genuinely saw as the group did. It seems that people will often falsify what they know, or squelch their doubts, in order to conform with the group. In debriefing sessions, subjects also reported a longing to be at one with the others in the group, and they often had a concern 'that they might appear strange and absurd to the majority' (Asch 1952: 465). Interestingly, the effect was 'markedly weakened' (1952: 477) when even one of the cooperating group was instructed by the experimenter to give consistently correct answers. It appears that any support at all from others greatly reduces the pressure on an individual.

Kuran likewise discusses the notorious Stanley Milgram experiment of the early 1960s, in which many experimental subjects were prepared to inflict what they understood to be high-voltage electric shocks to confederates of the experimenter. No such shocks were actually given, but the confederates acted convincingly as if they'd been received. The experimental subjects believed themselves to be involved in a study of how punishment affects learning, and – under instructions from the experimenter – most were prepared to escalate the level of the supposed shocks even in the face of severe pain and stress expressed by the 'students'. Milgram's work is especially relevant to the topic of human subservience to authority. Beyond this, however, as Kuran observes: 'The whole experiment testifies most vividly to our fear of social criticism' (1995: 29).

Kuran turns to the theme that motivates this chapter, the social rewards and punishments for expressing 'right' or 'wrong' preferences in our public interactions:

> Some public preferences elicit disapproving gestures, such as raised eyebrows and derisive stares. Others also generate negative remarks, which may range from guarded criticism to unmerciful vilification. Another form of punishment is the denial of opportunities. A person considered on the wrong side of an issue may be denied a job or turned down by a social club. Still another is physical. The individual may suffer harassment, incarceration, torture, even death. On the positive side, a person may receive various benefits for an expressed preference. The possible rewards include smiles, cheers, compliments, popularity, honors, privileges, gifts, promotion, and protection. (1995: 29)

Private Truths, Public Lies is fundamentally about preference falsification, which involves manipulating others' perceptions of our preferences and dispositions. It can include merely keeping quiet as well as deliberately projecting opinions that we don't hold. The phrase *living a lie* succinctly captures the meaning (Kuran 1995: 4).

In Chapter 2, I discussed Lord Devlin's comments, over half a century ago, that 'There are now in England men who secretly see nothing wrong with the homosexual relationship' (1965: 87) and, later in *The Enforcement of Morals*, 'I do not think that there is anyone who asserts vocally that homosexuality is a good way of life but there may be those who believe it to be so' (1965: 116). An important and troubling word in the first quotation is 'secretly'. Although he evidently saw nothing untoward about the situation, Devlin was describing a powerful effect of social conformity. If we trust his understanding of the society around him – and we probably should to some extent, since he was a man of considerable experience – those people of the time who saw nothing wrong with homosexuality were under pressure to keep their opinions to themselves.

In Kuran's terminology, *public opinion* is the distribution of publicly expressed preferences across individuals in a population. Thus it is not the distribution of the preferences actually held by members of the public: the distribution of whatever preferences they hold privately is, in Kuran's terminology, *private opinion*. We might say that public opinion is the distribution of the preferences that people purport to have, as opposed to those they hold genuinely. All of this can be distinguished from *public discourse*, 'the corpus of assertions, arguments, and opinions in the public domain' (Kuran 1995: 157).

On Kuran's account, preference falsification is not always negative in its consequences: it can sometimes prove beneficial in practice, by suppressing claims that really are false, restraining dangerous impulses, or enhancing social cooperation by smoothing over minor disagreements. Nonetheless, it is burdensome because it typically involves feelings of guilt, anger, and resentment when we feel the need to falsify our real thoughts. We may also fail to convey ideas and knowledge that would be valuable to others.

Preference falsification affects public discourse: when we conceal our true preferences we also conceal the knowledge on which they rest. Under social pressure, we can hide what we know, preventing it from entering public discussion where it might have been useful. Thus we reinforce our preference falsification with *knowledge falsification*. 'In so doing', says Kuran, 'we distort, corrupt, and impoverish the knowledge in the public domain. We conceal from others facts we know to be true and expose them to ones we consider false.' We can end up with 'the persistence of unwanted social outcomes and the generation of widespread ignorance' (Kuran 1995: 19). In short, public opinion tends to shape public discourse, while public discourse tends to shape private opinion, since it affects what knowledge is available to people and thus influences their beliefs and preferences.

This is all worrying enough, but it gets worse. Kuran discusses how people often feel a pressure to back up their expressions of support for one or another political position with something more. After all, merely stating support is easy even for someone who is not sincere. To show – or perhaps simulate – sincerity, people may engage in such activities as heckling opposed politicians, praising supportive op-eds, taking part in demonstrations, and giving donations. 'Taken by individuals for their own reputational needs, all such actions help shape the social pressures that influence the public preference choices of others' (Kuran 1995: 61).

There may be some limit to this, as Kuran explains, since not every participant in a cause will be expected to take part in all the rewards and punishments that it dishes out. As long as she engages in some forms of activism and her behaviour generally conforms to the relevant agenda, she'll be given the benefit of the doubt when needed. Nonetheless, there is always pressure to do more than assent to collectively favoured positions, and to do much more than merely keep silent. In many situations, even silent withdrawal may require more courage than we can reasonably expect of vulnerable people.

Public opinion tends to shape private opinion, but its power to do so is eventually constrained. After all, we each retain knowledge based on our own experience and our emotional and cognitive responses to it. Public opinion will reach an equilibrium where it is self-reproducing, but this is not necessarily the point where public opinion and private opinion are aligned. The pressures that produce preference falsification can thereby conceal widespread, though hidden, opposition to a status quo. With any shock to the equilibrium, an unexpected revolution can sometimes take place:

> at some point the right event, even an intrinsically minor one, can make a few sufficiently disgruntled individuals reach their thresholds for speaking out against the status quo. Their switches then impel others to add their own voices to the opposition. Public opposition can grow through a bandwagon process, with each addition generating further additions until much of society stands publicly opposed to the status quo. (Kuran 1995: 20)

Huge effects in shifting private opinion can take place under the surface of observable public opinion. As Kuran argues throughout *Private Truths, Public Lies*, these effects can be triggered in a kind of chain reaction by small events, depending on just how delicate the current equilibrium might be. Because opposition to the status quo is hidden, the revolutionary change cannot be anticipated, but it will become easier to explain in hindsight. Once the discontent is publicly revealed, its nature and extent can be investigated. (Even then, however, one complication is that many people who were content under the old regime will claim that they were suppressed revolutionaries all along.)

The dual preference model and pluralistic ignorance

Kuran refers to his model of the effects of preference falsification as the *dual preference model* because 'its central feature is the duality between private and public preferences' (1995: 21). On his approach, the pressures of public opinion and the sanctions it imposes do not constitute the entirety of what motivates us. The rewards and punishments for expressing certain preferences are its *reputation utility*, while there is also an *intrinsic utility* to a person as a result of one or another option's implementation. Thus, whatever I really think, I might have an interest in expressing loyalty to certain policies (reputation utility) even though the implementation of quite different policies would actually benefit me (intrinsic utility).

Even that is not the end of it, because we also gain some psychological benefit from acting authentically and honestly speaking our minds. In Kuran's terminology, the satisfaction that comes from publicly expressing true preferences is our *expressive utility* – not to be confused (as Kuran explains, 1995: 32) with mere anticonformism, a seemingly perverse pleasure in going against the crowd. 'As individuals', Kuran says, 'we are evidently prepared to endure some social conflict to say or do what we really want' (1995: 31). We find enjoyment in saying what we really think, acting as our real ourselves, resisting social pressures, and showing that we are people to be reckoned with, while we feel discomfort whenever we sense that we are suppressing our true selves. In discussing such cultural phenomena as Western movies, Kuran points out how we view uncompromising independence as a heroic trait, partly because 'it is the exception in human history, not the rule' and partly because 'we all identify, at some level, with personal independence' (1995: 34).

Most often, we conform – but a slightly complicated vector of forces controls whether and when we express ourselves honestly. In many cases, my intrinsic utility is pretty much fixed whatever I say or do. That is, I have little influence, as an individual, on social choices and outcomes, and thus on whether or not they will be to my benefit. In these cases, my expected intrinsic utilities from different options can be factored out of my choice as to whether I express my true preferences. If I'm deciding what to say (or whether to keep silent) based on my rational self-interest, there will be a trade-off between my expressive utility and my reputational utility. If the pressures of public opinion – and hence the reputational losses if I express myself honestly – are sufficiently powerful to override my expressive needs, I'll offer whatever opinion is safe for me to express (or better, an opinion for which I might even be rewarded) even though I privately disagree with it.

This suggests that people with strong expressive needs are the ones who are most likely to speak up honestly in the face of likely punishment. People whose expressive needs are not so strong will gain little psychological reward if they speak up, although basic honesty might at least drive them to keep silent rather than going overboard.

Students of psychology will see a link between Kuran's dual preference model and the phenomenon of pluralistic ignorance, which was first identified by social psychologists in the 1920s and 1930s, and has since generated an extensive body of academic literature. Pluralistic ignorance occurs when multiple individuals (at least two, but in practice usually many more) underestimate the degree to which others share their beliefs and sentiments. More broadly, the concept applies when multiple individuals are mistaken – one way or another – about the degree to which others agree with them (see O'Gorman 1975: 314).

Overestimating others' agreement with what we think and how we feel might have personally and socially undesirable consequences: for example, it might reinforce our acceptance of incorrect or harmful ideas. For many purposes, however, the narrower conception of the idea of pluralistic ignorance – that involving *underestimates* of others' agreement with our beliefs and sentiments – is more important. Such underestimates might have varied consequences. For example, we might become unnecessarily embittered, alienated from our group, or suspicious of those around us. We might be led to speak up in opposition to what we take to be the majority view, and in the extreme we might even leave the group. Far more likely, however, we'll retreat into silence or even misrepresent what we think or feel or want. We are likely to conform, in our speech and conduct – and perhaps eventually in our thought – to what we mistakenly take to be the majority opinion.

It follows that one powerful effect of pluralistic ignorance is to encourage preference falsification. In turn, an environment already pervaded by preference falsification provides each individual with false data about the beliefs, attitudes, and wants of others. It contributes therefore, to ignorance about the distribution of private opinion within a society or a group. Misrepresentation of group members' private views is, accordingly, recognized in the academic literature as the typical source of pluralistic ignorance about social norms (e.g. Prentice and Miller 1993: 244). Unfortunately, misconceptions about the views of others in our various groups can even lead, as Kuran suggests, to enforcing standards that we privately disagree with. The researchers Willer, Kuwabara, and Macy label this 'false enforcement', and they define it as 'the public enforcement of a norm that is not privately endorsed' (2009: 452, 460). Unfortunately, as Willer and his colleagues found in their experiments, human beings may not be adept at recognizing false enforcement when they see it (2009: 480–1). That is, they are likely to mistake false enforcement – enforcement of a view or standard that the enforcer does not privately accept – for enforcement that is motivated by sincere agreement with the group.

In summary, people often express preferences and views that positively contradict what they really think: they know that even silence can betray an element of dissent. They may go further and punish others for breaching group norms that they – those doing the punishing – do not genuinely accept. One implication is that, other things being equal, we should take it with a large grain of salt whenever we see others express preferences and opinions that seem inherently implausible but are locally safe options. This applies all the more if the others concerned are likely to be rewarded for enthusiastic demonstrations of conformity.

Against the pressure

I have not attempted in this chapter to sort out all of the precise factors that push us towards conformity in how we live, what opinions we express, and how we express them. However, many of the factors are well known to social and behavioural scientists and are largely agreed. We are conforming animals to an extent beyond what is genuinely needed for social functioning; we come under various powerful pressures to follow the lead of our various groups, and to look as much like prototypical group members as possible. We're pressured to live in socially accepted ways and to have socially accepted opinions (socially accepted, of course, within our own groups and tribes).

There are many situations where a particular view is the only safe one to express even though it might have flaws or have only weak empirical support. Perhaps it is approximately correct, and just needs some criticism and improvement. But even this might be too risky to say in the circumstances. I hope these situations will become less normal as we become more aware of alternatives. Meanwhile, this chapter – and this entire volume – can be viewed, in part, as my effort to boost readers' utilities in speaking honestly on difficult but important topics. If enough of us are more honest, this just might make honesty a safer option for everybody. If we conceive of ourselves as honest people with expressive needs, perhaps that will have its own psychological effect. If we connect with others like ourselves, and if we give each other support, the reputational downside of honesty can possibly be reduced. These strategies might not always work – but they are well worth trying.

6 IDEOLOGY, PROPAGANDA, AND OUTRAGE

Ideologies and the ideological ideologues who promote them

The common meaning of *ideology* in contemporary usage is captured by the fourth definition in the *Oxford English Dictionary* (*OED*): 'A systematic scheme of ideas, usually relating to politics, economics, or society and forming the basis of action or policy; a set of beliefs governing conduct' or 'the forming or holding of such a scheme of ideas.' As for *ideological*, the common meaning is undoubtedly the *OED*'s third definition, which is cross-referenced to the fourth definition of *ideology*: 'Of or relating to a political, economic, or other ideology ...; based on a principle or set of unshakeable beliefs.'

Our language also has the useful word *ideologue*, likewise with an *OED* definition: 'A proponent or adherent of a political, economic, or other ideology, especially one who is uncompromising or dogmatic.'

The historical examples of usage listed by the *OED* include liberal democracy itself as an ideology, and this seems fair. The ideas involved in the overall concept of liberal democracy can be developed systematically in one way or another, making it a political ideology (or a group of them) in the *OED*'s sense. In everyday discussion, capitalism and communism are often contrasted as rival 'ideologies', even though there might be doubt as to whether capitalism fits the definition well (is it a set of *ideas*, exactly?) and bearing in mind that this contrast is probably made less often than a few decades ago, prior to the collapse of the USSR and various other communist states. The People's Republic of China is a rising superpower with a nominally communist authoritarian government, but

I wonder how many people think of its current rivalry with the United States as essentially one between communism and capitalism.

It is difficult to pin down the nuances of any concept in a relatively brief dictionary definition, which inclines philosophers not to take dictionary definitions at face value. Still, I intend to keep fairly closely to the *OED* definitions when using the word *ideology* and its cognates. These definitions do seem to reflect contemporary understandings of the relevant words. I will not, therefore, be employing the words in more technical senses deriving from, for example, the work of Marx or theorists inspired by him. But I will give the words a slight spin – one that's in keeping with ordinary usage and hinted at in the *OED* definitions themselves. Note that the definition of *ideology* that I quoted from the *OED* sounds neutral: after all, there can be better and worse, or more and less accurate, systematic schemes of ideas relating to (for example) politics, economics, and the workings of society. Nonetheless, *ideology*, and even more so *ideological* and *ideologue*, carry some pejorative force in many everyday contexts.

We can find a suggestion of this in the *OED*'s reference – in defining *ideological* – to 'unshakeable beliefs'; likewise, it is present in the definition of *ideologue*, with its reference to proponents of ideologies who are 'uncompromising and dogmatic'. When we speak of someone's approach being ideological, then, we usually convey that it's based on dogma rather than being grounded in evidence and open to revision. If you accuse me of thinking ideologically, you're insinuating that I base my judgements on a system of ideas that I am not open to reconsidering, and to which I subordinate many of my conclusions, choices, and actions. And yet, so the suggestion goes, these are ideas about deeply contentious issues – particularly political issues – where even experts reasonably disagree. Someone who thinks and behaves like this is the sort of person whom we call an ideologue.

The word *ideology* is, I think, more neutral than *ideological*. Nonetheless, the implication when someone is said to be motivated by their ideology is often that they subscribe to a system of political, or similar, beliefs that they've adopted uncritically and cling to somewhat dogmatically. When we speak in a more abstract way of the influence of *ideology* (not a particular ideology, but, rather, the tendency to think ideologically) the implication is usually clear that we're concerned about dogma and uncritical thinking grounded in political, or similar, systems of ideas. We might also be worried that political beliefs are being applied outside what we regard as their proper domain, for example when artistic judgements are made through the lens of a system of ideas about politics (rather than being judgements of, say, creative intensity or formal artistic skill).

Ideologies, religions, and world views

Ideologies are not exactly the same as religions – but an ideology may play a similar role to a religion in a proponent's life. Religions are (very roughly) systems of belief and practice that include otherworldly or supernatural elements of some kind: they involve belief in something that transcends the observable world or eludes empirical inquiry. Further, religions teach that there is an otherworldly dimension to human lives, and that this has at least something to do with how we ought to act in this world. Religions almost always involve rituals of some sort, and they typically include moral norms that are given a supernatural or esoteric rationalization. (For more detailed discussion of the concept of religion, see Blackford 2012: 5–10 and the works there referred to; for a somewhat different, but arguably complementary, account, see Leiter 2013: 33–53.)

A religion may say nothing – or at least very little – about politics. But many religions have strong political elements. Likewise, social and political ideologies may include religious components. For example, a religion, or a particular interpretation of it, might tell its adherents that their ritual and moral practices must be imposed through secular political power. Some religions prescribe in detail how societies and economies should operate. Conversely, a political ideology might favour or disfavour particular religions. It might claim, for example, that the doctrines and moral standards of a particular religion should be enacted as secular law. Alternatively, it might claim that certain religions are threatening to the social order and should be suppressed.

Some otherwise-secular ideologies also have trappings strikingly similar to those of religions: they offer special knowledge to those who are taught the details of the system; they offer deep psychological transformations to committed adherents, analogous to religious conversions; and they sometimes predict, or even attempt to bring about, social transformations on a vast scale. These are not unlike the apocalyptic transformations that some religions promise.

Not everybody has an ideology – by which I mean an explicit and (at least somewhat) systematic scheme of political, economic, sociological, or similar, ideas that motivates her whether or not she's been taught all its details. Perhaps everyone has s*ome kind of world view*, even if its contents are not entirely transparent to her, but that's a different point. Whatever world view she holds, perhaps largely unconsciously, might include gaps where she suspends her judgement or is simply not interested. Indeed, she might have no settled views on politics, economics, and the workings of society. Her various beliefs about the world might be loosely integrated, rather than systematic, in which case altering or abandoning a particular belief might have little effect on the others. Again, many of her beliefs, outside of whatever her society or group considers common sense and experience, might not be held very dogmatically.

Thus, we don't all subscribe to ideologies or anything much like them, we are not all ideological, and we are most certainly not all ideologues. I often hear claims to the effect that all knowledge is ideological, but this is simply not true as long as we're using words in their ordinary English senses. For all that I can sort out here, all knowledge may be *based on some presuppositions* – perhaps presuppositions about ultimate standards of truth, or even presuppositions about certain widely accepted and seemingly commonsensical background claims – but even if that's so, it is another thing altogether.

Even someone who does subscribe to an ideology might subscribe to one that is relatively modest. Its contents might form much less than a total world view, and it might be rather open textured. It might, for example, maintain that some decisions should be left to individual choice or democratic deliberation, rather than being controlled in a more direct and specific way by the ideology itself. At the risk of labouring a point, ideologies are not always bad things, but we should worry about them when we see their proponents becoming ideological or outright ideologues. And allow me to underscore that some ideologies really are dangerous. At their worst, they demand enormously destructive and rapid change in an effort to usher in a perfect society. In practice, this is usually disastrous.

Note that even the ideas in this book might be systematic enough to count as a political ideology by my definition or the *OED*'s. If so, that's fine. I don't propose that we condemn anything and everything that could possibly be classified as an ideology. Rather, we should recognize the dangers that ideologies and ideological thinking can pose to individual liberty, democratic policy deliberation, and human (or even non-human) welfare. Ideological thinking is often destructive to art, culture, and our personal lives, but its destruction can be on a far greater scale than that, as with the atrocities of Stalin, Hitler, and Pol Pot.

John Kekes, in his 2008 book *The Art of Politics*, employs a similar conception of an ideology to mine (and the *OED*'s), though his is more specific:

> An ideology, then, is a systematic way of thinking about politics. It has a theoretical and a practical component. The latter is an application of the former. The theoretical component is a set of beliefs about human nature and another set about an ideal system of political goods. The two sets are closely connected because the ideal system specifies what the political goods are, given that human beings have a certain nature. There are and have been many ideologies, and they differ partly because they contain different beliefs about human nature and the ideal system of political goods. (2008: 9–10)

For Kekes, ideological politics is fanatical and personally intrusive politics. He does not, however, classify his own account of politics as an ideological one, since it is pluralistic and does not claim that any value or small set of values is overriding in all circumstances. Kekes values pluralism and flexibility, and he does not attempt to reduce his view of politics to a system. But even if his account did qualify as an *ideology* it would not automatically have all the dangers suggested by the words *ideological* and *ideologue*.

Propaganda

Like *ideology*, the word *propaganda* can be used in a somewhat neutral sense. In ordinary usage, however, it is unlikely to be anything other than pejorative.

In the 1950s, Solomon Asch devoted a short final chapter of his influential *Social Psychology* to the issue of propaganda – and both that chapter and the book as a whole contain much insight that is still of value sixty-five years later. Asch defines *propaganda* as 'the deliberate attempt by organized agencies to produce shifts in opinion and sentiment' (1952: 617). This matches up well with the original meaning of the word, in which it was not pejorative and the 'agency' concerned was the Catholic Church. The word referred to the church's work of *propaganda fide*: propagation of the faith. During the nineteenth century, however, *propaganda* acquired a wider meaning of systematic dissemination of information to the public. This was neutral in itself, but during the early decades of the twentieth century the word gained an unpleasant overtone in reaction to untruthful and outrageous stories spread during the First World War. It was claimed, for example, that the Germans ran a factory to boil down the battlefield corpses of their own soldiers, extracting the fat for use in household and military products (see Marlin 2002: 70–6).

In contemporary circumstances, the idea of some kind of falsity or dishonesty, combined with emotional manipulation, has become important to our concept of propaganda. There may, moreover, be no organized agency involved (perhaps just a political movement or a convergence of tribal thinking). Nonetheless, much of what we recognize as propaganda still comes from governmental sources, and much of the problem is that propaganda is amplified speech, aimed at a population that, as Asch states, does not have its own daily access to relevant data.

Nowadays, when we accuse someone of engaging in propaganda we are claiming that something false or dishonest is involved. We're suggesting that the relevant speech, writing, or other material has gone beyond a lack of nuance into one-sidedness about an issue that really has more than one side, and that it relies on emotional manipulation. As with *ideology*, the meaning of *propaganda* is slightly fuzzy. But it usually signifies one-sided, emotionally manipulative, and (most especially) misleading or dishonest efforts to influence public opinion and sentiment. If, for example, I refer to government anti-smoking advertisements as propaganda, I'm implying that the message has gone beyond information and encouragement into the realm of falsity or dishonesty.

In his 2015 book *How Propaganda Works*, Yale-based philosopher Jason Stanley discusses the example of over-the-top warnings on cigarettes, such as 'cigarettes kill'. These seem acceptable to us, he thinks, and we don't usually regard them as propaganda despite their being hyperbolic and emotive. By contrast, we'd take a harsher attitude to the political rants of a dictator. Stanley suggests that we have tacitly allowed bodies such as ministries of health to convey messages containing whatever we need to know when we don't have the time to do the relevant research. If, as citizens, we haven't given this tacit permission, health warnings and the like are 'democratically problematic' (Stanley 2015: 59).

There's some merit in this idea, although we might wonder why such a ministry could not give us *accurate* information rather than engaging in hyperbole and emotional manipulation. If these materials are not propaganda, they certainly verge on it. Depending on our individual value systems, we might regard them as a form of propaganda that is justified by overriding utilitarian considerations. We might, all things considered, approve of propaganda with sufficiently benevolent aims as opposed to propaganda aimed at fomenting, let's say, war, persecutions, or racial enmity.

Alternatively, we might think that the official messages sent to us about cigarettes are – although hyperbolic – accurate enough not to be greatly misleading. The hyperbole attracts attention, but (we might think) no one *really* believes that smoking kills in all cases or in isolation from all other influences on health. If we view them in this way, government anti-smoking campaigns are just honest enough not to count as propaganda efforts. What, however, if they included straightforwardly false information, such as claims that certain specified individuals died from smoking when it was actually not implicated in their deaths? Would *this* be more clearly a propaganda campaign? Yes, it would be. Beyond a certain point, propaganda is plainly propaganda, even if it has a truthful underlying message and was issued with benevolent intentions.

Though propaganda materials are commonly aimed at large populations, the relevant 'public' might be a smaller one. Thus, we can speak of propaganda intended to influence opinion in an industry sector, or within a quite small population such as the students of a university or the membership of a club. The pejorative label *propaganda* can be justified even if the audience is small, as long as its members are subjected to emotive, one-sided, and misleading or dishonest materials aimed at influencing their thoughts.

Though many atrocity narratives, such as that of the German corpse-rendering factory, have been thoroughly debunked, such tales of horror are often widely believed at the time. They stir powerful emotions, and political leaders, activists, and all varieties of ideologues rely on them for just that reason. Tales of atrocious conduct, whether true or false, can generate a sense of extraordinary urgency. They encourage an environment where voices of moderation will be ignored or punished. Even if we understand this in theory, most of us tend to believe stories that match our preconceptions. No one, I suspect, is totally immune to getting caught up in waves of popular outrage. It's not so hard to recognize a story as – most likely – atrocity propaganda when it supports a viewpoint that we regard with scepticism. It is far harder when the story supports our existing beliefs, suspicions, dislikes, and fears.

Although Asch's definition of *propaganda* was a neutral one, his chapter expresses concern about the overwhelming barrage of material that we're subjected to each day, trying to persuade us in one way or another. The problem has certainly not abated since the 1950s when Asch was writing – quite the opposite. Worse, it can be difficult to draw the line between outright propaganda and more accurate and honest messages. Since he used a neutral definition, Asch thought that there was a good kind of propaganda. But perhaps we should talk about *public information campaigns* or *publicity campaigns*, or something of the kind, when essentially correct and honest information is distributed by the government in circumstances of urgency. Even so, there can, as I suggested with hypothetical anti-smoking campaigns, come a time when a line into the realm of propaganda is plainly crossed.

Democrats versus Republicans: Accusations and mutual incomprehension

Throughout their recent book on the American political scene, *Asymmetric Politics* (2016), Matt Grossmann and David A. Hopkins distinguish the Republican Party, as a party of ideological commitment, from the Democratic Party as one devoted to coalition building and finding solutions to specific social problems. According to this account, Democrats tend to reflect views from mainstream academic research and scholarship, and from the ongoing political discussion in mainstream news media. Beyond this, no particular ideology or world view is required. By contrast, Republicans are less interested in developing specific policies and in assisting specific groups that experience social problems. But compared to Democrats, Republicans are more ideologically homogeneous.

With relatively little difference in emphasis among themselves, Republicans share a political ideology based on a set of non-negotiable values. They promote traditional Christian religiosity and its associated morality, maintain a strong faith in unregulated capitalist markets, and emphasize American military strength together with a readiness to fight foreign wars. All of this can be developed systematically by one or another conservative thinker or leader, but these core values are doubtless enough for most voters.

The Republican Party has shown a distrust of scientific consensus on issues such as anthropogenic global warning, though as Grossmann and Hopkins point out this does not follow from an underlying hostility to science. The situation is more the reverse: Republicans tend to reason backwards to reject science where its findings are inconvenient. In the case of global warming, for example, Republicans reject proposed solutions on grounds related to their dislike of government intervention in the market, and from here they 'work backward to reject evidence' supporting the despised interventionist solutions (Grossmann and Hopkins 2016: 194).

To a greater extent than Democrats, Republicans have established their own think tanks, located outside of more traditional universities and colleges, to provide a base of research. They then expect their chosen experts to be given equal deference to those employed in mainstream academic institutions, whether or not this can be objectively justified (some cases are surely more plausible than others). Again by contrast to Democrats, Republicans have come to view mainstream media outlets as biased, and so they rely on openly conservative outlets. Over the past two to three decades, they have been increasingly influenced by conservative talk radio programmes, Fox News Channel, and right-wing outlets on the internet. As a result, committed Republican voters are often cocooned in their own media universe, largely cut off from mainstream science, humanistic knowledge, and political opinion. To the extent that they are exposed to mainstream opinion in these areas, it is likely to be filtered and distorted

The stars of conservative media outlets in the United States sometimes criticize Republican politicians and each other. But they have enough commonality to create an overall picture of American society and international affairs that is dramatically at odds with opinion from mainstream media commentary and academic research. In recent years, the conservative media have painted a dystopian portrait of the state of affairs in American society. Not all conservative media stars approved of or endorsed Donald Trump's presidential campaign in 2016, yet their portrait of American society in crisis prepared the way for a slogan such as Trump's 'Make America Great Again'.

The Republican Party has moved sharply to the political Right over the past half-century. Increasingly, it is intertwined with conservative Christianity, as well as representing business interests and various traditional, though not necessarily sectarian, values. It has favoured politically reactionary candidates at all levels of government, and at the federal level in particular these individuals have frequently played the role of spoiler – more concerned to block (or reverse) Democratic initiatives than to pursue their own, and unwilling to accept even the democratic legitimacy of their opponents. Republican politicians who actually try to govern – making compromises and seeking workable solutions to problems – can find themselves punished by their own party and its electoral base. Against that background, it will be fascinating to see how President Trump relates to varied interest groups as his term of office continues. Trump does claim to have plans of his own, and he touts himself as a negotiator. As I write these words in early 2018, he has occasionally shown an inclination to wheel and deal with his opposition in the Democratic Party and to surprise his Republican colleagues. Overall, however, he shows few signs of deviating from the Republican Party's standard approach to policy and governance.

By contrast, the Democratic Party has moved less sharply in any political direction. Grossmann and Hopkins detect some net leftward movement since the 1960s, resulting from the defection of pro-segregation Southern Democrats (2016: 12; compare Haidt 2012: 362). But the Democratic Party is not a party of the Left by European standards. In particular, it is often hawkish on foreign policy and unwilling (compared to left-wing European parties) to regulate trading and financial markets. In liberal democracies outside the United States, it would be regarded as a relatively conservative, or centrist, pro-business party. It's noteworthy that the Democratic Party's emphasis is on assisting identifiable groups, rather than on 'universal' or Enlightenment concepts of, for example, liberty, individuality, and conjoined intellectual and social progress. This entails that no powerful political institution in the United States is motivated primarily by those concepts.

As Grossmann and Hopkins explain, the asymmetric nature of American politics leads to some of its ugliest features, and these play out in the wider public sphere of debate and discussion that stretches beyond politics in a narrow sense. Democrats and Republicans are inclined to attack each other in highly uncivil terms. Republicans view Democrats as subscribing to leftist or socialist political ideologies – though this is seldom the case with mainstream political candidates from the Democratic Party – and even as attempting to bring about the military and moral decline of their country. In many cases, Democrats, and especially their more straightforwardly left-wing voters and allies, view Republicans as motivated by racism, bigotry, and a cynical defence of the privileged and wealthy.

The latter accusations contain a grain of truth: even if Republicans are seldom bigots, bigots are more likely to vote for candidates from the Republican Party than those from the Democratic Party. But a grain of truth is only a grain. It is too easy to caricature Republican politicians and their voters, misunderstanding the values that actually motivate most of them. Those values are firmly grounded in American and Christian (especially Protestant) tradition.

In recent years, Jonathan Haidt has obtained prominence as a social psychologist specializing in the study of morality and the emotions related to it. His work is illuminating in its identification of different foundational moral values that appear to motivate people with different basic political orientations. Haidt's conclusions are controversial, and they doubtless require more discussion and critique than I can provide here. Nonetheless, he seems to be on strong ground when he identifies the most sacred value for American conservatives as 'Preserve the institutions and traditions that sustain a moral community' (Haidt 2012: 306). By contrast, Haidt identifies the most sacred value for liberals (so-called) as 'Care for victims of oppression' (2012: 297).

While a policy of caring for victims of oppression could easily be given an Enlightenment liberal rationale, it appears to have become an overriding value in itself for what I call revisionist liberals. In much current debate, it overrides such Enlightenment liberal ideas as reason, free inquiry and discussion, due process for those accused of crimes and misdeeds, epistemic humility, and the search for truth. We thus have a recipe for mutual incomprehension between Democrats and Republicans, but also between liberals in the tradition of Mill and revisionist liberals overridingly focused on helping demographic and cultural groups.

The Outrage Industry

Against the backdrop of American politics, political scientist Jeffrey M. Berry and sociologist Sarah Sobieraj discuss what they call an Outrage Industry in the United States, with a particular focus on the role of radio personalities such as Rush Limbaugh. One of the prominent examples in their book, *The Outrage Industry*, is Limbaugh's unmerciful belittling and vilification of Sandra Fluke in 2012. Limbaugh attacked Fluke for presenting to the House Democratic Steering and Policy Committee a statement prepared on behalf of Georgetown Law Students for Reproductive Justice. Among other toxic rhetoric, he repeatedly described her as a 'slut' and a 'prostitute'.

Right-wing outrage has become increasingly diversified and sophisticated. One manifestation is the news website *Campus Reform*, founded in 2009. This has made life difficult for many left-leaning academics in the United States. Though its stated goal is to expose liberal bias in American institutions of higher education, *Campus Reform* goes much further. In conjunction with other elements of the right-wing Outrage Industry, not least Fox News Channel, it often targets individual college and university professors. Right-wing outrage personalities have developed special skills in undermining the employment of academics whose public statements can be interpreted as calling for prejudice against white people. The cumulative result of their efforts is an apocalyptic image of American campus life. (There are real problems on American campuses, but they are not on such a scale and they will not be solved by racialized witch hunts against individual left-wing educators.)

One recent example of the Outrage Industry in action – in June 2017 – was the suspension, then dismissal, of an African American media commentator, Lisa Durden, from her position as an adjunct professor at Essex County College. This followed a heated interview with Durden on Fox News Channel, conducted by Tucker Carlson. Using unguarded and mocking language in response to Carlson's provocations, Durden defended a Memorial Day event held exclusively for black participants. Predictably enough, this led to a storm of outrage on social media.

Berry and Sobieraj observe that politicized outrage in the United States has taken on a new, far more prominent role in recent decades:

> Controversial content like this has always existed in small pockets of the media landscape, but in the past twenty-five years this form of commentary has come into its own, as a new genre of political opinion media that we term *outrage*. The genre has several distinctive attributes but is most easily recognizable by the rhetoric that defines it, with its hallmark venom, vilification of opponents, and hyperbolic reinterpretations of current events. (Berry and Sobieraj 2014: 5)

Berry and Sobieraj attribute the growth of the Outrage Industry to structural changes, including technological developments and new regulatory policies applying to the media (notably the removal, in the US context, of any legal requirement for political balance). These changes have made it more profitable for contemporary media organizations and individuals to adopt outrage as a model. Although Berry and Sobieraj focus on the American media landscape, it's likely that their analysis generalizes, at least in part, to the UK and other Western liberal democracies. In a more fragmented media environment, reward goes to those who are shocking rather than to those who are seen as inoffensive. Outrage personalities, and the media corporations that rely on them, do not aim at a wide cross-sectional audience but at attracting their own large, yet personalized, niche audiences.

Outrage personalities, whether working on television or in talk-back radio or seeking niches in the blogosphere or the YouTube community, create cults of personality around themselves. Whatever their specific political views – usually extreme in one way or another – they build audiences of admirers and acolytes, often with special in-group terminology, shared historical allusions, and a sense of themselves as a community of special people who know what's really going on.

The picture that emerges from Berry and Sobieraj, and from the research they cite, is that American society may not be more polarized than formerly in the sense of being more extreme in its overall range. There have always been people with extreme political views, and any greater tendency towards this, if it exists, does not explain the phenomenon of outrage and the flourishing of outrage warriors. At the same time, even if the *spread* of views is not expanding, American society is now more divided. The centre is hollowing out. People fit more clearly into rival groups, and so there is more tribalism and less toleration of rival tribes.

Berry and Sobieraj argue that outrage tactics harm meaningful political discussion. They 'make talking politics beyond our most intimate circles extraordinarily difficult, complicating our ability to have meaningful discussions about politics in our communities' (Berry and Sobieraj 2014: 6). Outrage rhetoric may undermine our individual tolerance of others' viewpoints and distort our understanding of the issues. On a larger scale, it undermines the spirit of moderation and compromise: 'At the institutional level, outrage is working to stigmatize compromise and bipartisanship, and undercutting the political prospects of more moderate voices' (Berry and Sobieraj 2014: 221). The whole process trends to social disharmony:

> When outrage hosts vilify and belittle people with whom we disagree and inflate our own sense of self-righteousness, different perspectives on the role of government in addressing public issues are inflated from policy preferences into litmus tests for human decency. This slippage between critique of ideas and those holding the ideas likely limits our openness to other perspectives and the people who hold them. Perceiving others as malicious and inept undoubtedly makes cross-cutting political conversations and collaboration even more difficult than they already are. (Berry and Sobieraj 2014: 222)

Though many of the most striking examples of outrage involve right-wing culture warriors, Berry and Sobieraj make clear that outrage can also be found on the political Left. They concentrate on right-wing outrage media – which they regard as more developed and (in that sense) mature than the outrage media of the Left (or whatever counts as the Left in American terms) – but they acknowledge that participation in the Outrage Industry is not confined to one side of politics. Moreover, though not discussed by Berry and Sobieraj, outrage now appears in debates over popular culture and other topical issues as often as those over more conventional party politics.

As we've seen, the Democratic Party is relatively non-ideological compared to the Republican Party, and it is not a true party of the Left with a socialist ideology. Nonetheless, there is plenty of room in the United States for more obviously left-wing ideologues to flourish. Even these, however, seldom think and speak in terms of social class. They often employ political and social analyses that theorize about the plights of historically oppressed groups, including women, minority racial groups, and those who form the LGBT (or perhaps LGBTQI) community. The industrial and rural proletariat is, however, conspicuously missing from these analyses. The thinking of US-based leftists may contain much that's correct or meritorious, but it can easily harden into inflexible ideology, supported by propaganda techniques and mechanisms of compliance that include punishment via focused outrage.

In the United States, the Outrage Industry has become sophisticated, institutionalized, and readily recognizable. Americans lead the field, if *leadership* is an appropriate concept here. Then again, they have long-standing competition from the writers and editors of the British tabloid newspapers; indeed, readers from many countries will recognize their own local Outrage Industries. The research programme of Berry and Sobieraj could be extended across all the Western liberal democracies. Meanwhile, it is safe to conclude that we live in an age of media outrage.

Propaganda techniques

What about the techniques of propagandists? Since Asch understands *propaganda* as a neutral word, he uses the expression *exploitative propaganda* for propaganda of a bad and dishonest kind. Among its hallmarks are deception, half-truths, deliberate omissions, simplification of complex problems, attacks 'on the personal qualities of individuals and groups' (Asch 1952: 626), insistent identification of a state of crisis, and fostering of a dualistic (good-versus-evil) style of thinking. All of this rejects causal complexity and moral nuance. Propaganda (exploitative propaganda in Asch's terminology) encourages moral and political Manichaeism – a moral/political world divided neatly into the houses of good and evil. All issues are viewed through a single lens: whatever ideology (and with it, whatever real or imagined crisis) motivates the propagandist. Multiple – and often very different – values, ideas, organizations, and individuals are fused together as a single opposition, which is then treated as an absolute enemy.

Haidt has described a strong trend to Manichaeism, amplified by propaganda efforts, in contemporary American politics in particular (2012, 361–6). The same tendency operates more generally in Western politics, if not always to the same extent as in the United States. Political disputants treat their disagreements as a struggle between absolute good and evil. Ideological purity is demanded, compromise is viewed as a sin, and the result is a poisoned political environment (Haidt 2012: 309–12). Asch observes that propaganda (again, exploitative propaganda in his terminology) undermines any spirit of compromise. In its place, the prevailing principle becomes: 'He who is not with me completely is completely against me' (Asch 1952: 632). The atmosphere of real or faux crisis becomes one of zealotry. Independence and moderation are viewed with distrust:

> Moderate independence, which under more settled conditions would have every earmark of being thoughtful and responsible, acquires the

character of recklessness if not of treason. Eventually lack of opposition or independence no longer suffice; to be above suspicion one must account for what one has not said and done. (Asch 1952: 632)

As Asch also identifies, propaganda is often backed by censorship and more forceful reprisals: where propaganda is issued by the state, it both supports and is supported by police power. In my own understanding of propaganda, it is not necessarily a state activity, but something very similar applies when it is used by non-state organizations, political movements, and the like. Although these lack the powers of the state, they do possess weapons of a kind. They often have the power to ostracize dissenters, smear their reputations, and jeopardize their jobs and careers. As Asch notes, however, propaganda is not always effective, especially if those who are propagandized have some independent access to relevant facts. Thus, silence in the face of propaganda does not always indicate agreement or a lack of inward resistance to its message: 'When fear of reprisal reigns, silence or outward approval may appear to be consent, although it may actually represent stark skepticism or disillusion' (Asch 1952: 634). This is, in essence, the phenomenon of preference falsification discussed in the previous chapter.

One significant achievement of recent academic philosophy has been its development of subtle tools for analysing what is communicated by language: not only its literal semantic content, but also what is conveyed pragmatically by words in their varied contexts. These tools might help philosophers to analyse, understand, and explain the techniques of propagandists. In *How Propaganda Works*, Jason Stanley has taken the lead in using contemporary pragmatics for exactly that purpose. He concentrates on a narrow, though undoubtedly significant, part of the phenomenon: a style of rhetoric that he associates with the American political Right. He analyses the ways in which right-wing rhetoric that invokes worthy-sounding ideals – such as humanity, liberty, equality, objective reason, and democracy itself – can be employed to serve goals that undermine those very ideals.

Stanley prefers not to emphasize the role of falsehood in propaganda, since many statements can be false without amounting to propaganda, but this is a rather weak point. We can readily distinguish between everyday lies and the sorts of false or misleading material that are used to manipulate us in various kinds of public campaigning. Again, Stanley rightly points out (2015: 42–3) that not all statements used for propaganda purposes are literally false. Some might not have any literal content at all, and so cannot be literally true *or* false, but merely convey emotion. Others, such as 'There are Muslims among us', may well be true when interpreted literally, but in context they are recognizably propaganda. Such a statement trades on false beliefs – such as a belief that Muslims are inherently dangerous – in order to manipulate the audience's emotions. Of course, there actually are Muslims 'among us' in the populations of Western countries. But not much follows from that bare demographic fact.

Stanley condemns what he calls 'demagogic propaganda', which consists in the use of flawed ideology 'to cut off rational deliberation and discussion' (2015: 47). But this is a confusing move, since much propaganda need have little to do with demagoguery as that concept is normally understood (purveyors of propaganda are not necessarily demagogues, although some notable ones, such as Adolf Hitler, definitely were). More fundamentally, it is not necessarily flawed ideology that cuts off rational deliberation and discussion. The corpse-rendering factory story, for example, did not depend on anything that could meaningfully be considered false or flawed ideology: it depended on nothing more ideological than a vague suspicion of Germans, or of foreigners more generally, plus the emotional power of the lie itself.

For clarity, we should take note that Stanley's conception of ideology is a technical one that he attributes to the twentieth-century British philosopher Susan Stebbing (Stanley 2015: 196); similar accounts are common in much discourse within political theory. The idea is that ideological beliefs are cherished beliefs that we are emotionally resistant to giving up: from our viewpoint, it would be dreadful (or so it seems to us) if they turned out to be false, perhaps because their truth is important to our sense of identity or to the ways in which we justify how we live and act. These beliefs may be closely connected to much-loved social practices: practices in which we are immersed, and which we would not abandon lightly. It does not follow from any of this that an 'ideological' belief, so understood, is false – many such beliefs might actually be true – but they are crucial to how we understand ourselves and the world even if we don't consciously articulate them. If they are false, we might find ourselves living on the basis of a lie and impeded from gaining a better understanding.

Stanley shows little interest in ideology in the more popular sense discussed earlier in this chapter, but he argues that we are all scripted in our practical and moral expectations – and in the ways that we tend to act

– by networks of deep-seated, cherished, and often not explicit, beliefs. On this account, flawed networks of beliefs arise from, and are reproduced by, flawed social structures. All of this may be correct, but nothing so specific or controversial is required for propaganda to operate as it does, or for ideologues – as that label is more popularly understood – to use it as a tool for control. As long as human beings have emotional tendencies at all, we are vulnerable to campaigns to manipulate our emotions.

Nonetheless, Stanley makes important points: he summarizes, for example, how propaganda (in our classical understanding of it) involves appealing to emotions to close debate by bypassing the rational will. In some cases, this involves whipping up emotional reactions that are out of proportion in their intensity to whatever evidence might justify them. According to Stanley – and again this seems to be correct – propaganda may be used to support a good, bad, or neutral idea. But its distinguishing feature is that it uses emotions – such as 'nostalgia, sentiment, or fear' (Stanley 2015: 53) – to cut off rational consideration of other possibilities.

How Propaganda Works is useful in showing how political rhetoricians can appeal to prestigious values even while distorting, misunderstanding, or outright opposing them. It's unfortunate, however, that its author does not acknowledge a conspicuous aspect of contemporary politics: the fact that left-wing or liberal ideologues do much the same as their right-wing counterparts. For example, many ideologues in the Western nations now employ conceptions of safety, diversity, and freedom in the service of projects that actually undermine important kinds of safety, diversity, and freedom. Thus, a 'safe space' is often one where it is *not* safe to dissent from certain locally orthodox ideas. Even the concept of diversity is distorted when used merely of demographic and cultural diversity (a mixture of sexes, racial and ethnic backgrounds, sexualities, and so on) without valuing a diversity of viewpoints, opinions, ideas, attitudes, characters and temperaments, and chosen ways of life. No political party, movement, or side of a debate holds a monopoly on the propagandist abuse of noble language.

Conversely, much propaganda does not take this form. Much of it consists of nothing more than false claims about past achievements and current successes. Much of it is false claims about the moral character (or the cluelessness) of opponents, and about the evil deeds (or sometimes the clueless blunders) that they have perpetrated.

Consider, yet again, the atrocity narrative of the German corpse-rendering factory. In this case from the First World War, no particular ideal was relied on, only to be subverted by, the Allied propagandists. The power of the narrative did not come from values that it appealed to with explicit and noble language. Rather, the Germans were made to seem callous and inhumane because of their willingness to treat the bodies of their own dead as mere physical raw material for recycling. Somewhere in the background, perhaps, were appeals to kindness, compassion, and respect for human dignity, but it would be procrustean to portray the story's importance as lying in a subversion of those ideals. The more straightforward point to make is that a false story was used during the Great War to arouse strong emotional responses. As is usual with propaganda, the most obvious value that was being undermined was simple honesty.

At this point, we should take note that propagandists are often sincere about their overall positions, while showing a recklessness with the truth about any particular situation and a willingness to bypass the rational faculties of their audience. Thus, the perpetrators of the German corpse-rendering factory story doubtless believed that there was an imperative to oppose the Kaiser's regime. However, they relied on an outrageous falsehood in an effort to persuade. As Stanley points out, even Hitler and his followers were honest at one level: they doubtless believed that the Jews were a threat (2015: 44–7). However, the Nazis' efforts to shore up their own popularity, and to kindle anger and hatred against the Jews, employed a wide variety of powerful methods to bypass reason.

In principle, there might be circumstances so urgent that they justify the use of propaganda techniques to mobilize public opinion. Perhaps almost *anything* could be justified in response to an ongoing catastrophe of vast extent and great urgency. An idea similar to this motivates Herbert Marcuse's essay 'Repressive Tolerance' (1969), one of the key texts of the 1960s social revolutions. Marcuse, a leading theorist of the Frankfurt School of critical theory and a darling of the era's New Left, openly argued for toleration of radically left-wing ideas – accompanied by intolerance for the ideas of right-wing and hence, in Marcuse's view, regressive elements of society. He did not imagine that this policy would, or in the prevailing circumstances could, be pursued through state power. Rather, he called for radical activist groups to engage in intolerant, including violent, action:

> If they use violence, they do not start a new chain of violence but try to break an established one. Since they will be punished, they know

the risk, and when they are willing to take it, no third person, and least of all the educator and intellectual, has the right to preach them abstention. (Marcuse 1969: 131)

Marcuse justified such acts of intolerance, up to and including violence, precisely by his claim that he lived in a morally catastrophic political and cultural environment, and by his further claim that civil discussion was futile as a means to bring about change. In his essay, Marcuse states that 'extreme suspension of the right of free speech and free assembly is indeed justified only if the whole of society is in extreme danger.' However, he immediately adds, this is precisely the situation in which he finds himself: 'I maintain that our society is in such an emergency situation, and that it has become the normal state of affairs' (Marcuse 1969: 123).

This rationale could be employed to justify rioting and violence aimed at shutting down right-wing speakers, or indeed *any* speakers, however moderate in their views, who might be regarded as supporters of the political and social status quo. Accordingly, Marcuse's essay offers a rationale for today's violent anarchist and Marxist groups that try to prevent a wide range of what would otherwise be considered democratically legitimate speech. Whether or not Marcuse is widely read by present-day campus activists, they offer similar rationales for their actions. Note, however, that a structurally identical rationale is available to right-wing activists, demagogues, and outrage warriors. Trump's 2016 presidential campaign was focused on the idea that the United States was in an ongoing emergency situation, but one requiring drastic action from the populist Right.

Sometimes we really are confronted with political and social emergencies, but if we make that judgement too quickly we might be impelled to atrocious conduct that cannot be justified by any defence of necessity. Even if the situation around us does seem to have reached a point of crisis in one or another regard, extreme acts – such as attempts at suspension of others' ability to speak, listen, and assemble – are more likely than not to worsen the situation. *Pace* Marcuse, it is naive to think that violent actions, carried out by self-selected activists dealing with what they interpret as emergency situations, will break an established chain of violence. On the contrary, their violence will inevitably be seen by their more radical opponents as justifying retaliatory violence, which will lead to an escalation with no obvious stopping point.

Whenever we're told that we live in a sociopolitical state of crisis in which civil, honest discussion has become futile, we'll do well to examine just how bad things really are. In doing so, we need not deny that our society has significant problems that should be addressed. Unfortunately, propaganda techniques can be used for exactly the purpose of bypassing rational deliberation about how catastrophic our situation has become. There's a temptation for controversialists – especially those on the political extremes – to depict each and every situation that they care strongly about as involving some enormous crisis, a state of emergency.

A cautionary example for liberals – the *Rolling Stone* case

On 19 November 2014, freelance writer Sabrina Erdely published a sensational feature article of some 9,000 words in the high-circulation magazine *Rolling Stone*. Entitled 'A Rape on Campus: A Brutal Assault and Struggle for Justice', the story was evidently intended to highlight the existence of a 'rape culture' – an environment where sexual violence is prevalent and culturally enabled – on US college campuses. Such a culture may well have a presence on those campuses, or some of them, fuelled by alcohol and machismo. But to whatever extent that is true, Erdely failed to shed any light. Instead, she inadvertently provided us with an example of mainstream investigative journalism morphing into a confection of ideology, propaganda, and outrage.

She claimed that a young woman, identified throughout by the pseudonym *Jackie*, had experienced a brutal gang rape during a party held by the Phi Kappa Psi fraternity at the University of Virginia. This supposedly happened in September 2012. Erdely represented the rape as an initiation rite – making her story reminiscent of the widespread 1980s and 1990s panics about Satanic ritual abuse. But the allegations were so out of the ordinary, and the level of viciousness described was so extreme (Jackie was repeatedly raped by seven young men over a period of three hours – so Erdely claimed), that 'A Rape on Campus' displayed obvious hallmarks of atrocity propaganda.

We should acknowledge clearly that some atrocities really do take place. Consider, for a start, the Nazi Holocaust and numerous other horrors perpetrated by totalitarian, ideology-driven governments.

Consider, too, the undeniably brutal and outrageous treatment of many Indigenous groups as a consequence of European colonialism. At first, then, immediately after its publication, there was no basis to dismiss Jackie's story out of hand. But nor was it wise to assume that such an extraordinary account was actually true, whether in its detail or its essentials. And yet, a rush to judgement took place on the internet, with viral sharing of the story itself and international shaming of the Phi Kappa Psi fraternity and its members. Journalists who should have known better accepted the narrative at face value. Rowdy demonstrations were organized to denigrate the fraternity and demand changes to the fraternity system.

As *Rolling Stone*'s account came under external investigation over the following days and weeks, it totally collapsed. Cautious readers might have expected an element of truth to remain – perhaps that Jackie had been sexually terrorized and abused in some way rather different from what was narrated by Erdely – but no grains of truth emerged. *Rolling Stone* formally retracted the story on 5 April 2015, though by this time much damage had been done, including physical vandalism to the fraternity's chapter house, psychological harm to fraternity members – at least some of whom were ostracized and threatened – and the trashing of numerous individuals' reputations.

Whatever happened to Jackie that night in 2012, nothing like the protracted gang rape luridly described in *Rolling Stone* ever took place. It appears that Jackie's allegations were entirely fabricated. (As far as anything seems clear in such circumstances, the gang-rape claim may have been an attempt to gain the sympathy of another student to whom Jackie was romantically attracted.) Erdely believed the false narrative pretty much unquestioningly, clearly enough because she was predisposed to do so. She appears to have done little in the way of checking, and then, in turn, she received no real oversight or guidance from staff employed by the magazine. In December 2014, *Rolling Stone* published a disclaimer about the story's veracity, and it subsequently asked the Columbia University Journalism School to investigate what went wrong. The school's formal report, published by *Rolling Stone* in April 2015, shows a depressing record of ideologically motivated reasoning and careless journalistic practice (see Coronel, Coll and Kravitz 2015).

A number of lawsuits were issued against *Rolling Stone*, Erdely herself, and others, including a defamation suit by Nicole Eramo, the associate dean who was responsible for handling sexual assault allegations at the University of Virginia. Erdely's article was scathing about Eramo's handling of the case, with devastating impact on Eramo. In evidence given during the trial of her lawsuit, she testified to suicidal thoughts while curled in a ball under her desk. In November 2016, a jury found Erdely and *Rolling Stone* liable for defamation. Eramo was awarded $1 million in damages to be paid by *Rolling Stone* and $2 million to be paid by Erdely. The case was eventually settled confidentially prior to the hearing of an appeal. Phi Kappa Psi's separate litigation against *Rolling Stone* was settled in June 2017 for a sum of $1.65 million. In December 2017, *Rolling Stone* settled a claim by a small group of individual members of Phi Kappa Psi, thus concluding the litigation against it.

Irresponsible journalism has done great harm in this instance. One obvious consequence of the fiasco was to undermine the credibility of women who actually do suffer violent sexual assaults on US college campuses. For our purposes, however, the most important point relates to the combination of gullibility and zeal displayed by Erdely, by *Rolling Stone* staff, by many individuals associated with the University of Virginia, and by a much wider audience who accepted the original story uncritically and passed it on. These readers showed none of the scepticism that such extraordinary, too-bad-to-be-true claims should immediately provoke.

Erdely herself seems to have set out to make a point, rather than to follow the facts wherever they led. If not outright dishonest, this is at least a failure of journalistic skills and intellectual rigour. It seems that she looked for the ultimate narrative: she wanted a story involving an innocent victim brutalized in the most outrageous, devastating, and unambiguous way. She was motivated, it seems, by her belief in a Marcusian situation of emergency on American campuses. This, however, clouded her judgement. There must have been genuine stories that she could have investigated: more than sufficiently horrible on-campus rapes that really happened in 2014 and the few years immediately beforehand. But if so, apparently none was sensational enough for her purpose.

How not to be outrage warriors

Cass Sunstein has discussed how our prior beliefs, hopes, and fears can make the rumours we encounter seem either believable or baseless.

One example is a false claim (accepted uncritically by many) made in 2008 that American politician Sarah Palin believed Africa was a country rather than a continent (Sunstein 2009b: 6; see also Brogaard 2015). For those who believed this, Sunstein remarks, Palin's supposed cluelessness fitted with what they already believed about her. Likewise, it was easy for many people who read Erdely's *Rolling Stone* story to believe even the most extreme and vile things about the behaviour of frat boys on college campuses in the United States. There have, after all, been many incidents of male fraternity members behaving badly. Thus, the pseudonymous Jackie obtained much credence even though her story was bizarre. It fitted with pre-existing assumptions and ideologies.

One reason why we might believe, or not believe, rumours and propaganda narratives is how well they fit with information (true or otherwise) that we already have. A related reason is that accepting some claims makes us feel good, or better than we did, whereas rejecting them makes us feel bad. In particular, we are likely to deny claims, however well supported they are by the evidence, if they contradict our political or social ideologies, our religious or moral views, or (to adopt some of Jason Stanley's terminology) simply our cherished beliefs. Conversely, we are likely to accept ugly rumours about people we disapprove of – and to pass them on to others – even if they're poorly evidenced and their content stretches human credulity.

The Outrage Industry described by Berry and Sobieraj (2014) – and all too obvious to observers – both feeds upon and feeds a sense of crisis. Sometimes this sense might be justified, at least by the lights of the outrage warriors' own values. If, for example, you view abortion as murder, you live in a world (or think you do) where murder is being committed on a mass scale in every Western country. If this were really so, it would surely be a crisis to be faced, and you might say or do almost anything to bring it to an end (even voting for anti-abortion political candidates whom you otherwise despise). As I stated in Chapter 1, I see nothing wrong with abortion, and I celebrate (and seek to further) women's reproductive freedom, but those who disagree with me must experience the world very differently. This is something I try to keep in mind when I find them exasperating.

By many measures, things are often not as bad as they look. Western societies have significant and entrenched problems, and solving them won't be straightforward. Yet they won't be solved by angry rivals who (for their very different reasons) see themselves as caught in a state of perpetual crisis, examine each other through opposed world views, ideologies, and systems of values, and always think the worst of each other. A state of Manichaean politics encourages ideologues, propagandists, and outrage warriors (and people who seem to be all three in one obnoxious package). In the extreme, it produces violence and civil unrest. It does little, however, to heal divisions, solve social problems, or advance human knowledge and understanding.

7 YOU CAN'T SAY THAT! IDENTITY POLITICS AND ITS VICTIMS

Threats from all sides

We might expect that the greatest threats to individual freedom in post-Christian liberal democracies – and especially to the freedom to express and discuss our ideas – would come from church and state. The Christian churches might be motivated to suppress heretical speech, including challenges to traditional *mores*. Government officials might try to crush anything they regard as sedition or subversion of the political order.

It often works out like this, and I'll return to the point in Chapter 9. Too often, however, supposedly liberal or left-wing individuals and organizations are at least complicit in attacks on freedom. They use a wide array of tactics involving propaganda and outrage. Sometimes they are not above appealing to the power of the state to censor political enemies. A relatively recent case in Australia involved a hard-line anti-abortion campaigner from the United States, Troy Newman, who was denied entry to the country to give a scheduled lecture tour under the auspices of a pro-life group.

Newman has defended some genuinely outrageous ideas: in particular, he regards abortion as murder, and he has asked, rhetorically, why it should not be a capital crime in jurisdictions with the death penalty. He has even expressed sympathy for a convicted murderer, Paul Jennings Hill, who was executed in 2003 for killing a doctor and his bodyguard. However, no evidence has ever been produced that Newman posed a threat to Australian society in the sense of being likely to incite violence during his visit. His opponents campaigned for his exclusion by government action largely, if not entirely, because they wanted to keep his opinions from being expressed, heard, and discussed in Australia. I submit that Australia should *not* have denied him entry, and his opponents should never have sought such a thing.

(As events turned out, Newman arrived illegally. After making an unsuccessful application to the High Court of Australia to be permitted to stay, he was deported in early October 2015. See Blackford 2015b for a lengthy blog post that I wrote during the heat of the debate.)

This should have been a straightforward case. While Newman's substantive views were, in my opinion, wrong, ugly, and bizarre – and of course, offensive to many people – he should have been allowed to express them in a liberal democracy such as Australia. Conversely, those who wished to hear him in person should have been able to. From a strictly prudential viewpoint, the fracas inevitably ended up giving *more* publicity in Australia to Newman's views. Furthermore, he carried out at least some of his plans by speaking from abroad, using modern communications technology. It's not clear, at least from any information available to me, whether Newman and his organization ended up worse or better off overall.

Newman is himself a highly illiberal individual. Very often, however, the victims of efforts such as these – campaigns to silence or punish opponents – have good credentials of their own as liberal or left-leaning thinkers.

An increasingly evident phenomenon in recent years, although it dates back to the 1970s, is what is known as no-platforming. In case after case, speakers who have been invited as guests at conferences or university forums have had their invitations rescinded. In these situations, even when an invitation remains in place there may be continuing attempts by pressure groups to force a last-minute cancellation. When events do finally take place in a highly politicized atmosphere, they are sometimes turned into chaos by protestors who try to shout down speakers and otherwise disrupt proceedings. No one can complain if peaceful protests are held outside a venue, but we have every reason to complain about hecklers' vetoes over speech.

Violent demonstrators have sometimes smashed property and physically hurt people. That risk climbed markedly during 2017 with the increasing involvement of black-masked 'Antifa' (anti-fascist) activists armed with makeshift weapons. Indeed, a separate book could be written on the escalating political violence in the United States in particular – especially since Donald Trump took office in January 2017, which no doubt gave heart to many far-right groups while simultaneously giving many left-wing activists a sense of living in the sort of 'emergency situation' described in the 1960s by Herbert Marcuse (1969: 123).

The idea of no-platforming was originally aimed at actual fascists involved in propaganda and recruitment for violent organizations such as the National Front in the UK. In that narrow form, and especially in the explosive racial environment of 1970s Britain, the idea made sense. During no-platforming's original heyday, student unions frequently extended the policy to individuals and organizations with ties to South Africa. But no-platforming has now been used well beyond the UK, well beyond a policy of keeping out fascist thugs, and certainly beyond the 1970s and 1980s campaign against apartheid. On various occasions, undoubtedly left-wing speakers, such as Peter Singer, Julie Bindel, and George Galloway – and many others too numerous to list – have found themselves blacklisted or disinvited from giving specific speeches.

Singer is an interesting example, since he has opponents on both the Left and the Right for his views on medical decisions at the beginning and end of life. Some of his opponents support traditional religious morality and 'pro-life' views on abortion and related topics. Others, however, are disability advocates who would see themselves as liberal or left-wing figures. When a high-profile speaker such as Singer receives a conference disinvitation, as happened at the Cologne Philosophy Festival in mid-2015, he will have other outlets to express his viewpoint. But others with similar opinions and lower profiles get the message: keep your opinions to yourself or you will be punished.

In this chapter, I'll describe a range of cases that ought to cause us concern. As a result, the chapter will be something of a litany of horrors – but I could adduce many more examples. I occasionally encounter scepticism about such cases from people who have not personally encountered them, so I will document some of the more recent cases in detail (perhaps more than is strictly needed). I emphasize, however, that new cases come to public attention almost daily. While some individuals might be sceptical that the more extreme cases exist, or at least that they are reported fairly, many others who speak to me in confidence have had sufficient experience of their own to recognize the sort of mayhem involved.

Don't talk like that! The case of Philipp Jenninger

In his article 'Self-Censorship in Public Discourse', Glenn Loury discusses the case of Philipp Jenninger, who was forced to resign in November 1988 from his position as president of the Parliament of the West German Republic. Jenninger's transgression was to make what was widely seen as an improper speech about events leading to the horrific *Kristallnacht* fifty years before, when Nazis attacked German Jews in a devastating pogrom that can be seen as the beginning of the Holocaust. As Loury puts it: 'An uproar was created by the fact that many in his audience construed Jenninger's brutally frank account of prevailing attitudes among Germans in the 1930s as a disguised defense of National Socialism' (1994: 438).

There was no doubt at the time (or now) of Jenninger's long-standing anti-Nazi credentials and opposition to totalitarianism. There was no evidence whatsoever that he harboured anti-Semitic feelings. Indeed, he was a forthright supporter of Israel. Moreover, 'virtually all reviewers who examined the speech concluded that he had said nothing untrue, malicious, or defamatory' but had uttered truths 'that some people did not want to hear in a manner they were unwilling to accept' (Loury 1994: 439). While condemning the barbarity of *Kristallnacht*, Jenninger dramatically conveyed the widespread admiration among Germans of the time for Hitler and the Nazi leadership, and the routine 'suspicion and contempt' felt towards the Jews (Loury 1994: 439).

In short, Jenninger confronted the German people of his own time with vivid, honest, necessary speech designed to expose the brutal truth about Germany during one of the most shocking periods in European and world history. In doing so, he chose words that conveyed the thought processes of Nazis and Nazi supporters in ways that could, taken out of the controlling context, be understood as expressing sympathy with them. He broke a taboo against such open expression, failing to restrict himself to platitudes and sanitized speech, although the taboo operated to preclude an 'honest examination of history and current circumstance from which genuine moral understanding might arise' (Loury: 1994: 44). He proved unable to create – in the minds of his accusers – a space between the words that he used to indicate the mindset of pro-Nazi Germans and his own thoughts on the subject.

Conveying the way those Germans of the 1930s thought and felt about Hitler, the Nazis, and the Jews was socially forbidden. When Jenninger broke the taboo, he was harshly punished.

The betrayal of Salman Rushdie

Salman Rushdie's novel *The Satanic Verses* was published in 1988, the same year as Jenninger's political downfall. It is a major literary work from one of the great authors of our generation. Please read it for yourself, if you haven't already done so. However, it soon became notorious because of threats that drove the author into hiding. In February 1989, Ruhollah Khomeini, a Shi'ite Grand Ayatollah and the Supreme Leader of Iran, issued a ruling on Islamic law – a fatwa – against Rushdie. It called for the novelist's death for allegedly blaspheming Islam, the Qur'an, and the prophet Muhammad. This extraterritorial death sentence extended to all who were involved in the book's publication and aware of its contents.

Though Rushdie has survived, his Italian translator, Ettore Capriolo, was severely wounded in a knife attack in July 1991. In the same month, Hitoshi Igarashi, the Japanese translator of *The Satanic Verses*, was stabbed to death. In 1993, its Norwegian publisher, William Nygaard, was shot outside his home. Nygaard survived, fortunately, but only after a lengthy time in hospital with serious wounds. Many others were threatened, hurt, kidnapped, or killed. Meanwhile, the novel was banned in many countries. Worse, many supposedly moderate Muslims defended the fatwa. Even worse, many Western religious leaders, public intellectuals, and political commentators turned against Rushdie for his alleged insensitivity to religious and cultural feelings. Even those who criticized the fatwa often greeted the book itself with distaste or disdain.

The great European author Milan Kundera makes a similar observation:

> With mysterious unanimity (I noticed the same reaction everywhere in the world), the men of letters, the intellectuals, the salon initiates, snubbed the novel. They decided to resist all commercial pressure for once, and they refused to read a work they considered simply a piece of sensationalism. (1995: 25)

Kundera goes on to describe the response of politicians, which he summarizes, snarkily but aptly, as follows: 'We condemn Khomeini's verdict. Freedom of expression is sacred to us. But no less do we condemn this attack on religious faith. It is a shameful, contemptible attack that insults the soul of peoples' (1995: 25).

Major world leaders of the time, including UK prime minister Margaret Thatcher, US president George H.W. Bush, and leading members of their respective cabinets, offered only weak responses to the fatwa. The British foreign secretary, Geoffrey Howe, went out of his way to distance himself and the government from Rushdie, in what approached denunciation of the book. As Kenan Malik observes in *From Fatwa to Jihad*, 'Western politicians seemed incapable of taking an unequivocal stand in defence of free speech and against the threat to Salman Rushdie's life' (2010: 34, and see generally 32–5).

Thatcher and Bush were right-wing political figures, but the Left was no better. In his giant-sized memoir of those years, *Joseph Anton* (2012), Rushdie laments the number of people on the Left who denounced him, many of them writing columns for major British newspapers such as *The Guardian*. Some of these pieces called on him to be humbled by what had happened, or to learn from it and atone for the offence he'd caused. Meanwhile, he was leading a difficult, cramped, furtive life, constantly beset by housing and other crises. He was denigrated by his enemies as a bastard and a dog, fit only to be killed.

In a recent article published in the *Journal of Religion and Society* (2016), Paul Cliteur examines the unsympathetic responses to Rushdie of two eminent academic philosophers, Charles Taylor and Michael Dummett. Cliteur pays particular attention to an early response by Taylor. This is an astute choice, since Taylor's article manifests some important elements in current academic thinking about Islam and intercultural disputes. It concludes with an admonition to Westerners to be more understanding of authoritarian religion:

In Rushdie's book, one has the comfortable sense that exactly the things which repel him from religion (or at least arouse ambiguous reactions in him): its authoritarian certainty, the childlike security it offers; that these are the things its devotees cherish. They experience exactly the same spiritual realities, and just reverse the sign. Rushdie's book is comforting to the western liberal mind, which shares one feature with that of the Ayatollah Khomeini, the belief that there is nothing outside their world-view which needs deeper understanding, just a perverse reflection of the obviously right. To live in this difficult world, the western liberal mind will have to learn to reach out more. (Taylor 1989: 122)

Although much in Taylor's article is considered and provocative of thought, I agree with Cliteur that Taylor draws an extraordinary conclusion. At a time when Rushdie's life was in serious danger, Taylor saw fit to lecture him, and others of a 'western liberal mind', about the need to 'reach out' to authoritarians. One might have thought it more incumbent on the authoritarians to do their share of non-violent reaching out.

Part of the problem is a degree of cultural relativism in Taylor's approach, in that he is unwilling to accept an obvious liberal response: the literary language employed by Rushdie was not harmful, or at least any harms it caused were of a socially accepted and legitimate kind. Instead, Taylor asks us to adopt an understanding of harm that is relative to cultures. On his approach, if we attempt to find a more universal concept of harm, we thereby endorse 'the superiority of the West' (Taylor 1989: 120).

In this article, Taylor is attempting to avoid tribalism and to take a more objective view of the issues arising from the Rushdie affair. As far as it goes, that's commendable. He emphasizes his own opposition to laws against blasphemy, but he attributes this partly to his Christian, and more specifically Catholic, background. In this respect, he seems to have a point. Christianity was a persecutorial religion for as long as it dominated Western culture and politics. It was, however, considerably tamed by the major events of European modernity: the Protestant Reformation; the sixteenth- and seventeenth-century wars of religion, and the backlash against them in modern political thinking; the Scientific Revolution; the European Enlightenment; and other upheavals such as those associated with colonial imperialism, industrialization, and urbanization. The Islamic world experienced all of these very differently, and Islam has never been tamed in quite the same way.

Likewise, as Taylor highlights, Christianity and Islam draw upon different theological resources. It is easier to imagine a warlord such as Muhammad employing organized political and military might to strike down blasphemers – thereby upholding the honour of his deity – than to place Jesus of Nazareth in such a picture. Still, this takes us back to the issues about harm and offence. Pious Muslims may, indeed, be offended by different things – and for different reasons – from those that bother pious Christians like Taylor or non-believers like me. It does not follow that Muslims thereby experience *harm* – or at least a kind of harm that should be cognizable by the law.

As an example, Taylor states that it might be harmful in some cultures, or at least seriously insulting, to have doubt cast on the legitimacy of your birth. He understates this, since, until not very long ago, illegitimacy was a serious impediment to social acceptance even in Western countries. But the difference is not that the *harm* – being treated as an outsider, ostracized, denied certain legal rights, and so on – is different. It's that different things, once revealed about you, will produce such consequences in different societies. In some cases, it might be difficult for people from different cultures to understand each other's claims as to what is harmful, but very often this is not so much because they have different conceptions of harm. It is more that they have different world views, and with them very different expectations of the consequences of certain acts.

Note, however, another deep issue. Taylor accuses Westerners – that's me, and probably you – of believing in the superiority of our own culture if we attempt to define intercultural standards of what counts as harm. This sounds as if we are guilty of some kind of bigotry, but are we? Of course, it's almost impossible to compare two entire cultures with a view to deciding which is, all things considered, superior to the other. There are too many dimensions of comparison; there is no overall (much less agreed) metric for the comparison; and so, in many cases, an all-things-considered attempt to rank cultures will be a futile exercise. All that said, one culture may be clearly superior to another in a particular respect.

Think of different historical periods in the development of a single culture. Whether or not the contemporary culture of the American South is superior, all things considered, to that of the antebellum South might be difficult to prove to everyone's satisfaction. Still, it seems fairly obvious to me: if a culture very similar to the Old South existed somewhere in the contemporary world, I'd have no hesitation in considering it inferior to the southern states of the United States in their current form. At the least, those states would be superior in the particular respect that they no longer rely on slavery.

If Western culture is superior to Islamic culture in its greater emphasis on secular government, individual liberty, spontaneity, free inquiry, gender equality, and certain other principles and values, so be it. We're entitled to conclude, based on our best investigations, that these are true, or at least useful, principles and values. If so, a culture that embraces and emphasizes them is, other things being equal, superior to a culture that does not. It might or might not be superior *overall*, since numerous other aspects might need to be considered, but we should reject the idea that all cultures are as good as each other and that denying this is bigotry. (If this is enough to make us cultural imperialists, then there's nothing wrong with being cultural imperialists. So be it.)

Taylor is probably correct that *The Satanic Verses* contains elements that are anathema to religious authoritarians. He identifies three stances or attitudes towards religion in contemporary secular thinking:

> One, defiant unbelief, affirming the dignity of humans alone in the universe; two, courage before a universe which is in itself meaningless; and three, an acceptance of human limitation, of the irremediable unspirituality of human beings, or of the weakness, sensuality, self-referentiality of everything they call 'spiritual', not seeing this as 'fallenness' anymore. (Taylor 1989: 119)

According to Taylor, these stances or attitudes can, in turn, be used to ground a threefold critique of religion as a purveyor of false submission ('all the worse because it can be used to underpin human exploitation'); false, childish hopes; and impossible standards that 'can only lead to endless self-torture' (1989: 119). He locates all of these critiques in Salman Rushdie's novel, even if expressed with some ambivalence, and perhaps he's right to find them there. But what follows?

Taylor expresses sympathy with the view that religion merits special protection, such as via blasphemy laws, since it 'is the locus' of a believer's 'stand on the deepest and most fundamental issues – death, evil, the meaning of life' (1989: 118). From another viewpoint, however, this is exactly why we should subject religion to sceptical scrutiny and *not* give it any special protection. It makes very large claims, including claims about how we should live our lives. It demands subjection from us; and if it cannot persuade us as to why we should abase ourselves, we have every reason to resent its demands and to meet it with a defiant response. As Cliteur expresses the point, Taylor makes precisely the wrong call for understanding. He does not call for understanding from 'religious fanatics', but for understanding from 'the side of the critics of religion, the satirists, and the proponents of free speech' (Cliteur 2016: 5). Unfortunately, bad calls of this sort are too common, and they all too commonly come from sources – such as many of Rushdie's detractors, including Taylor and Dummett – strongly identified with liberal or left-wing politics.

A genuinely liberal alternative would look very different: we'd permit speech that might offend, while protecting those who give offence from the vetoes of hecklers and worse – where 'worse' in this case includes jihadist murderers. The long-term aim is to impart a valuable lesson: groups with opposed ideas must each make their own way, enduring criticism, and even satire, from their opponents. Whether or not they survive depends on how they fare in the cut and thrust of debate, and how far they remain attractive to adherents.

Since the Rushdie affair there have been many other examples of theoterrorism (Cliteur's word) directed at authors and artists. Among the most shocking incidents were the murders committed in January 2015, when two masked jihadists attacked the Paris offices of *Charlie Hebdo*, a satirical weekly magazine. They murdered twelve people in all, including eight *Charlie Hebdo* staff and two police officers, and left eleven other victims wounded. Among the dead were the beloved editor and cartoonist Stéphane 'Charb' Charbonnier. In the aftermath of the attack on its office, many people expressed solidarity with the magazine's remaining staff and their loved ones, yet many left-wing Western commentators and public intellectuals turned against the victims. Most commonly, they expressed the sanctimonious advice not to 'provoke' Muslims. Often they accused *Charlie Hebdo* of racism or something similar (for more on these responses, see Blackford 2015a; Cliteur 2016).

In the face of theoterrorist violence, many voices on the political Left demand that Westerners show more understanding of religious, and especially Islamic, ways of thinking. They do not, however, call for charity and understanding in assessing the work of victims such as Rushdie and the *Charlie Hebdo* cartoonists. At the end of his 2016 article on the Rushdie affair, Cliteur observes that Rushdie never wrote another book like *The Satanic Verses*, published in 1988, and that Danish cartoonist Kurt Westergaard never drew another cartoon like the one that famously made him a marked man in 2005. Dutch filmmaker Theo van Gogh is dead, murdered by a jihadist fanatic in 2004, as is Charbonnier, along with many of his colleagues. And yet, we seem to acquiesce:

The most haunting specter is not that people write religious satire (as has been done, against all odds, throughout European history), but that many people will stop doing so because they feel unsupported by their government, which is unable to guarantee their safety, and because their intentions are mischaracterized by the greatest intellectuals of our time, who pontificate about 'respect', 'dialogue', and 'wise judgment', but in fact play into the hands of the terrorists. (Cliteur 2016: 17)

Galilean personalities

Much of Alice Dreger's 2015 book, *Galileo's Middle Finger*, recounts the experiences of scientists and scholars who have come under attack for one or another sort of political nonconformity. One of them is J. Michael Bailey, a psychology professor at Northwestern University whose research relating to transgender people led him to reject an account frequently used by transgender advocates. Dreger describes this account as follows:

> Everyone is born either male or female in the brain. But a person might accidentally be born with the 'wrong' sexual anatomy – be born with an essentially female brain in a male body, or vice versa. If this happens, the person will know from early childhood that a terrible mistake has been made. If fortunate, such a person will eventually be able to come out of the closet and use surgery, hormones, and the legal system to end up with the body and social identity he or she should always have had. (2015: 54)

I have no view, one way or the other, about the substance of this account. I am not at all qualified to assess the evidence. Note, however, that if it's accepted it makes the basics of contemporary transgender issues seem straightforward. The implication is that each of us has a true male or female self from birth – and gender reassignment sorts things out correctly when needed. In his 2003 book, *The Man Who Would Be Queen*, however, Bailey rejected this as simplistic and unscientific. At the same time, as Dreger emphasizes, he also supported the right of transgender people to whatever hormone treatments and surgeries they wanted and needed in order to feel whole. Bailey thus rejected a particular theory, but he lent his support to transgender people on compassionate and more or less libertarian grounds. See for yourself: I recommend reading *The Man Who Would Be Queen*.

(I should add, in an effort to head off any misunderstandings, that I likewise extend transgender people my full support. I in no way support or advocate transphobia, whatever I might ultimately conclude about the scientific merits of Bailey's work.)

Bailey's account draws on the views of Ray Blanchard, who identified two kinds of individuals who seek male-to-female gender reassignments: those who are traditionally feminine in personality and presentation and grow up to become, or appear as, very feminine gay men; and those who do not present as feminine, or find themselves attracted to men, but nonetheless sense a powerful feminine component in themselves, with part of that sense involving erotic arousal from the idea of being (or becoming) a woman. Blanchard coined, and Bailey subsequently employed, the term *autogynephilia* for the psychological phenomenon involving a love of oneself as a woman or, in Blanchard's phrase, *amour de soi en femme*. Blanchard and Bailey saw culture as affecting decisions about whether to transition: for example, an ultrafeminine gay man might not feel a need to do so in an environment where he was safe and accepted with that identity.

Whether or not this account should be accepted in preference to others involving 'male' and 'female' brains (or whether some other account again will ultimately prevail scientifically), Bailey's programme of inquiry was not aimed at undermining transgender people politically. Nor does it appear to have been driven by any hatred or disgust directed to them – if anything, quite the opposite. However, Dreger suggests that one aspect of *The Man Who Would Be Queen* that caused upset was its emphasis on sexual desires, whether those of gay men or those attributed to autogynephiles. She argues, I think plausibly, that trans advocates have wished to underplay issues of sexuality in an attempt to avoid ideas of mental illness and sexual perversion, and to resist any thought that only gay femme men should be permitted to transition. At this point of her discussion, Dreger makes an astute observation relevant to a wider desexualizing of social advocacy:

> Before Bailey, many trans advocates had spent a long time working to *de*sexualize and *de*pathologize their public representations in an effort to reduce stigma, improve access to care, and establish basic human rights for trans people. The move to talking about trans*gender* instead of trans*sex* was motivated in part by a desire to shift public attention away from an issue of sexual orientation (sexuality always being

contentious) to an issue of gender. This is similar to how gay rights advocates have desexualized homosexuality in the quest for marriage rights, portraying themselves in living rooms and kitchens instead of bedrooms, in order to calm fearful heterosexuals. (Dreger 2015: 63)

It seems, indeed, that ideas of sexual liberation no longer drive much left-wing advocacy. Even support for gay rights is more typically couched in terms of gay men and lesbians being oppressed groups who deserve the same kinds of rights (such as a right to marry) as society's more privileged group, other things being equal: heterosexuals. The rhetoric is one of care rather than one of liberation. It seldom relies on ideas of freedom for gay men and lesbians – and everyone else – to live in their own ways, finding pleasure in activities that are essentially harmless to others. Perhaps this retreat from sexual liberation as a left-wing value was a reaction to the AIDS crisis of the early 1980s, or perhaps it represents an accommodation to the permanent sensibilities of straight society. Whatever the reasons, there are now relatively few voices advocating sexual liberation as a value in itself. If anything, the idea is now widely viewed as outdated and a bit distasteful.

Dreger describes a campaign to smear and destroy Bailey, and so discredit his ideas. She provides the details of threats of violence, attempts to get him fired, and much other abusive behaviour. The campaign involved dubious, or just plain false, allegations of ethics breaches. Early in her investigation of Bailey's circumstances, even Dreger thought there must be some substance in the accusations, but after almost a year of research she concluded that it was all a sham:

Bailey's sworn enemies had used every clever trick in the book – juxtaposing events in misleading ways, ignoring contrary evidence, working the rhetoric, and using anonymity whenever convenient, to make it look as though virtually every trans woman represented in Bailey's book had felt abused by him and had filed a charge. (Dreger 2015: 100)

Dreger emphasizes that Bailey's publications do, indeed, contain ideas and passages that she finds obnoxious or grating, and she offers the thought that he is 'tone-dumb', lacking an ability to sing in tune to the political music around him (2015: 71). I also cringed at some passages in *The Man Who Would Be Queen*, though not necessarily those that

Dreger singles out. Bailey sometimes states his claims very directly and tactlessly, as in this straightforward statement: 'Two types of men change their sex' (2003: 145). He also shows an unnerving confidence in his own judgements and predictions about other people (as I read his book, I sometimes wondered whether he's right about them as often as he thinks). Nonetheless, his sympathy towards the trans women who are the main topic of his book is palpable.

At any rate, Bailey was evidently innocent of the allegations made against him. Rather, '[the accusers] didn't want to hear what Bailey said, so they had to make him just go away – and make sure no one else ever tried it again' (Dreger 2015: 100). Furthermore, Dreger herself received a torrent of abuse and smearing when she published a long article defending him in the journal *Archives of Sexual Behavior* (Dreger 2008).

Once again, my purpose here is not to adopt or defend Bailey's substantive views. Perhaps they are open to genuine scientific criticisms, based on the state of the available evidence, and any individuals who have merely criticized Bailey's views, without going further into smear campaigning and related attempts to punish or silence Bailey himself, have not thereby done anything to their discredit. It would not be democratically legitimate to retaliate against them with comparable efforts to punish them or intimidate them into silence. The point, then, is not to identify the adherents of rival views as good guys and bad guys. It is, rather, to call for a rational, fair debate over the intellectual merits of the views themselves.

Among Dreger's other examples of unfairly treated scientists and scholars, she discusses the furore over *A Natural History of Rape* (2000) by Randy Thornhill and Craig Palmer, which went against a common political narrative by arguing that rape is (at least usually and predominantly) about sexual gratification, rather than power, anger, misogyny, and a male wish to dominate and control women. On Dreger's account (2015: 115–27), Thornhill and Palmer were characterized, falsely and unfairly, as apologists for rape because they saw biological and sexual elements to it, and they were subjected to misrepresentation and abuse including numerous death threats. Of course, the Thornhill–Palmer thesis is fair game for examination and criticism – but many of its opponents have, it seems, been unable to consider it on its merits. Their objective, rather, has been to demonize its proponents and so deter expressions of support for their ideas.

As they make clear throughout their book, Thornhill and Palmer are far from being apologists for rape. On the contrary, they set out to understand it for the purpose of eradicating it from human societies or at least greatly reducing its frequency. However, they argue strongly against current academic understandings of rape which, as they see it, have been distorted by politicization of research: 'The ability of ideology to blind people to the utter implausibility of their positions is perhaps the greatest threat to accumulating knowledge necessary to solve social problems' (Thornhill and Palmer 2000: 152).

The Thornhill–Palmer thesis that rape is generally motivated by desire for sexual gratification seems to accord with folk belief and cultural experience, or simply with common sense. This, however, does not make it correct; many scientific findings have produced revisions of our pre-scientific intuitions. Furthermore, the thesis flies in the face of much social science research and feminist literature, and in that sense it is inconvenient to many people. If it's generally accepted, it will require reconsideration of much current scholarship and activism. That said, nothing about the Thornhill–Palmer thesis need be inconsistent with the basics of feminist thought, such as insistence on gender equality and (more specifically) the cognitive equality of men and women.

Thornhill and Palmer do not, of course, seek to vindicate rapists, reveal them as morally good people, or justify their actions. Even if they are usually motivated by sexual desires, as Thornhill and Palmer conclude, based on a wide range of evidence, rapists are not helplessly *in the grip* of their desires. Merely possessing desires – even powerful ones – does not license anybody to act upon them in ruthless, brutal ways. Indeed, much of the point of the core criminal law is to deter people from satisfying their desires in ways that harm others. Thornhill and Palmer are clearly well aware of this.

Dreger also introduces the ordeal of Napoleon Chagnon, a distinguished anthropologist whose unsentimental vision of our evolved human nature was part of what got him into trouble with colleagues. Serious allegations were made against Chagnon (and the late James V. Neel Sr.) by the journalist Patrick Tierney, particularly in the latter's book, *Darkness in El Dorado*, published in 2000. The most serious, and central, of Tierney's accusations involved gravely unethical and harmful medical practices relating to a measles epidemic among the Yanomamö people of South America. These accusations were quickly shown to be false, and in the end Chagnon was cleared of all charges of misconduct. In June

2005 the American Anthropological Association (AAA) rescinded its acceptance of a task force report, critical of Chagnon, from three years before. However, the impact on Chagnon and his family was devastating, to the point that he was hospitalized on one occasion in 2000 after collapsing with stress.

In his 2013 autobiographical work, *Noble Savages*, Chagnon portrays the bitter campaigning against him, even within his own professional organization, the AAA, as prompted by his tough-minded Hobbesian understanding of human nature, as opposed to what he'd see as more sentimental accounts of human nature and the lives of native peoples. Whether or not he is entirely correct about the source of the hostility, it seems clear that at least some of it related to Chagnon's views on these large anthropological issues, grounded in many years of research in the form of field work among the Yanomamö.

Chagnon writes that 'anthropologists should be the most likely people to arrive at a highly informed, empirically defensible view of human nature using the evidence from generations of anthropological research' (2013: 8). His general complaint is that contemporary anthropology is, instead, dominated by individuals who see themselves as activists on behalf of native peoples, and who insist upon politically motivated theories that lack empirical support or even run counter to the scientific evidence. To such people, Chagnon seems a dangerous heretic.

Chagnon's personal style may have attracted some of the attacks. In discussing his ordeal, Dreger introduces her idea of the Galilean personality:

> But exacerbating tensions was the fact that Chagnon had the classic Galilean personality, complete with political tone dumbness – that inability (or constitutional unwillingness) to sing in tune. Indeed, descriptions of Chagnon provided to me by both his friends and enemies sounded eerily reminiscent of Galileo: a risk-taker, a loyal friend, a scientist obsessed with quantitative description, a brazen challenger to orthodoxy. (2015: 141)

Later, recounting what she said at a meeting of the Human Behavior and Evolution Society in 2009, Dreger refers to 'Galilean types' as 'men and women who are smart, egotistical, innovative, and know they're right' – saying that they 'tend to get in trouble, especially when there's a narcissistic nemesis around' (2015: 180). These people insist on the truth, at least as they see it, even if they pay a price in their own suffering. Dreger ultimately acknowledges that the 'Galilean personality' description applies also to her:

> *Yes.* Pugnacious, articulate, politically incorrect, and firmly centered in the belief that truth will save me, will have to save us all. Right in the fight but never infallible. Yes, I thought: In Chagnon, I have met the ghost of Galileo. And he is me. He must be all of us. (2015: 175)

In turn, Dreger has herself been treated in some quarters as an unacceptable author to publish. As she tells the story, in early 2016 she was contacted by the blog site Everyday Feminism seeking to republish her essay 'What If We Admitted to Children that Sex is Primarily About Pleasure?' (see Dreger 2014). After some routine negotiations, together with an exchange over possible editing to make the piece 'more inclusive' in its wording, it was actually published on the site around the end of May 2016. Soon after, however, it was taken down with no explanation until Dreger wrote to ask for one. In her post on the issue, Dreger quotes an explanatory email from the site's programme director, Josette Sousa:

> When we asked permission … we weren't aware of some of the articles you've published on trans issues and after a reader brought it to our attention and we looked into them. We then realized that while we very much valued the information in the article on teaching children that sex is about pleasure, the views expressed in several of your other articles directly conflicts with the work we're trying to do in Everyday Feminism. For that reason, we decided to pull the article. (Dreger: 2016 [syntactical oddities in the original email as quoted by Dreger])

I'm tempted to exclaim that this is extraordinary, but in fact it is not so extraordinary in today's world of political Manichaeism. Here we see an essay being denied publication, but not because of its quality or its suitability for publication on the site concerned (it was actually *solicited*!). Rather, it was taken down because, *in other work*, its author expressed views that the publisher disagreed with. Like Peter Singer, Dreger is a well-known author with a range of publishing opportunities. But other people who share her opinions on various issues might not have her level of bargaining power. The cumulative effect of events such as

Dreger's online no-platforming by Everyday Feminism is to produce an intellectual climate where free, honest discussion is stifled.

Whatever this is, it is not liberalism as that was historically understood. It's a good example, however, of what I call *revisionist liberalism*.

The Christakis affair at Yale University

The Christakis affair was remarkable in many ways, but not least for the lack of support – and even the outright betrayal – encountered by the victims. This alone would be a reason to consider the case carefully. I'll do so in this section and the next.

On 28 October 2015, Yale University's Intercultural Affairs Committee sent an email to all undergraduate students asking them to exercise cultural sensitivity when choosing Halloween costumes. The email immediately became the subject of controversy, and it can easily be found on the internet (e.g. Intercultural Affairs Committee 2015). In itself, a request for sensitivity appears reasonable, but there is also room to question just how much micromanagement young adults really require from their elders. This is a legitimately debatable issue.

While the email's concerns about costumes amounting to forms of 'blackface' are understandable, given the history of the practice to denigrate and mock people of colour (especially those of African descent), this had not been a problem at Yale. In any event, the email goes much further. It appears to discourage any costume that could possibly offend anybody about anything, even inadvertently. The email's language suggests a particular concern to avoid offending others on religious grounds, by mocking or belittling 'someone's deeply held faith tradition'. This admonition is especially worrying. Admittedly, Halloween parties and events are not the best forums for anti-religious satire. But we might wonder, judging from the email's choice of words and self-righteous tone, whether the Intercultural Affairs Committee would recognize *any* forum at Yale to be appropriate for anti-religious speech. Religions exert power and influence. They are fair targets for sceptical scrutiny, and even for satire and mockery; in that sense, they do not merit special protection – and universities should not give it to them.

All things considered, the Intercultural Affairs Committee's email was at least well-meaning. It was, however, wordy and prescriptive to an extent that could reasonably seem officious. Part of the problem was its provision of very detailed dos and don'ts when a short, general reminder to be tactful and kind might have been more than enough. The Intercultural Affairs Committee even provided a link to a site with anodyne costume ideas and some sanctimoniously expressed suggestions about costumes to avoid. The site provides further links to other such lists of semi-forbidden costumes. If we take this all literally, it seems that students at Yale should not (among many other things) dress up as the dragon-riding *Game of Thrones* character, Daenerys Targaryen, or as the heroine of *The Hunger Games*, Katniss Everdeen. Perhaps the administrators concerned did not think this through.

After midnight on 30 October 2015, Erika Christakis responded by sending an email of her own to the students at Silliman College, a residential college at Yale where she was Associate Master. Her husband, Nicholas Christakis, held the position of Master of the college (that position is now known as 'Head'). The email from Erika, as I'll call her to distinguish her from her husband, is (like the email it responded to) easily found on the internet (e.g. Christakis 2015). It reveals its author's worry about adults' exercise of control over children and young people. Erika states, almost at the outset, 'I don't wish to trivialize genuine concerns about cultural and personal representation, and other challenges to our lived experience in a plural community.' Among other issues that she raises, however, she wonders exactly where to draw the line between a costume that shows admiration for a fictional character – for example, the Disney heroine Fa Mulan – as opposed to one that seems insulting to a racial or cultural group. Who should decide where to draw the line? As she continues, Erika adopts a tone that is far from aggressive or incendiary. On the contrary, the voice that comes across seems quiet, tentative, and exploratory. Erika wonders why young people don't deserve more trust, and even some room to make small misjudgements and transgressions.

This concern about the freedom of young people to make their own decisions fits with Erika's academic and professional expertise in child development. The issues she raises are obviously important to her; she dwells on them in her thoughts, as recorded in the email. Towards the end, she reports that her husband takes a rather libertarian line on Halloween: 'Nicholas says, if you don't like a costume someone is wearing, look away, or tell them you are offended. Talk to each other. Free speech and the ability to tolerate offence are the hallmarks of a free and open society.' Without exactly adopting or rejecting this view (she leaves it dangling, available for others to mull over), she concludes on a slightly different note:

> But – again speaking as a child development specialist – I think there might be something missing in our discourse about the exercise of free speech (including how we dress ourselves) on campus, and it is this: What does this debate about Halloween costumes say about our view of young adults, of their strength and judgment?
>
> In other words: Whose business is it to control the forms of costumes of young people? It's not mine, I know that. (Christakis 2015)

There is more to Erika's October 2015 email, and I have not covered every issue that it raises. Overall, it is somewhat inconclusive – evidently by design. Its wording suggests the thoughts of a careful, honest person confiding in a trusted audience. There is room to argue against some of its ideas and suggestions, but it defines a legitimate topic for discussion in a liberal democratic society: adults' anxieties about the decisions of young people, and, with the anxieties, an urge to constrain and control. A fair-minded person reading the email for the first time might, therefore, hope that anyone disagreeing with it, or with any of its various strands of thought, would respond with similar humility and self-interrogation. That might have led to sincere, reflective dialogue, approached less as a political contest and more as a cooperative exploration of the issues.

Instead, all hell broke loose at Yale.

Erika's intervention was greeted with outrage, including letters denouncing her (and distorting her views), calls for her and her husband to be removed from their jobs, and much personal hostility that went far beyond civil – or even forthright and not entirely civil – debate. They found hateful graffiti scribbled on their doorstep. In one incident, enraged students surrounded Nicholas Christakis, some of them screaming abuse, using language that I suspect they'd never had chosen outside their participation in an angry mob; this was captured on video and widely circulated online.

For Nicholas and Erika, working at Yale, and particularly in their positions as Master and Associate Master of Silliman College, became unmanageable and deeply unsetting. Erika resigned from her teaching position at Yale in December 2015, judging it impossible to continue to teach in such a vitriolic environment and with no real support from the university administration. Erika and Nicholas resigned from their positions as Master and Associate Master in mid-2016, staying on as long as possible in what had become an impossibly hostile work environment. Nicholas retained his tenured professorship at Yale and his position as Director of the Yale Institute for Network Science. However, Erika, who had been a popular and successful teacher, severed all her ties with the university. This was a lamentable outcome for her, for Yale, and for the students who had flocked to her classes.

Betrayal at Yale

Erika and Nicholas Christakis seem like empathic, forgiving people, so perhaps they don't hold grudges. But they'd have every right to feel betrayed by their own academic colleagues at Yale University. Whether out of fear or otherwise, most of their colleagues offered little defence or support.

To be fair, the University President – Peter Salovey – and the Dean of Yale College (Yale's undergraduate liberal arts college) did send an email to students of Silliman College. This was entitled 'Moving Forward Together', and it expressed support for Nicholas and Erika in their respective roles as Master and Associate Master. Notably, however, this email did not go to the whole university. It was sent, moreover, on 17 November 2015, almost three weeks after Erika's original email about Halloweeen costumes, by which time the Christakises' circumstances had become very difficult. Moreover, the email was weakly worded – and it was brief to the point of being perfunctory. See for yourself: like much else in this case, it is readily available on the internet (see Salovey and Holloway 2015).

In addition, an open letter defending the husband-and-wife team – drafted by A. Douglas Stone, professor of applied physics – was signed by ninety-one Yale colleagues (Letter of Support 2015). But far more colleagues were either silent in public or outright hostile to Erika and Nicholas. One unsympathetic response to their plight came from Zareena Grewal, an associate professor at Yale teaching American Studies, Religious Studies and Ethnicity, Race and Migration. Her contribution to the *Washington Post* (Grewal 2015) is little more than a propaganda piece.

Grewal insists that the students and others who campaigned against Erika were not attempting to suppress the free expression of other students. Really? On any interpretation they were agitating in opposition to Erika's email, and in support of the original email from the Intercultural Affairs Committee (with all its officious, condescending detail). Admittedly, the committee's email did not have the status of a directive, but it carries the signatures of twelve senior figures in the Yale community and it appears plain enough that any student who ignored it would have done so at her peril. In this respect, Grewal's approach is a blend of the merely pedantic and the outright Orwellian. Yes, *of course* the students who went after Erika wanted to restrict expression. The only issue is how far this and the methods they employed were justified.

Keep in mind that nobody, least of all Erika, was suggesting that students dress with complete insensitivity to the feelings of others. The question Erika had raised was, in the first instance, where the line should be drawn between the clearly innocuous (perhaps dressing as Mulan, though even that would doubtless attract criticism from some quarters) and the clearly insulting. Grewal mentions blackface as one example of inappropriate costuming, but (to repeat) this had not been a problem at Yale. Moreover, Erika made it clear that she was not encouraging anyone to appear at Halloween parties in egregiously insulting or offensive costumes. Instead, her email states her understanding that there were 'genuine concerns about cultural and personal representation, and other challenges to our lived experience in a plural community'. The questions in Erika's mind were about where to draw a reasonable line, who should draw that line, and whether administrators and other adult authority figures ought to show more trust in the ability of students to do so themselves.

So, why was it necessary for so many students (and even faculty) to react to one thoughtful, gentle email sent by a female teacher expressing her concern over adults' distrust of young people? Erika could have done far worse than send her email, and the reaction would still have been out of proportion to the occasion.

Yet, Grewal goes so far as to assert: 'we shouldn't demand that our students coddle professors' – as if treating Erika Christakis and her husband with ordinary human decency would have been *coddling* them! At one point, Grewal refers with disdain to what she calls 'a few seconds of viral video footage of a black student shouting at a calm, white professor', but this trivializes a serious event. On the occasion concerned,

Nicholas was physically surrounded by students, perhaps 150 of them, layered far too deep for him to escape unaided. The students subjected him to abuse for well over two hours. Enough has been documented on the internet to put these facts beyond serious doubt (see, for example, the videos embedded in Kirchick 2016).

However, Grewal does make one worthwhile point. The young woman shown screaming abuse at Nicholas Christakis in the best-known video of events at Yale was subsequently subjected to harassment and reportedly one or more death threats (compare Kirchick 2017). Grewal states:

> And yes, the widely viewed video in which a student curses at Nicholas Christakis ... is difficult to watch. But the antipathy toward our students from afar has been disturbing – it's been less widely reported that the woman in the video has received a death threat. (Grewal 2015)

This exemplifies a recurrent problem with debating issues on the internet. Any misconduct that is revealed online, however unrepresentative it might be of the person's usual behaviour, is likely to shape public perceptions of her (see Chapter 8). This can lead to indefensible forms of retaliation from outraged members of the public. Death threats and other abusive communications must be condemned, and I do condemn them. Grewal, however, uses the abuse received by the student to downplay what had happened to Nicholas. He was subjected to protracted abuse in a frightening real-world situation after having done nothing wrong at all.

Again, the young woman should not have received death threats or other abusive communications. Nonetheless, she and many other students disgraced themselves. To excuse them, Grewal employs a propaganda tactic that I discussed in Chapter 6: portraying an emergency situation that justifies extreme measures such as shutting down or punishing others' speech. But she provides no evidence that students residing at Yale's Silliman College were living in such an apocalyptic zone of racial hate and violence as to justify what would be unacceptable conduct in any other circumstance.

Grewal does refer to an unrelated allegation that came up for investigation about the same time: it was claimed that one member of a Yale fraternity had been overheard at an off-campus Halloween party saying words to the effect of 'We're only looking for white girls.' A more sensational version was that the fraternity actually ran a whites-only party. Even if this had been true, however, it would in no way have excused the treatment of the Christakises for Erika's email written prior to any Halloween parties. In fact, the allegation was ultimately not substantiated and was likely a total fabrication.

One year later, Erika published an article (Christakis (Erika) 2016) in the *Washington Post* to mark these events' anniversary. Here, she presses a point that should have been obvious from the start: the views that she expressed in her October 2015 email 'fell squarely within the parameters of normal discourse' and deserved consideration and discussion on their merits. Erika also deals with the ludicrous claim that what happened to her was nothing more than unpopular speech being met with legitimate disagreement (see for example Manne and Stanley 2015). The record shows that her opponents did not merely disagree and criticize. They radically escalated. They moved straight to declaring Erika's views beyond the pale of toleration, treating them as a modern-day form of heresy and trying to get her fired.

The attempts to drive Erika and Nicholas out of their jobs, together with on-campus incidents of abuse and harassment, do not amount to mere disagreement. This was an aggressive, intolerant, and largely successful effort to punish Erika and Nicholas for expressing forbidden ideas. When others on campus were intimidated into silence, while privately sympathizing with the Christakises or their views, *their* speech was also effectively suppressed. As a result, such discussion as took place at Yale was unimaginative and intellectually impoverished. Erika received no good-faith response to the concerns that she'd raised about young people's maturation and assumption of autonomy. No interlocutors dealt with any of this seriously, and there is still an important cultural conversation to be had about how far adults ought to control children's – and young adults' – behaviour.

For Erika and Nicholas Christakis, the final betrayal came when two of the most abusive students – two who were prominent among the many who'd surrounded and harassed Nicholas – were ultimately made the recipients of the Nakanishi Prize, awarded by Yale for 'enhancing race and/or ethnic relations' (Kirchick 2017).

No individual's life should be destroyed over a single action that falls short of a major crime or act of dereliction. It would have been a step too far to have expelled students from Yale for their roles in just this single event. Perhaps their behaviour that day was out of character, intoxicated as they were by participation in a mob. At the same time, there must be some limits to forbearance. In the absence of any expressions of remorse for their poor conduct, these students should not have been considered for such an award.

In a lengthy article that appears to me a fair summation of the Christakis affair, Conor Friedersdorf wrote in *The Atlantic*:

> Yale activists felt failed by their institution and took out their frustration on two undeserving scapegoats who had only recently arrived there. Students who profess a belief in the importance of feeling safe at home marched on their house, scrawled angry messages in chalk beneath their bedroom window, hurled shouted insults and epithets, called for their jobs, and refused to shake their hands even months later, all over one email. And the couple's ultimate resignation does nothing to improve campus climate.
>
> What a waste. (Friedersdorf 2016)

Islam, again, and the smearing of Maajid Nawaz

In October 2016, the Southern Poverty Law Center (SPLC), an organization originally devoted to opposing hate groups such as the Ku Klux Klan, issued its 'Field Guide to Anti-Muslim Extremists'. This strange document enjoined media organizations to deny public platforms to the named and profiled 'extremists', or at least to present them to the public in hostile, undermining ways. Some of the individuals concerned do, indeed, appear to have very strongly anti-Muslim viewpoints, although it is not clear whether any of them fit the picture of an *extremist* as someone who urges extreme, especially violent, measures directed towards political ends.

The cherrypicking nature of the accusations – not to mention their irrelevance or triviality in many cases – made it difficult to determine from the Field Guide alone just how extreme the various individuals are. Some, such as the anti-Islamic activist Pamela Geller, may be sufficiently hostile to Islam as a belief system – and sufficiently public in their hostility – to qualify as extremists in some sense. Geller might well be an anti-Muslim bigot, but even she does not appear to advocate violence against Muslims. Be that as it may, the SPLC document also included Ayaan Hirsi Ali and Maajid Nawaz. Hirsi Ali has sometimes been inflammatory in her anti-

Islamic rhetoric, but it is absurd to describe her as an extremist. In recent years, she has been closely associated with the New Atheist group of authors that includes Richard Dawkins, Daniel Dennett, Sam Harris, and the late Christopher Hitchens (see Chapter 10). She has been involved in public debate through somewhat intellectual books reflecting on her own eventful life (from her early years growing up in Somalia, through her rocky political career in the Netherlands, to her eventual flight to the United States). Her books, other writings, and speeches engage with the Enlightenment legacy of political ideas, and it is fair to conclude that she displays an ongoing hostility to Islam as a belief system. However, this does not amount to hatred of individual Muslims.

More bizarre than Hirsi Ali's inclusion in the Field Guide, was that of British author, broadcaster, and sometime political candidate for the Liberal Democrats Maajid Nawaz. Nawaz is a former Islamist (and activist in the Islamist group Hizb-ut-Tahrir) who has since abandoned political Islam and positioned himself as a liberal Muslim who calls for moderation. His views are concisely summarized in a short book that consists of courteous dialogue with Sam Harris: *Islam and the Future of Tolerance* (2015). Nawaz opposes Islamism – theocratic views connected with Islam – and its more radical manifestations in acts of terrorism; however, he does not seek to destroy Islam. He argues, instead, for theological reforms and non-literal interpretations of Islam's sacred texts. These reforms and interpretations would, he maintains, assist Muslims to embrace secular government and, more generally, the political principles and values of liberal democracies.

The SPLC's listing of Nawaz, in particular, caused something of an outcry on the internet – justified on this occasion. Painting any individual, particularly an ex-Muslim such as Hirsi Ali or a liberal Muslim such as Nawaz, as an anti-Muslim extremist is an effective way of identifying her, or him, as a target for actual violent extremists. In truth, Hirsi Ali's life was already under constant threat from jihadist would-be assassins. Nawaaz, too, had already received many death threats. It is regrettable that the SPLC acted in a way that made these individuals even more obvious targets for violence.

In its final form before it was removed from the SPLC's website in April 2018, the Field Guide contained about 640 words of accusations against Nawaaz, none of them adding up to any sort of demonstration that he is an extremist. One of the accusations was that he once tweeted a cartoon (it was actually a T-shirt with the cartoon) from the Jesus and Mo website (see Jesus and Mo n.d.).

Nawaaz took this action even though, as the Field Guide put it, 'many Muslims see it as blasphemous to draw Muhammad'. As the Field Guide acknowledged, however, Nawaz tweeted the cartoon to express his opposition to the concept of blasphemous speech. In fact, the tweet stated, 'This is not offensive and I'm sure God is greater than to feel threatened by it' (Perry 2014). By the standards the SPLC employed on this occasion, the use of 'Jesus and Mo' cartoons thoughout my own book, *50 Great Myths About Atheism* (2013), co-authored with Udo Schüklenk, is evidence that Schüklenk and I are anti-Muslim extremists.

It does not seem to have occurred to the author of the Field Guide – apparently one Mark Potok (Cohen 2016) – that individuals who are in no way prone to violence, or motivated to harm Muslims, might wish to take a stance against the concept of blasphemy, or that they might wish to satirize the extraordinary truth claims of traditional Christianity and Islam. The Jesus and Mo website is a source of good-humoured, almost affectionate, anti-religious satire, and Schüklenk and I had no compunction about using cartoons from the site in our book (with the permission of their author).

Some of the accusations against Nawaz were arguably more serious, but none, separately or in combination, added up to anti-Muslim extremism. At worst, they might have shown some episodes of opportunistic and otherwise questionable conduct. In particular, the use of brief excerpts from newspaper interviews with Nawaz did not resemble the overall position that he has developed in his writings. Nawaz has every right to feel that his views were quote-mined and misrepresented.

Among its many claims, the SPLC alleged that Nawaz's organization, Quilliam, had produced a list demonizing a wide range of Muslim organizations operating in the UK as potentially jihadist – but this appears to be simply false. In a scathing article in *The Spectator*, Nick Cohen (2016) demonstrates the apparent ignorance of the Field Guide's author about Nawaz's actual views on Muslim organizations and the overall situation relating to Islam in the UK.

In the upshot, the SPLC made various accusations against Nawaz, some of which were simply ridiculous and worthy of being dismissed out of hand – as with the Jesus and Mo incident. An early version of the Field Guide even tried to employ Nawaz's attendance at a raunchy stag night as evidence of anti-Muslim extremism. The Field Guide placed Nawaz in a false light. It misrepresented his actual views on Islam, Islamism, and Islamist violence. Those views lie well within the boundaries of democratically legitimate speech. Indeed, they include much that is worthy of public discussion. *Islam and the Future of Tolerance*, in particular, deserves a wide readership.

In a letter to the SPLC, Katrina Lantos Swett, president of the Lantos Foundation for Human Rights and Justice, protested against the naming of Ayaan Hirsi Ali and Maajid Nawaz as anti-Muslim extremists. She described Nawaz as follows:

> Maajid Nawaz is a British-Pakistani former Islamist who has become one of the most eloquent and effective campaigners against violent jihadist ideologies. He is the founder of Quilliam, a London based think-tank that counters extremism, promotes greater democracy within Islam, and seeks to empower moderate Muslim voices. Unlike Hirsi Ali, who proudly proclaims her atheism, Nawaz continues to identify as a Muslim and seeks to reform the faith that he practices. However, Nawaz has also faced death threats and violence in his efforts to champion freedom of expression and fundamental human rights. (Lantos Foundation 2016)

Most relevantly to the themes of this book, the SPLC's action in issuing the Field Guide was a blatant attempt to undermine the speech of opponents through smearing, hostile framing, and denial of platforms. As so often, we can see a frightening message – this time from a powerful organization with an endowment of over 300 million dollars – that you can be punished for expressing certain views, even if they're as moderate as those expressed in Nawaz's writings and presentations.

This case underlines a tendency on the contemporary Left to treat Islam as sacred – not in the sense that its tenets are regarded as *true*, but in the sense that it nonetheless lies beyond any criticism or satire. Islam is seen as entirely a 'religion of peace', though it has been, in many times and places, a religion of war; Muslims are viewed as beyond moral reproach, unless they take critical stances towards Islam such as shown by Nawaz; critical commentary on the religion's history, tendencies, or doctrines has become a form of secular blasphemy. From this secular, left-wing viewpoint, the blasphemy is not against Islam's god. It is, rather, blasphemy against an oppressed, and therefore sanctified, demographic group. All of this helps deter rational debate about the merits, and the real problems, of Islam and other religions.

To be fair, there is cause for sensitivity here. Islam merits critique, and it is not surprising that it receives harsh criticism from ex-Muslims such as Ayaan Hirsi Ali and the Iranian–British activist Maryam Namazie. For such individuals, Islam functioned in their lives as an oppressive system of beliefs and practices. (It should not be surprising, however, that critics of Islam such as Hirsi Ali and Namazie disagree about some issues among themselves; they are not an undifferentiated mass, but thoughtful individuals who might each have something valuable to say.) At the same time, the civil rights of Muslims are increasingly vulnerable in many Western nations, and this suggests a need to oppose anti-Muslim bigotry while *also* supporting the right to criticize Islam. There's a fine line to tread, but this should not be beyond the skills of liberal-minded people. It should not have been beyond the abilities of the SPLC.

And on it goes ... Rebecca Tuvel and Bret Weinstein

As I complete this manuscript, the immediate past year (2017), saw far too many unfortunate episodes and situations to identify and list. In this section, I will comment on just two. Both involved liberal academics whose views got them into trouble in ways that are becoming familiar. The victims in these cases were, respectively, Rebecca Tuvel (an assistant professor of philosophy at Rhodes College in Memphis) and Bret Weinstein (at the relevant time, a professor of biology at the Evergreen State College in Olympia, Washington).

In early 2017, the feminist philosophy journal *Hypatia* published an article by Tuvel entitled 'In Defense of Transracialism' (Tuvel 2017). Here, the author argued for the theoretical possibility of racial transitioning by analogy to the experience of transgender people. Whether or not her argument is ultimately successful, Tuvel employs a standard philosophical approach in offering her analysis of difficult concepts and a delineated logical path from stated premises to a conclusion. One aim of contemporary analytic philosophers is to clarify confusing issues, which includes identifying crucial points where disagreement may be intellectually legitimate. Tuvel does this using a methodology that is entirely orthodox within her discipline, while engaging with an impressive range of prior literature. Her article is of high quality, and it manifestly deserved publication.

In essence, Tuvel develops a traditional liberal rationale for accepting the genuineness of gender transitions, while arguing that the same approach would appear to require that we accept the genuineness of at least some claimed transitions between races. Her examination of this issue was provoked by public controversy about the racial identity of a high-profile civil rights activist, Rachel Dolezal, whose ancestry was revealed in 2015 to be European (mainly German, Dutch, Swedish, and Czech). Dolezal nonetheless identified as African American.

All of this is politically sensitive as well as conceptually difficult. There is a very large body of scientific and other literature on the concept of race, exploring its meaning and its legitimacy as a biological, sociological, or other category. No single view prevails in the same authoritative manner that evolutionary theory prevails in contemporary biological science. We can be comfortably sure that sub-species and 'lesser breeds' of humans do not exist in the way once imagined by racial theorists. In that sense, race is an unscientific concept. Beyond that, however, there is much complexity to studies of population-level genetic differences within *Homo sapiens*. Likewise, there is much complexity to studies of the social construction of perceived 'races' (which do not track neatly with any genuine population-level differences identified by geneticists). This is a minefield; all the same, Tuvel's article shows the awareness and sensitivity that we might reasonably demand of an academic philosopher venturing into such controversies. Anyone who disagrees with the article is, of course, at liberty to produce a scholarly rebuttal.

Instead, over 800 individuals signed an open letter to the editors of *Hypatia*, demanding, among other things, that the article be retracted and that the journal issue an apology for its publication (Open Letter 2017). This document was sent to *Hypatia*'s editors around the end of April 2017. It seems to have been formally received by the journal's editor-in-chief in early May, by which time it was already the subject of widespread contention. The open letter makes numerous dubious claims and accusations, and its clear intent is to insist on an academic orthodoxy.

Astonishingly, *Hypatia*'s Board of Associate Editors used the journal's Facebook page to issue its own unauthorized 'profound apology' for publication of the article (Hypatia Board of Associate Editors 2017). This statement included detailed reference to the supposed 'harms' caused by an article that does no more than subject a difficult social issue to philosophical analysis. As with the open letter itself, the obvious intent was to impose an orthodoxy on the discussion of controversial, but socially important, topics relating to gender identification and racial identity. The open letter and the associate editors' apology amounted, therefore, to condemnations of Tuvel for a secular equivalent of heresy. Conversely, the politicized and highly contentious writings of trans theorists and critical race theorists were treated in these documents as incontrovertible.

Fortunately, *Hypatia*'s editor-in-chief and board of directors eventually stood by the decision to publish Tuvel's article (Board of Hypatia 2017). The board's statement strikes me as overly conciliatory to Tuvel's (and *Hypatia*'s) critics, but reasonable people might differ about that. In any event, this sequence of events showed that many educators, students, and others were prepared to subject a young and relatively powerless scholar to an academic witch hunt (compare Singal 2017) in order to insist on particular ideas that do not have the status of robust, authoritative science.

Bret Weinstein's situation has much in common with the ordeal suffered by Erika Christakis. As background, the Evergreen State College has a long-standing tradition of conducting a Day of Absence during which students, academic faculty, and non-academic employees from minority backgrounds absent themselves from campus. The idea is to emphasize the significant contributions of non-white members of the college community. In 2017, however, this arrangement was altered, with encouragement for white students and staff to stay off campus for the day. The college planned on-campus events 'especially designed for faculty, staff, and students of color' and 'a concurrent program for [white] allies' to be held off campus (Orenstein 2017).

Weinstein objected to this change of format. In an email dated 15 March – addressed to the director of the college's First People's Multicultural Advising Services programme, and copied to all staff and faculty at the college – he registered his 'formal protest'. He stated that the right to speak or be present on a college campus 'must never be based on skin color'. Weinstein supported this stance with a distinction between the previous arrangements and the 2017 plans for the Day of Absence:

> There is a huge difference between a group or coalition deciding to voluntarily absent themselves from a shared space in order to highlight their vital and under-appreciated roles ... and a group or coalition encouraging another group to go away. The first is a forceful call to consciousness which is, of course, crippling to the logic of oppression.

The second is a show of force, and an act of oppression in and of itself. (Orenstein 2017)

Was Weinstein correct about this? In fairness to the college, participation in all scheduled events was voluntary and there was no compulsion on anybody to stay away from the campus. It is at least arguable that Weinstein overreacted, though it is also likely that he felt social pressure to stay away from the campus on the Day of Absence (compare Zimmerman 2017). All this is, however, rather beside the point. It is not necessary to conclude that Weinstein's position on this substantive issue, or on other campus issues that arose at Evergreen during 2016 and 2017 (Zimmerman 2017), was the correct, or most reasonable, one. For our purposes, it is enough that he contributed to discussion in a way that – like the email that got Erika Christakis into trouble at Yale – fell within the range of normal, democratically legitimate expression of ideas. Weinstein's language could scarcely have been more remote from the kinds of serious dehumanization and hate propaganda whose democratic legitimacy is questionable (see Chapter 4).

Little eventuated from Weinstein's email until late May 2017, well after the Day of Absence had come and gone. At this point, student activists held demonstrations that shut down the college campus. Their activities were partly focused on Weinstein, and particularly his one-person, purely verbal, 'protest' from two months before. One of Weinstein's classes was physically disrupted. His opponents agitated for him to be fired from his job, and he conducted some classes off campus in response to police advice about his physical safety.

At a minimum, this is yet another case of intolerance for ideas that are viewed as, in essence, heretical. Some students placed Weinstein's opinions beyond the pale of toleration and sought that he should lose his employment. It appears that some faculty members sided with them. Yet, Weinstein appears to be a straightforward Enlightenment liberal; he is by no means a racially intolerant or right-wing figure.

In the end, Weinstein did leave the Evergreen College. He and his wife, Heather Heying, an anthropologist also employed by Evergreen, sued their employer for its failure to provide them with a safe working environment. The lawsuit was settled in September 2017, on the basis that the couple would resign from their positions while receiving a sum of $500,000 (including $50,000 towards their legal costs) (Spegman 2017). In settling the claim, the college continued to deny any legal liability, as is common when such settlements are reached. However much we might blame the college itself, or its administrators, for the course of events, the response of many students and others to Weinstein's democratically legitimate speech was illiberal and deplorable.

As we've seen (Chapter 6), liberal and left-wing educators have something to fear from right-wing outrage personalities and their media platforms. On a day-to-day basis, however, a more persistent and ubiquitous pressure for conformity comes from their own colleagues and students.

Purity policing YA novels

Pressures to conform are not confined to the academy – they are widespread within the cultural Left, particularly affecting the literary world. During 2017, public attention was drawn to an environment of bullying and purity policing in the professional and fan communities associated with Young Adult (YA) fiction. The general situation was already well known to writers, critics, and editors, and in my own experience a similarly fearful environment can be found in parts of the literary scene well beyond the YA field. In this section and the next, however, I'll focus on YA, where there is now significant documentation of the role played by what appears to be a small group of activists with a large social-media following.

The journalist and author Kat Rosenfield revealed the problem in an article published by *New York Magazine* in August 2017 (Rosenfield 2017a). Here, she conveys the power that can be wielded by well-connected online outrage warriors. In this case, the target of their outrage was Laurie Forest, whose debut novel, *The Black Witch* (2017), had just been widely denounced as racist, ableist, and homophobic, despite being a critique of racial bigotry in particular. Forest's publisher was inundated with hate mail, most of it undoubtedly from individuals who had not read the book but wished to join the campaign.

The Black Witch depicts the psychological journey of its protagonist from a mindset of unreflective prejudice against the 'heathen' and supposedly degenerate 'races' on her world (such as the Lupines, Fae, Kelts, Elves, and Icarals – or winged people) towards a better appreciation and understanding. Although Forest depicts characters who show bigoted attitudes and use grossly bigoted language, they are clearly not held out as figures to emulate. Rather, the main character, Elloren Gardner, gradually frees herself of bigotry when she leaves her home and encounters Lupines, and the rest, for herself. Through a series of crises, she eventually joins the resistance to the oppressive, even genocidal, regime established by her own race of Gardnerian Mages.

No esoteric reading skills are required to follow the novel's moral trajectory. Though the plot is complex and the book is the first of a series, its adolescent readers could not possibly miss the point. It appears, however, that Forest's detractors were unwilling to countenance any literary depiction of bigotry, even for the purpose of exposure and critique.

As Rosenfield (2017a) observes, campaigns against books such as *The Black Witch* seldom lead to their cancellation. Nor, however, are they totally ineffective. Apart from the traumatic effect upon authors who are targeted, this sort of campaign can overwhelm the positive discussion of a book in the lead-up to its publication. Cyberbullies can silence the buzz for an anticipated title, grossly distort the consumer rankings on key sites such as Goodreads, and undoubtedly reduce sales. Even when they fail or backfire, as might be the case with *The Black Witch*, these campaigns display an illiberal mentality. They are attempts to punish authors and prevent their reach to readers who might find their work valuable.

A similar campaign was launched in 2017 against Laura Moriarty, a more seasoned author whose most recent book, *American Heart*, appeared in January 2018. *American Heart* depicts a near-future America in which Muslims are confined to detention camps in Nevada. It expresses the author's fear of where anti-Muslim bigotry might lead, and her concern at the growing confidence of fascist leaders and groups. In short, *American Heart* shows an obviously humane motivation and sensibility. Yet, it was subjected to a negative campaign, organized among online social justice activists and designed to undermine the book's reputation and sales. This campaign took place in October 2017 – well before the book's release date, at a time when few of those involved could have read advance copies.

What was Moriarty's literary crime? *American Heart* is written from the viewpoint of a 15-year-old white girl, Sarah-Mary Williams, who lives in Missouri with her fundamentalist Christian aunt but is herself a thoughtful and principled atheist. Sarah-Mary befriends Sadaf Behzadi – an Iranian Muslim immigrant and a fugitive from American 'justice' – and helps her efforts to escape to Canada. This seems much like an updated version of Mark Twain's classic *Huckleberry Finn*, and indeed the narrative references Twain and his work (even in the book's final paragraph). To some readers, however, the decision to tell the story from the viewpoint of a non-Muslim character is socially intolerable, while any portrayal of assistance offered from a white character to one who could be classified as a person of colour must be condemned out of hand as a 'white saviour narrative'.

Narratives that portray white saviours are, indeed, frequently open to criticism. One prominent example is the Hollywood movie *Avatar* (directed James Cameron, 2009), which currently holds the record for the largest all-time box-office takings for any film. It falls slightly down the list of box-office hits when an adjustment is made for inflation, but by any measure it has achieved gargantuan commercial success. I have discussed *Avatar* elsewhere (Blackford 2017: 184–5), but on this occasion I will sharpen up some criticism that I previously left more or less implicit.

Avatar depicts the activities of the Resource Development Administration (or RDA) in mining for a valuable mineral on Pandora, the moon of a gas giant planet distant from us in space. As the action commences, we learn that the RDA has located a deposit beneath the 'Hometree' worshipped by one clan of Na'vi, a humanoid alien species with whom we are invited to sympathize. The Na'vi are blue skinned and somewhat feline in their appearance and movements. They show a more-than-human agility and grace, but they are close enough to human in their appearance for audience identification. In many ways, they also suggest Native Americans, at least as portrayed in classic films of the Western genre. Although the Na'vi are superb hunters, and although they are much taller and stronger than humans, they seem for most of *Avatar* to be almost helpless against the heavily militarized RDA's array of weaponry.

Avatar eventually treats its audience to an apocalyptic battle between good and evil, with the Na'vi cast as good – along with a few humans who choose to side with them – and the oppressive human colonists/ miners of the RDA as evil. The Na'vi are successful in repelling the RDA, but it's notable that one human, Jake Sully (played by Sam Worthington), becomes a messianic figure for them, rallying their forces across Pandora and leading them into the climactic battle. Though it was doubtless unintended, this suggests that the Na'vi were unable to find a leader of their own equal to Sully in courage and competence. Further, the various human characters are depicted vividly, with some marvellous performances by the actors. By contrast, the Na'vi tend to be de-individuated, with only one performance of note: from Zoe Saldana, who plays Neytiri, a beautiful Na'vi woman.

One effect of *Avatar*, therefore, is to make the Na'vi seem incompetent and undifferentiated compared to the human invaders. By extension, this suggests a certain incompetence and lack of individuality in the colonized and dispossessed Indigenous peoples that the Na'vi so obviously allegorize. The implication is clear enough to be noticeable – at least if we watch the movie after being sensitized to the issue – but it is obviously not the intended message and it is far outweighed by more overt themes. On balance, the values successfully conveyed to any random audience member by *Avatar* are likely to be anti-colonialist, anti-imperialist, and environmentalist. For all that, *Avatar* is a clear-cut example of how white saviour narratives can go wrong, conveying secondary and unintended ideas that partly undermine their progressive messages. It is fair to identify this whenever we encounter it.

It does not follow that any particular narrative merits condemnation, or even serious criticism, as soon as it can be pigeonholed as an example of the white saviour trope. Rather, criticism of particular novels, movies, and other cultural products should be careful, accurate, well-informed about relevant traditions and techniques, and appropriately responsive to issues of detail, context, thematic weight, and tone. It is lazy, distorting, and anti-intellectual to point to certain superficial characteristics to identify a trope, and then condemn a novel or a movie merely on the basis that the trope is intolerable. This caution applies to *Avatar*: the undercurrent created by its use of the white saviour trope does merit discussion, but it is only one aspect of a complex movie with wide appeal. Part of the problem is that Sully appears to be so much more effective than the Na'vi at their own game: that is, he achieves so much on their behalf without calling on resources not available to them. This impression would have been obviated, or at least reduced, if (for example) he'd provided the Na'vi with human military technology or inside information about its weaknesses.

Laura Moriarty was evidently well aware of the artistic and political risks in writing *American Heart*, a novel that could easily be pigeonholed and condemned as a white saviour narrative. Indeed, she and her publisher went to considerable lengths to address the risks. According to a post by Ruth Graham on *Slate*'s culture blog (2017), Moriarty sought advice about the Iranian character, Sadaf, from two friends who were

Iranian immigrants. She obtained additional feedback from another friend: a practising Muslim of Pakistani and American descent. She also asked a senior academic at the University of Kansas – someone with a record of criticizing racist narratives – to check the manuscript 'with a particular eye toward avoiding another narrative about a "white savior"'. On accepting the book for publication, Harper arranged for several 'sensitivity reads' to identify potential problems.

American Heart obtained a starred review from the influential book-review magazine *Kirkus Reviews*, which is heavily relied upon by booksellers and librarians. A favourable review from *Kirkus Reviews*, with an appended star to indicate high quality, can be crucial to a book's success. It is coveted by any author, and Moriarty had every reason to be thrilled by it. However, subsequent to publication of this review, Moriarty's detractors took to social media sites to campaign against *American Heart* and its starred review. One activist in the YA community, Dublin-based Adiba Jaigirdar, posted a screed entitled 'Books by Muslims to Read Instead of *American Heart*'. She accused Moriarty's novel of 'Islamophobia and erasure of Muslim voices' (Jaigirdar 2017).

Kirkus Reviews caved in to the pressure. Taking an unprecedented step, it replaced the original review with a much-muted version by the same reviewer, this time without a star. The review in its original form (no longer available on the site) concluded as follows:

> By turns terrifying, suspenseful, thought-provoking, and touching, this book is so rich that the coincidences in the plot are easily forgiven. A moving portrait of an American girl discovering her society in crisis, desperate to show a disillusioned immigrant the true spirit of America.

Despite the passing reference to plot coincidences, this peroration would encourage booksellers and librarians to order the book. Compare the ending of the revised review:

> Sarah Mary's ignorance is an effective worldbuilding device, but it is problematic that Sadaf is seen only through the white protagonist's filter. Still, some will find value in the emotionally intense exploration of extremist 'patriotic' ideology, the dangers of brainwashing and blind spots, and some of the components of our nation's social fabric

that threaten to destroy us, such as segregation, greed, mistrust, and mob mentalities.

A thought-provoking, chilling read with a controversial premise. (*Kirkus* 2017)

In this version, some praise remains, but *Kirkus Reviews*, in consultation with its anonymous reviewer, gave the mob what it wanted: a statement that the book's structure and viewpoint are 'problematic'. What had been a glowing recommendation was watered down to the point of saying only that, despite the book's allegedly 'problematic' aspect, 'some will find value' in its content.

It is most unfortunate that *Kirkus Reviews* bowed to pressure from a mob. Weak-kneed responses like these will encourage more such incidents. Though the magazine had not previously acted like this, its editor-in-chief, Claiborne Smith, defended its decision when interviewed by Kat Rosenfield. He signalled that *Kirkus Reviews* would become more aggressive about recommending for or against books on simplistic and essentially political grounds. Judging by Rosenfield's acount, he could not have been much clearer about this: 'When I ask if the book's star was revoked explicitly and exclusively because it features a Muslim character seen from the perspective of a white teenager, Smith pauses for only a second: "Yes"' (Rosenfield 2017b).

None of this demonstrates that *American Heart* is a flawless novel. In particular, Sarah-Mary is sometimes so quick-witted and resourceful for a 15-year-old as to stretch credulity. On the other hand, she learns by the end of the book that her wits and resourcefulness can carry her only so far: rescuing Sadaf is beyond her individual abilities. The precautions taken by Moriarty and her publisher show that they were alert to the 'white saviour' issue and made a good-faith effort to deal with it intelligently and sensitively. Sadaf does need help, since she cannot speak without her accent giving away her Middle Eastern origin, but she is a rounded character who is shown to us as cultured, educated, gracious, and an advocate of secular government – she is not at all a Muslim stereotype. Notwithstanding her considerable reliance on Sarah-Mary's street wisdom, youthful chutzpah, and American accent, she also sets Sarah-Mary straight numerous times.

American Heart is complex, suspenseful, and – in the best sense – uncomfortable to read. I hope it will attract the attention of critics who can handle its complexity. Its first-person narration from a white, non-

Muslim girl provides a bridge between Sadaf and the book's most likely audience: mainly white teenagers. As the narrator examines and sets aside her own prejudices, *American Heart* challenges whatever prejudices its young readers might start out with. Ultimately, this novel is also deeply moving and it deserved its starred review.

I hope I've been clear in this section about what I am – and am not – claiming. I don't mean to claim that all talk of white saviour narratives, cultural appropriation in literature and art, and so on, is nonsense that we should wave away dismissively. I am making the milder – but important – claim that these issues require nuance, particularity, and trained critical discernment. Unfortunately, the worst, most rigidly politicized, criticism often drives out the good.

Identity politics and purity policing

It is worth pausing to recall that Philip Jenninger was not a Nazi or a Nazi sympathizer. Salman Rushdie has a long record of opposing racism – even using some vituperative rhetoric – and supporting the rights of immigrants to the UK. He has every reason to feel that much of the British Left betrayed him in 1989 (and thereafter). The contributors – deceased and surviving – to *Charlie Hebdo* have been bitter opponents of racism in France, and particularly of the *Front National*, the far-right political party currently headed by Marine Le Pen.

Napoleon Chagnon is not an enemy of the Yanomamö, and J. Michael Bailey is not an enemy of transgender people – neither is Alice Dreger or Rebecca Tuvel. Nor is Tuvel motivated by racism, and likewise for Bret Weinstein. Whatever the merits of their controversial book, Randy Thornhill and Craig Palmer are not rape apologists, misogynists, or even, as far as I can discern, anti-feminist.

Erika and Nicholas Christakis are not right-wing figures or enemies of progressive social change. Quite the opposite. Nicholas comes from a multi-racial family, and he served part time for several years as a hospice physician, largely to indigent patients in Chicago's south side, while teaching at the University of Chicago (for more, see Sharlet 2000). Erika has helped vulnerable people including battered wives and homeless substance users. As a couple, they have – and already had at the time of their problems at Yale in 2015 – a proud record of supporting college students from minority groups.

Their tribulations highlight an important problem. In its current form, what passes as the political Left eats its own, or if not exactly *its own* (since Bailey, for example, may be more a political libertarian than anything else) at least people who could be helpful in the Left's contemporary social struggles. Responding to the illiberalism so often evident on US college campuses, Nicholas Christakis wrote an article for the *New York Times* in June 2016, emphasizing the importance of liberal institutions and principles. As he stated, students attending American universities thereby join 'traditions that revere free expression, wide engagement, open assembly, rational debate and civil discourse' – and these very ideas underpin the demands of disadvantaged groups. It is self-defeating to reject liberal ideas in the process of social justice activism:

> Conversely, it is entirely illiberal (even if permissible) to use these traditions to demand the censorship of others, to besmirch fellow students rather than refute the ideas that they express and to treat ideological claims as if they were perforce facts. When students (and faculty) do this, they are burning the furniture to heat the house. (Christakis (Nicholas) 2016)

I could have used many other examples in this chapter, for as I've stated there is no shortage. The examples I've discussed are illustrative, but they are not isolated. I'll introduce even more of them in Chapter 8, where I focus on uses and abuses of the internet. Meanwhile, *What on earth is going on here?* Why have the people whose stories I've briefly told received so much grief? In each of these cases and more, the answer is obvious. In each case, a taboo was breached: a taboo somehow involving historically oppressed groups.

Jenninger did not support the Nazis' campaigns against Jews and others, but he spoke frankly about how the Nazis' supporters probably thought. That broke a taboo in 1980s Germany.

Rushdie was not an enemy of Muslims, but he wrote of Islam critically and not with reverence. Much the same applies to *Charlie Hebdo*, and in a different way to Maajid Nawaz. Chagnon is not an enemy of Indigenous peoples, but he studies them and thinks about them in a way that, again, does not show the kind of reverence – or the outright political activism – demanded by some of his colleagues. Bailey supports transgender people, but on a broadly libertarian basis that is unacceptable to some trans activists.

Rebecca Tuvel's *Hypatia* article spelled out its author's support for transgender people, while claims by the article's detractors that it was somehow racist are clearly risible. Tuvel's mistake – seen from a certain viewpoint – was to ground her support for transgender people in Enlightenment liberal thinking. When applied to so-called transracialism, this style of thinking might imply acceptance of at least some claims along the lines of Rachel Dolezal's. For Tuvel's opponents, that was an unacceptable conclusion with the appearance of a reductio ad absurdum argument against trans rights.

Thornhill and Palmer found themselves in a similar situation. They sought to understand rape in order to combat it – but not on a basis that is orthodox among current feminist activists and scholars. For their opponents, this looked almost like an attempt to justify rape, though nothing of the kind followed from their scientific arguments. Unfortunately for these authors, their analysis was inconsistent with an interpretation of rape that carries much political investment from the Left. Even the Christakises questioned revisionist liberal orthodoxies about cultural appropriation and insensitivity, though Erika's real and deeper aim was to raise issues about freedom and control relating to young people.

In each case, something was said that was viewed as *offensive* to certain groups (and in some cases, inconvenient to activists working on their behalf). In each case, the problem was not merely that the victim's speech was seen as inaccurate: rather, something about what was said, or how it was said, was viewed as politically unacceptable. But in each case, I submit, something of value had been placed on the table for discussion. The views expressed by Jenninger, Bailey, Chagnon, Thornhill and Palmer, the Christakises, Nawaz, Tuvel, and Weinstein were all worth consideration. Each of these views might contain elements of truth. Rushdie's magnificent novel and the uninhibited satire of *Charlie Hebdo* are significant and valuable contributions to modern Western culture. YA authors Laurie Forest and Laura Moriarty have employed their talents to oppose bigotry, nativism, and fascism, but using literary techniques not approved by the YA community's purity police.

In short, the victims described in this chapter did not deserve the betrayals they received. Rather, they deserved support, and of course they received it from some quarters. But they were policed for ideological purity.

Today, left-wing and liberal thought (in the American sense of *liberalism*) is often in flight from Enlightenment liberal ideas. In their place we can see something remarkably different: a social and political ideology, perhaps historically continuous with liberal traditions, that is increasingly centred on identity politics. To be more precise, it is built on glorifying or sanctifying (not merely assisting) historically oppressed cultural and demographic groups. Referring to contemporary hate speech laws – many of which are potentially very broad and range well beyond dehumanizing propaganda – Kenan Malik compares the traditional crime of blasphemy:

> Traditionally, the sacred was a means by which to ensure that institutions, beliefs and practices could not be publicly challenged. Blasphemy laws were simply the most visible of such means. In today's more secular age, it is culture and identity, rather than simply religion and God, that the law seeks to protect from public assault. Even laws that ostensibly protect faith ... are framed in terms of protecting a community's culture and identity. In today's world, identity is God, in more ways than one. (2010: 161)

Thanks, in part, to group polarization, this revisionist ideology goes beyond a liberal-minded concern to break down legal and social barriers that disadvantage people from certain groups, preventing them from living as they wish and realizing their potential. That concern would be a natural outgrowth of Enlightenment liberalism, and it is something that I fully support. Instead, an ideology based upon demographic identities has adopted many of the trappings of religion. It has its own esoteric doctrines, its own definitions of non-belief and apostasy, its own approved boundaries of doctrinal orthodoxy, and its own conceptions of heretical and blasphemous speech.

8 CYBERSPACE AND ITS DISCONTENTS

Trouble in cyberspace

The rapid development of electronic communications has been liberating in many ways, opening up new possibilities for individual speech and cooperative work. The internet offers alternative sources of information, outside of mainstream media coverage of news and current affairs. At the same time, it has brought its own problems. Unfortunately, ideologues, propagandists, outrage warriors, malicious provocateurs, and individuals who carry grudges all exploit the internet's resources.

We can distinguish several problems, but in actual situations that arise on the internet more than one is usually involved. First, the internet expands the potential for ordinary forms of smearing, invasion of privacy, and other abuse. Malicious individuals of all kinds have obtained new opportunities to harm others – sometimes for revenge but sometimes just out of bitterness, immaturity, or cruelty. Second, the internet exacerbates problems of group polarization and encourages extreme viewpoints. Third, it enhances the ability to punish people for nonconforming conduct, especially for disliked or offensive, but democratically legitimate, speech. This can escalate as rival individuals or groups look for tactics to shut each other down.

I'll turn first to the problem of malicious individuals and the websites that support them. The take-home point here is just a reminder that abusive conduct towards individuals has little value as speech – and in principle there is every reason to act against it.

Presence of malice

In Brian Leiter's terminology, many sites on the internet are cyber-cesspools:

> I shall use the term 'cyber-cesspool' to refer to those places in cyberspace – chat rooms, websites, blogs, and often the comment sections of blogs – which are devoted in part to demeaning, harassing, and humiliating individuals: in short, to violating their 'dignity'. Privacy is one component of dignity – thus its invasions represent an attack on dignity. (2010: 155)

Note that Leiter is not invoking any metaphysical or otherwise esoteric concept of dignity. It's clear enough what kinds of abuse he has in mind, and to spell it out further he adds other categories in addition to invasions of privacy: 'implied threats of physical or sexual violence'; 'non-defamatory lies and half-truths about someone's behavior and personality'; 'especially demeaning and insulting language'; and 'tortious defamation and infliction of emotional distress' (Leiter 2010: 155). Thus, cyber-cesspools inflict a mix of tortious harms (harms for which there could be redress in the civil courts) and dignitary harms (for which no legal redress is normally available, but the victims are nonetheless treated in ways that violate ordinary ideas of decency).

Leiter describes two cyber-cesspools that he has encountered through the blogosphere: one a chat room called AutoAdmit catering to discussions of law school and legal practice, but mainly engaged in extreme sexist, racist, and anti-Semitic abuse, including vile lies and/or invasions of privacy relating to identified female law students; the other a blog devoted to harassing, vilifying, defaming, and generally abusing Leiter himself (complete with threats to him and his family). Leiter's larger point, though, is that incalculable numbers of internet sites take this form in respect of some or even all of their content. Furthermore, it is almost impossible to obtain assistance from the civil courts, partly because of the inherent expense and uncertainty of going to court, partly because much of the material may not be legally actionable, and partly, in the United States, because of the effect of section 230 of that country's Communications Decency Act. Section 230 absolves anyone of legal liability for material published on the internet except for the person who actually provides the content. For example, it is not possible to sue a blog owner for defamatory accusations made by others in the blog's comment section.

We can contrast the usual situation with newspapers, for example, where the proprietors bear legal liability for tortious speech in such forms as letters and advertisements. Unfortunately, abusive material that appears on the internet is likely to be more damaging than material in other forms, since it is widely available and can be discovered easily by anyone – such as a potential employer or a potential romantic partner – who knows how to use a search engine. In other words, it's available to almost anyone at all in most countries. As a further contrast, Leiter points out, character assassination by mere word of mouth meets various obstacles before it is widely spread and believed. It is common human experience that vicious gossip can be harmful, but at least the harm is likely to be confined in one way or another. The equivalent via the internet is likely to be more damaging.

As Cass Sunstein explains in his 2009 book *On Rumours* – though it should be obvious from even the most casual acquaintance with the internet and its workings – it is now straightforward to isolate, select, and manipulate data to create a destructive and essentially false picture of a person or a situation, and this can then create a cascade of repetition that defines wider perceptions. Through cascade effects and group polarization, immense audiences can be induced to form ideas about us, as individuals, that are damaging and wrong. The internet is full of reports about what people (allegedly) did and believe, but these can be fictions. Incidents taken out of context, then reported as if they are somehow typical of an individual's behaviour, 'can produce a palpably incorrect impression'. They can be crushing and unfair even if they are not totally false: that is, even if they contain 'a shred or a kernel of truth' (Sunstein 2009b: 63).

Leiter argues – I think incontrovertibly – that the types of abuse found in cyber-cesspools have no significant value as speech. For example, lies or revelations about the sexual conduct of a particular law student do not contribute to the sort of human knowledge that Mill (for example) had in mind; and they do nothing to assist voters to deliberate about political candidates and their proposals. As for self-actualization or autonomy, Leiter gives this short shrift: the abusers may gain some preference-satisfaction from what they do, but it's not plausible that it could outweigh the harm done to others. I might place more emphasis than Leiter on the ability to speak our minds as especially important to human self-actualization – not as just another way among many to satisfy certain preferences. But my analysis would come to essentially the same conclusion (see my discussion of defamatory and invasive speech in Chapter 4). Even if the ability to speak our minds is vitally important and should not be interfered with lightly, we can demand that people restrain themselves when spurred by malice, or when it's obvious that their speech might have a seriously harmful impact on others.

Men and women both receive abuse in cyberspace, but the patterns are gendered. Women are more likely to be victims of revenge porn from angry ex-partners and lovers, and they are often abused in specifically misogynist ways involving threats of rape or calls that they be raped (see generally Citron's *Hate Crimes in Cyberspace*, 2014). Men are, of course, also frequently threatened with violence. Both men and women receive death threats to themselves and their families. (I have had some of these myself, for my criticisms of religion. The threats were not credible, but they were unsettling, especially at a time when I was receiving them day after day.) None of this is socially tolerable speech, and for much of it there should be legal redress.

Mill would not disagree. He did, of course, defend a liberty to express unpopular views on topics of general importance. Although he counselled some basic fairness and self-restraint, he was also prepared to accept a degree of incivility in public debate. But he did not imagine a right to engage in defamation, invasions of private lives, menacing communications up to and including credible threats, campaigns to get opponents fired, or any related forms of abuse. Mill did not defend any of this. Neither should we.

Going to extremes

The rapid development of the internet has greatly increased the social effects of group polarization. A generation ago, in the depth of the 1980s, the phenomena of trolling (online provocation in all its forms) and flaming (angry, insulting disputation) were associated with a relatively small subculture of computer enthusiasts, and especially with participants in Usenet news groups. During the 1990s, more and more of us used email and participated actively in online forums of one kind or another: among them, list-serves, bulletin boards, and blogs. Trolling, flaming, hacking, and spamming (unsolicited online advertising) became increasingly familiar to anyone with a computer.

The emergence of 4chan (established 2003), YouTube (2005), Reddit (later in 2005), Facebook (open to the public since 2006), Twitter (2006), Change.org (2007), and Tumblr (also 2007) – along with many other popular and varied online outlets for self-expression – then transformed our experience of the World Wide Web. The ubiquity of social media has profoundly altered the character of public debate. Large-scale cultural warfare can now be fought in cyberspace.

Cass Sunstein succinctly describes how extreme ideas thrive online:

> With the Internet, it is exceedingly easy for each of us to find like-minded types. Views that would ordinarily dissolve, simply because of lack of social support, can be found in large numbers on the Internet, even if they are understood to be exotic, indefensible, or bizarre in most communities. (2009a: 81)

In a guest post on Leiter's prominent 'Leiter Reports' philosophy blog, Berit Brogaard (2015) offers no less than six factors that encourage this trend, which we can summarize as follows:

1 Online sites and forums attract people who already have similar social and political agendas;

2 The swift flow of information encourages the formation of rival outgroups in response to provocative viewpoints;

3 Exit from an online group is easy, which encourages less like-minded members to leave with relatively minimal consequences;

4 The internet quickly disseminates information about emotionally charged events, which tends to spur groups to react very strongly one way or another;

5 Anonymity tends to erase within-group individual differences, encouraging loyalty to the views of leaders or the majority, and provoking one-upmanship in offering extreme perspectives; and

6 Search engines facilitate selective searches motivated by the impulse to confirm group viewpoints, with a resulting pressure on group members to become more dogmatic and extreme.

As a result, Brogaard argues, relying on studies by Sunstein and other researchers, group identity is exaggerated on the internet, group positions become more extreme and potentially fanatical, and objectively implausible rumours about opponents are believed uncritically. One prominent example that gained the limelight in 2016 was the fiasco of 'Pizzagate' – in which wildly implausible rumours were spread about a Satanic paedophile ring run out of a (specifically identified) pizza restaurant in Washington, DC, and involving high-level figures associated with the Democratic Party (see, for example, BBC Trending 2016).

Brogaard acknowledges that there can be settings where group polarization is beneficial, even if it involves the group adopting dubious beliefs – for example, an Alcoholics Anonymous group (or similar) with extreme and exaggerated beliefs about alcohol can reinforce an alcoholic's determination not to drink. In most settings, however, hypertrophied kinds of group polarization are unreliable for generating true or useful beliefs. At the same time, the process can easily stigmatize innocent people with an impact that can be 'painful, damaging, or even devastating' (Brogaard 2015).

Ron Rosenbaum is one of many commentators who especially blame anonymity for what he calls the 'noxious and polarizing' character of online political conversation:

> The online conversation in particular has become a vicious internecine civil war, noxious and polarizing. And I think I know why: the snake in the garden is the cyber-disinhibition – the loss of restraint, the rhetorical race to the bottom – that is both enabled and encouraged by the use of anonymous screen names. (Rosenbaum 2010: 241)

Some of Rosenbaum's own rhetoric seems overwrought, but I sympathize with it based on my experiences of online social and political discussion. His comments react to a disturbingly high level of abuse on the internet, and he provides examples of angry commenters, from varied political perspectives, who evidently perceive their opponents as ugly, evil, and Nazi-like. The internet provides havens for extreme ranters, while the mask of anonymity protects commenters not just from exposure but from any accountability, responsibility, or sense of shame that might restrain them.

The role of anonymity is apparent from any experience with sites that permit anonymous comments and are not heavily moderated. Anonymity can disinhibit online commenters, enabling them to express a degree of anger and bitterness that they would hide, at least partly, if using their real names. Then again, online commentary can be rough enough even when real names are used, and the tendency for the internet to create communities of like-minded people who already have similar ideas and grievances creates a strong tendency towards group polarization.

As a result, ideas that would seem extraordinary at a meeting in the offline world quickly come to be accepted as the local norm, and dissenters with more mainstream or moderate views are treated as heretics with all that this entails. People who have done nothing wrong by ordinary moral standards can find themselves 'called out': ritually denounced and shamed in public. Rather than supporting the victims, many onlookers choose to pile on in attacking them, perhaps to signal their own ideological purity.

The online moral police

Thanks to social media platforms, it has become easy to organize campaigns against disliked individuals in order to punish nonconforming conduct and (especially) speech. Public shamings, various kinds of boycotts, the practice of no-platforming speakers, and campaigns to have individuals fired can all be used to disrupt even quite powerful opponents. As Greg Lukianoff writes, the process never seems to end: 'It seems as if every day brings a new controversy regarding the purportedly offensive remarks of a celebrity, an official, or an ordinary citizen, followed by irate calls for the speaker to suffer some sort of retribution' (2014: 1).

As a consequence of the internet, any protective effects of physical distance have been largely erased. At one point in *Joseph Anton*, Salman Rushdie reflects on the rise of the internet and the popular search engine Google. He first heard the word *Google* spoken in his presence in 1999, and he reflected then on how deadly it would have been to his chances ten years earlier. Speaking of himself in the third person, since he presents himself more or less as a character in *Joseph Anton*, Rushdie says:

> If this 'Google' had existed in 1989 the attack on him would have spread so much faster and wider that he would not have stood a chance. He had been lucky to be attacked just before the dawn of the information age. (2012: 582 [italics in original])

Rushdie was, of course, especially vulnerable, having incurred what amounted to an extraterritorial death sentence from a religious leader with a global following. But *many* of us should be fearful. The internet greatly expands the opportunities for surveillance, and hence for many kinds of abuse. Online forms of policing and shaming have created an environment with new pressures to conform. Sunstein warns how vulnerable each of us can be:

> To an increasing degree, your silly, confused, flirtatious, angry, and offensive moments, on Facebook or in an email or in daily life, are subject to being recorded and stored (forever) and, potentially, mischaracterized. At one or another time, those moments may come back to haunt you and perhaps seriously injure you. (2009b: 62)

Almost everyone has done something that can, if isolated and disseminated to the world, be made to seem objectionable or even point to something sinister in the person's character. When public figures are involved, this can distort serious deliberation about political choices, but we can all be presented unfairly to friends, family, employers, and others in our lives who matter to us. In a book-length critique of the culture of taking offence, British–Australian writer Richard King acknowledges the power of the internet to extend our speech far more widely, but he adds an important caveat. The effect on free discussion can be counterproductive:

> But it's also true that internet technology vastly increases the opportunities for both giving and taking offence, and that it can engender an atmosphere that works against if not the letter then at least the spirit of freedom of speech. The social networking site Twitter connects people from all over the world, but since its creation in 2006 it has also served as an echo chamber for those who have an axe to grind. Taking offence at some newspaper article, or off-colour comment in an interview, or the musings of a fellow tweeter, the Twitter user is able to raise an instant mob. And so a technology that seems, on the face of it, to increase the scope for freedom of speech is frequently used to close it down. (King 2013: 196)

As in the previous chapter, I could recite a litany of examples, but I'll try to be sparing. I'll include some examples of policing by the political Right, but first let's consider a nasty case discussed by Daniel Solove in *The Future of Reputation*. In 1998, right-wing shock-jock Laura Schlessinger had less success in stopping the appearance on the internet of highly explicit nude photos of herself, taken about twenty-five years before, when she was young, than did the company with copyright in the photos. So, copyright law ended up in this case being more powerful than privacy law. Solove comments:

> While some might cheer this comeuppance of the harsh champion of family values, Internet Entertainment Group obtained the photos through [Bill] Ballance's breach of confidentiality. It seems fairly clear that Schlessinger believed that the photos were to be kept by Ballance in confidence and not sold for profit. (2007: 184)

These circumstances bring together several common features of online punishments. There was doubtless a political element in targeting Schlessinger, but it is also an example of targeting a disliked woman by using nude images without permission in an attempt to humiliate her. Something similar can happen to men, as with Hulk Hogan's treatment by Gawker (apparently with the collusion of Heather Clem, the woman in the Hogan sex tape). But this particular kind of abuse is more typically aimed at women, and it reflects a callous attitude towards women that remains all too prevalent online and elsewhere. Often there is no political element, and the practice is used for revenge or out of simple malice. The large-scale leaks of nude celebrity photos in August 2014 ('the Fappening', as it was soon called, based on a slang term for masturbation) were presumably for sexual gratification and to display hacking prowess.

A more recent case, this time with right-wing culprits, involved Scott McIntyre, a sports reporter with the Special Broadcasting Service in Australia. On 26 April 2015, it was announced in the Australian media that McIntyre had been dismissed from his employment over a series of tweets that he'd made the day before, on Anzac Day. Anzac Day (the first word stands for 'Australian and New Zealand Army Corps') is an important day of national commemoration in both Australia and New Zealand. It marks the anniversary of the Allied landing on the Gallipoli Peninsula, in Turkey, during the First World War, which began on the morning of 25 April 1915. This became a protracted and tragic campaign, with horrific losses on both sides.

Anzac Day thus recalls the first participation by soldiers from Australia and New Zealand in major military conflict. More generally, it is a day of solemn reflection on war and its sacrifices. Australia's participants in the Gallipoli landing are revered as heroes, and their sufferings during the carnage are undoubted. For readers who are unfamiliar with Anzac Day, I hope I've conveyed something of why Australians take it seriously. There is a secular sacredness about it, and any violation of this is understandably offensive to most Australians, especially those with family connections to the events at Gallipoli.

What, then, was McIntyre's crime that supposedly justified his dismissal from employment? He published a series of trenchant tweets criticizing the Anzac Day mythos. Taken as a sequence, these read as follows:

Remembering the summary execution, widespread rape and theft committed by these 'brave' Anzacs in Egypt, Palestine and Japan. Wonder if the poorly-read, largely white, nationalist drinkers and gamblers pause today to consider the horror that all mankind suffered. The cultification of an imperialist invasion of a foreign nation that Australia had no quarrel with is against all ideals of modern society. Not forgetting that the largest single-day terrorist attacks in history were committed by this nation & their allies in Hiroshima & Nagasaki. Innocent children, on the way to school, murdered. Their shadows seared into the concrete of Hiroshima.

Many of us might disagree with McIntyre's sentiments, or at least feel uncomfortable with their emphasis. Even if we understand his critique of war and imperialism – surely he has a point! – we might raise our eyebrows at his particular focus on a solemn national day for remembering those who died or suffered in war. We might also deplore McIntyre's tone, including his apparent contempt for many of his fellow citizens ('poorly-read, largely white, nationalist drinkers and gamblers'). In short, McIntyre might be open to some legitimate criticism for the tweets, their wording, and their timing. Nonetheless, his views lie well within the usual boundaries for toleration in a liberal democracy.

As I discussed in Chapter 4, *some* viewpoints may lie beyond the pale of liberal toleration. Viewpoints involving the advocacy of genocide – perhaps characterizing the targets as vermin – are obvious candidates. Staff who are closely identified with their employer, such as its senior managers or individuals who provide its public face in one way or another, inevitably bring the employer into disrepute if they publicly express seriously dehumanizing and genocidal views. Even if those views ought not be subjected to government censorship, we cannot expect employers to retain closely identified employees who've publicly expressed them. But nothing in McIntyre's tweets was remotely of that kind.

Despite the aggressive language he chose, McIntyre expressed opposition to violence, not advocacy of it, and irrespective of his timing he sketched a familiar left-wing critique of war and its frequent glorification. Nor, moreover, did he take advantage of his large social media platform to single out individuals for attack. Whatever hurt he may have caused to feelings, he did not damage anyone's ability to function in society. McIntyre may have felt exasperated by the large volume of material commemorating Anzac Day – material that he evidently viewed as celebrating imperialism and warfare – but it's unlikely that he set out heartlessly to offend war veterans and their loved ones. Yet, the SBS moved swiftly (with 'decisive action', as its senior managers expressed it) to fire him with immediate effect. This followed an outcry on Twitter that included denunciation of McIntyre by a government minister, Malcolm Turnbull (who became Australia's prime minister later in 2015).

In this case, an employer blatantly punished its employee for expressing an unpopular point of view. Defenders of the SBS might claim that disciplinary action was appropriate on this particular occasion because the individual concerned was a public face for his employer, and therefore needed to avoid expressing opinions that would alienate its audience and harm ratings. For all I know, something along these lines might have been in McIntyre's contract of employment (any sharp employment lawyer would make sure of that). The case was not tested in court, although McIntyre lodged a Federal Court claim for unlawful termination of employment. In the event, the parties reached an out-of-court settlement prior to a scheduled trial. But here is an obvious question. How far would the SBS, which appeals to a multicultural and sophisticated audience, really have been damaged by McIntyre's tweets, absent the storm in reply and particularly the intervention by a powerful politician?

Even if *some* action by the SBS could have been justified, why not something much less extreme, such as publicly dissociating itself from McIntyre's views and cautioning him to exercise tact in future public comments, given his association with the employer's brand? I wonder, finally, how many people who attempt to justify the SBS's actions would take the same approach to cases where the victim was from their own political tribe.

As I discussed in Chapter 6, right-wing outrage warriors in the United States are especially willing to target academic faculty who can be interpreted as calling for prejudice against white people. A case with some similarities to these American campus controversies, as well as to Scott McIntyre's situation in Australia, involved an online statement by the British model Munroe Bergdorf. In August 2017, Bergdorf was signed by the cosmetics firm L'Oréal for its marketing campaign in the United Kingdom. She was the first transgender model to be chosen to front such a campaign in the UK. Within a few days, however, she was fired over a statement that she'd made on Facebook.

Bergdorf had written the following sentences, which I've taken from a report in *The Daily Mail*:

> Honestly I don't have energy to talk about the racial violence of white people any more. Yes ALL white people… Because most of ya'll don't even realise or refuse to acknowledge that your existence, privilege and success as a race is built on the backs, blood and death of people of colour. Your entire existence is drenched in racism. From micro-aggressions to terrorism, you guys built the blueprint for this s***. Come see me when you realise that racism isn't learned, it's inherited and consciously or unconsciously passed down through privilege. Once white people begin to admit that their race is the most violent and oppressive force of nature on Earth… then we can talk. Until then stay acting shocked about how the world continues to stay f***** at the hands of your ancestors and your heads that remain buried in the sand with hands over your ears. (Moodie and Tingle 2017)

Interpreted literally, Bergdorf's first two sentences are inflammatory and incorrect. It is simply not true that all white people are guilty of racial violence as that is commonly understood. However, three points can be made in her defence.

First, her statement as a whole amounts to the claim that white people are beneficiaries of past acts of racial violence and/or of current social structures that perpetuate racial violence. That much is surely correct. Read fairly, Bergdorf was not conveying that every individual white man and woman has personally committed violent, racially motivated assaults. Second, the intemperate wording is understandable, coming as it did in the immediate aftermath of the far-right Charlottesville, Virginia, rally of August 11 to 12, 2017, which involved the violent death of one counterprotestor and injuries to many others. Third – and perhaps this is most important – Bergdorf's statement would have received little attention if it had not been disseminated to a huge and hostile audience by *The Daily Mail*. This was, I submit, a vigilante attack by a sensationalist British tabloid upon the reputation of a relatively powerless individual.

Like Scott McIntyre, Bergdorf was a public face for her employer. It was understandable, therefore, that L'Oréal executives would feel concern about her use of social media. But how far would L'Oréal really have been damaged by Bergdorf's intemperate rant on her Facebook page without *The Daily Mail*'s intervention and the inevitable storm that it provoked? L'Oréal could have acted with restraint. It could have emphasized that Bergdorf had expressed only her personal views, and at a time when feelings were running high over racial issues.

Another deplorable episode in recent years related to Sir Tim Hunt, a seemingly gentle British scientist who (with two collaborators) was awarded the Nobel Prize in Physiology or Medicine in 2001. Hunt's record in science and science administration over several decades has been especially notable for the support he's given to women making careers in the scientific disciplines. Yet he was subjected to a McCarthy-style smear campaign, complete with a Twitter mob with its own hashtag – #DistractinglySexy – all in response to what appears to have been a warm, funny, irony-laced speech delivered at a conference in Seoul, South Korea, on 8 June 2015. The gist of the speech was to offer support for women in the sciences, though it was falsely reported that Hunt called for sex-separated laboratories to protect men from the distraction of having attractive women around them at work.

As so often, there was an online rush to judgement: many credulous Twitter users assumed, without further evidence, that Hunt really had said such a ludicrous thing in all seriousness. The Twitter smear campaign and the #DistractinglySexy hashtag went viral before Hunt, or his defenders, had any opportunity to put his side of the story, and this provides a good example of the way participants in social media go on the attack with indecent haste.

In their partial defence, although I did not join in the cybermob against Hunt, I initially assumed that the vast volume of smoke surrounding him was evidence of some kind of fire. Surely, it seemed, Hunt must have said *something* that deserved condemnation. But it soon became clear that I was wrong. When it comes to internet smears and shamings, smoke can be caused by no fire at all. Hunt's mistake – if it was one – was to engage in some amateurish (but apparently well-received) stand-up comedy about his own romantic experiences with women in the workplace. Such complexities of modern life are staples of situation comedy on television and elsewhere. They are not a reason to have segregated labs, and Hunt did not claim that they were.

It seems that it's taboo with some journalists and other ideological purity police to mention the funny side – and the occasional awkward moments – of mixed-sex workplaces. Seeing the funny side – and yes, the occasional awkwardness – is completely consistent with being glad that women began, in the 1960s and 1970s, to enter in large numbers into predominantly male places of work, with considering this a social improvement, and, indeed, with being strongly supportive of women in the sciences and other male-dominated fields. Hunt takes socially progressive positions in respect of women's roles in science and the modern workforce more generally. Despite early claims that his short speech was met with a disapproving silence, it received applause – and his actual viewpoint was evidently conveyed clearly enough to most people in his original audience.

The content and meaning of Hunt's speech were distorted, either in the genuine perception of some who heard it – which cannot be ruled out when events happen quickly – or more deliberately. Either way, the interpretation provided to the public immediately thereafter was astonishingly uncharitable. We can easily draw the inference that Hunt was sacrificed for political ends. He lost his honorary position with the University College of London (UCL), following a phone call from the institution that was answered by his wife, the distinguished scientist Professor Mary Collins. At one stage, according to reports, he even contemplated suicide.

Hunt's eventual exoneration, at least in the court of public opinion in the UK, owes much to the tenacious, perhaps even obsessive, detective work of one woman who took on his case: the journalist and former Conservative Party politician, Louise Mensch (see, for example, Mensch 2015). Mensch is, in my perception, not always credible. I doubt that I would agree with her about many issues, and – frankly – I'd ordinarily take her journalism with a grain of salt. In this case, however, her work withstood scrutiny. Her role in defending Hunt's reputation provides a positive example.

Much has been written about the Tim Hunt controversy, and readers will need to google for themselves to test my interpretation of the main facts. But one sympathetic and essentially accurate summary can be found in a *Guardian* article by Robin McKie (2015), published six months after the original dispute. At this stage, Mary Collins had been appointed as Dean of Research at the Okinawa Institute of Science and Technology, a position for which she'd applied before her husband was smeared and pushed out of UCL. The future currently seems bright for the couple, but they should never have been put through this.

Ronson on public shaming

In recent years, the trend to an online call-out culture has continued and even intensified, but something changed during 2015, when mainstream journalists and public intellectuals finally began to express unease. In his book published that year, *So You've Been Publicly Shamed*, Welsh journalist Jon Ronson identified 'The terror of being found out': each of us has something we fear being publicly exposed, even in a world where 'nobody cares' anymore about masturbation and the like (2015: 28).

Ronson discusses a wide range of cases, and an evident problem is that they vary considerably, making it difficult to draw overall conclusions or to frame exact principles. Some individuals who've been publicly shamed clearly enough 'started it', in one sense or another, but even people who are partly at fault can sometimes suffer from a cruel and disproportionate backlash. Some victims have been public figures who genuinely acted badly, as with Jonah Lehrer, a journalist who fabricated quotes to make his stories appear more impressive. But even in his case, the shaming process was disproportionate and – as described in detail by Ronson – almost sadistic.

Other victims of public shaming are more innocent than Lehrer. Prominent among them is Justine Sacco, whom Ronson views with sympathy. Sacco's career and personal life were ruined after a single ill-advised tweet that she made on 20 January 2013. She was, at the time, flying from New York to Cape Town, stopping at Heathrow Airport in London. Sacco was then thirty years old, and she was already the senior director of corporate communications for the media and internet company IAC. She was not, however, in any sense a public figure. She had a mere 170 Twitter followers, so her various 'acerbic little jokes about the indignities of travel' as Ronson calls them (2015: 63) would have been seen by only a small number of people – mainly, we might assume, people who would have understood her sense of humour.

The tweet that she sent while at Heathrow said, 'Going to Africa. Hope I don't get AIDS. Just kidding. I'm white!' She was then subjected to a viral Twitter attack. It evidently began when Gawker journalist Sam Biddle retweeted the Sacco tweet to his 15,000 followers at the time, after it was sent to him by one person among Sacco's much smaller group of followers. From there it spiralled out of control into an orgy of spite and glee. Justine Sacco's name was googled 1,220,000 times from that day until the end of December. She lost her job and became an international laughing stock. In January 2018, Sacco obtained a job with an IAC spin-off company, Match Group. This might seem to be a happy ending, but it hardly undoes the ordeal she endured unnecessarily five years earlier.

Ronson offers his own interpretation of the Sacco Tweet: 'It seemed obvious that her tweet, whilst not a great joke, wasn't racist, but a self-reflexive comment on white privilege – on our tendency to naively imagine ourselves immune to life's horror. Wasn't it?' (Ronson 2015: 69). To be honest, it is *not* obvious to me just how to interpret the tweet, and of course I can't read Sacco's mind. If it comes to that, I doubt that she pondered the wording carefully while stopping between flights and adding what must have seemed like just one more of her 'little jokes'. Still, the joke was aimed only at her small circle on Twitter, and it probably did convey to them something along the lines of what Ronson suggests.

Much satire and humour is, as we know, unstable in its meaning – simultaneously saying something outrageous and testing our emotions as we find ourselves laughing at it. It can make us squirm with uncertainty. This applies (sometimes) to high literary satire, but also to much ordinary badinage among friends. In this case, charitable interpretations – if not a single straightforward one – were plainly available for Sacco's tweet. And yet, through a cascade effect, the Twitterati lost their perspective, their sense of charity, and their basic goodwill and decency towards another human being.

Ronson also describes the case of Lindsey Stone, whose life was ruined for a childish (at worst) photograph taken in Arlington National Cemetery. In the photo she is mocking a 'Silence and Respect' sign by miming a shout and making an obscene gesture. Even interpreted at its worst, this is surely not behaviour that merited the consequences: she lost her job; her reputation was trashed; and her life morphed into one of ongoing shame, humiliation, and fear. Like Sacco, Stone was a victim of ideological zealots, though Sacco's attackers came mainly from the political Left while Stone's were firmly based on the Right. When Stone's case was handed to a reputation rehabilitation agency, its strategy was to generate bland, likeable online material associated with her name and likely to be picked up in a Google search. Ronson comments on this with dismay:

> The sad thing was that Lindsey had incurred the Internet's wrath because she was impudent and playful and foolhardy and outspoken. And now here she was, working with Farukh [an operative for the agency] to reduce herself to safe banalities – to cats and ice cream and Top 40 chart music. We were creating a world where the smartest way to survive is to be bland. (2015: 254)

Soon after, he quotes Michael Fertik, from reputation.com (the reputation rehabilitation agency handling Stone's case): 'We're creating a culture where people feel constantly surveilled, where people are afraid to be themselves' (Ronson 2015: 256). More generally, Ronson concludes:

> We see ourselves as nonconformist, but I think all of this is creating a more conformist, conservative age.
> 'Look!' we're saying. 'WE'RE normal! THIS is the average!'
> We are defining the boundaries of normality by tearing apart the people outside of it. (2015: 269)

Despite all its promise, *this* is what the online world has come to.

Forking his repo

In her book *Hate Crimes in Cyberspace*, American law professor Danielle Keats Citron discusses a more complex case that also appears in Ronson's book. This is the experience of Adria Richards, an American technology developer. Unfortunately, Citron discusses it in tendentious terms that illustrate a more general problem when people take sides in a messy conflict. Citron states that Richards 'overheard two men making sexist jokes' (2014: 112) at a conference for Python coders – but she gives no account of the nature of these 'sexist' jokes, even though there was much discussion of them on the internet in March 2013. In fact, Richards' tweet of 17 March 2013 makes pretty clear what the problem was: 'Not cool. Joking about forking repo's in a sexual way and "big" dongles. Right behind me #pycon'.

Unlike Citron, Ronson gives the other side of the story from 'Hank', including his view of the notorious dongle joke: 'It was about a fictitious piece of hardware that has a really big dongle – a ridiculous dongle. We were giggling about that. It wasn't even conversation-level volume.' Immediately prior to that point, they were joking about 'forking someone's repo' (see Ronson 2015: 105–6). (In the world of IT, *forking* means copying and then developing for one's own purposes; as Ronson explains, *repo* is short for *repository*.)

Richards took a photograph of the two men, uploading it onto Twitter with her 'Not cool' tweet, and they were cautioned soon thereafter – by the conference administrators – about making sexual comments. There seems to be no allegation that they were disrupting proceedings around them by talking loudly, and it's clear enough that the jokes, while perhaps carrying sexual overtones, were not straightforwardly sexist. They consisted, at most, of bawdy plays on words, using IT terms that could easily sound like sex organs or sexual acts. This kind of humour is, of course, a mainstay of Shakespearean theatre, and it can be found in Western literature at least as far back as the plays of Aristophanes in classical antiquity. Both men and women engage in – and enjoy – this kind of humour, and there is nothing inherently sexist about it even if we view it as puerile.

We should note for the record that Hank does not deny the bawdy nature of the dongle joke – obviously a play on the slang word *dong* for *penis*. Indeed, he has publicly apologized for this. He appears, however, to maintain that the joke about forking was not intended as a pun on *fucking* but merely a running gag through the conference about 'forking his repo' as a form of flattery. (See the comment by mr-hank made on Hacker News in March 2013.) I see no reason to disbelieve this, since Hank concedes that the humour was bawdy at least in part. It's also not clear why the (seemingly) heterosexual Hank would praise other men by saying, in effect, 'I'd have sex with his repository'. The running gag explanation sounds just as plausible. But who knows? On any interpretation, it was all rather mild. For British readers, the humorous banter of Hank and his friend – a couple of puns about dongles and (perhaps) forking – must seem tame compared to the ribaldry on any random episode of the BBC television series *QI*.

The discussion on Hacker News also reveals that Richards engaged in some vulgar dialogue of her own, on Twitter, only days before the dongle-joke incident. In her case, the joke was advice to a man to stuff socks into his pants. This doesn't, in itself, excuse jokes about dongles and forking (if they need to be excused). But it's one more piece of evidence as to how (in)offensive such banter really is in contemporary life.

To her credit, Citron notes of Richards: 'Her initial tweet might give us pause because it prematurely turned a private conversation into an act of public embarrassment' (2014: 112). Yes, exactly so. As far as the online battle goes, Richards was the aggressor – the one who publicly shamed Hank and his friend, using a Twitter account that had a large audience. Richards dragged the rival culture warriors of cyberspace into an otherwise trivial dispute that could, and should, have been handled confidentially. Whatever else Hank and his friend might have done, they did not target, abuse, or harass Richards, online or otherwise, at least not in the everyday meaning of the word *harass*. (They may, however, have violated the conference's conduct code, with its own stipulative definitions of words; in that sense, the conference organizers themselves were at least within their rights to investigate the issue, and perhaps even to act as they did by issuing a caution.)

Also to her credit, Citron continues:

Richards did not tell the two men how she felt in real space, nor did she tweet their remarks without identifying them to see what others thought. She instead posted the men's picture, sparking an even more disturbing chain of events. (2014: 112)

Hank was soon subjected to the familiar kind of social media shaming – and then fired by his employer. Citron claims that what was alleged in Richards' tweet dovetailed with other problems he was having at work (2014: 112), but she provides no evidence for this. For the record, I am unaware of any such evidence; if it exists, it does not appear to be well known on the internet. Even if Hank had already been in some other trouble in his workplace, we have no way of knowing from Citron's account how serious or otherwise it might have been. The word *dovetailed* suggests some kind of overall pattern, but there is no public evidence of any such pattern.

Thereafter, Hank made a brief public statement in the form of a comment on the discussion board Hacker News (Ronson 2015: 110 – although Citron [2014: 112] refers to a 'blog post'), in which he apologized for any offence given by his jokes, while placing blame for the outcome (his firing) on Richards. His comment included the words: 'She gave me no warning, she smiled while she snapped the pic and sealed my fate' (Hacker News 2013; the comment is also quoted by Ronson 2015: 110). Though obviously composed in an aggrieved tone, those words signed by mr-hank appear to be factually accurate.

By this point, much online opinion was turning against Richards. That is understandable in itself: her behaviour in publicly shaming Hank had caused him harm in his real life. Much of the backlash was, however, unacceptable by any standards of decent online conduct: it included death threats, rape threats, and revelations ('doxxing') of Richards' home address. Denial-of-service attacks were made on Richards' own site and her employer's site (see Citron 2014: 113; Ronson 2015: 114). Richards was herself fired as a result of the internet firestorm. This turn of events is itself, as Citron states, 'shocking' (2014: 113). Two people were now out of work over a very minor incident at a conference.

It appears that Richards' employer considered its own position – for as long as it continued to employ her – to be untenable. This was, however, just the sort of situation where we should look to employers to do whatever they can to exercise moderation and to resist external pressures to harm their employees. The outcome for Richards was out of all proportion to her initial conduct, and much of the reaction that she suffered was vile. Unfortunately, however, she later displayed what seems a lack of empathy and self-awareness. As recorded by Ronson, she denied, when asked, that she felt 'pretty bad' about Hank's firing. She further denied to Ronson that she didn't know what she was doing in making her tweet – that is, creating a threat to Hank's job: 'Yes, I did' (Ronson 2015: 112). In speaking on the record to Ronson, Richards asserted her right to be offended by bawdy jokes, but jokes about a man stuffing socks into his pants evidently didn't offend her at all.

Angela Nagle on the wars in cyberspace

There is no definitive history of the online cultural wars of the past six to ten years, but Angela Nagle's *Kill All Normies* (2017) is the closest thing we have. Nagle writes clearly and well, provides a large amount of information in a very short book, and displays a gift for apt and acidic turns of phrase. Her main theses are thought provoking and contain more than a grain of truth. As I'll discuss in Chapter 10, her research shows flaws, but *Kill All Normies* makes a valuable contribution to current debates.

Nagle tells a story of Manichaean online politics in which bizarre, paranoid subcultures of the Right and Left attack, provoke, and react to each other in a spiral of escalating craziness that bears no resemblance to rational debate. Referring to purity policing and public shaming from the online Left, Nagle writes that 'the dreaded call-out, no matter how minor the transgression or how well intentioned the transgressor, could ruin your reputation, your job or your life' (2017: 8). Nagle's only mistake in the relevant passage of her book is to suggest that online call-out culture has passed its height; that appears far from true.

Nagle plausibly suggests that much of what we now see of the online Left and Right has been produced by – or in reaction to – the exaggerated ideological purism of left-wing call-out culture and 'cry-bullying'. She describes this as 'a vicious culture of group attacks, group shaming, and attempts to destroy the reputations and lives of others within their political milieu' (Nagle 2017: 75). On Nagle's account, this has done enormous damage to the reputation of left-wing politics:

There is no question but that the embarrassing and toxic online politics represented by this version of the left, which has been so destructive and inhumane, has made the left a laughing stock for a whole new generation. Years of online hate campaigns, purges and smear campaigns against others – including and especially dissident or independent-minded leftists – has caused untold damage. (Nagle 2017: 117)

Nagle laments that few public figures not on the political Right have criticized left-wing call-out culture. In fact, this changed somewhat in 2015, with the efforts of Jon Ronson and others, but the point remains largely correct. Nagle writes approvingly of Mark Fisher, a British cultural theorist, writer, and publisher, as one honourable exception, especially for his essay 'Exiting the Vampire Castle' (Fisher 2013):

During the period examined in this book, Mark Fisher stood out as one of the few voices not on the right who had spoken out against the anti-intellectual, unhinged culture of group hysteria that gripped the cultural left in the years preceding the reactive rise of the new far right online. (Nagle: 117)

As *Kill All Normies* describes in saddening detail, Fisher was himself treated badly by left-wing outrage warriors in response to his critique. His depression-related suicide in early 2017 was greeted by some of them with unseemly gloating.

Nagle may exaggerate the extent to which online call-out culture produced – in reaction – the toxic right-wing culture that has become prominent online. She does not make this case with rigour. In her support, however, a practice of excluding and shaming dissident group members is always likely to turn some individuals radically against the group. Recall the finding by Catanese and Tice (2005) that individuals who've been rejected by a group are likely to respond with hostility to the group and with a general propensity towards aggression.

Online call-out culture enabled right-wing provocateurs, such as Milo Yiannopoulos, to push back recklessly, thrive, attract acolytes, and become celebrities. Yiannopoulos is a flamboyantly camp British journalist with a mission to oppose call-out culture by any means necessary – however cruel to the individuals he targets. Though he evidently regards himself as a cultural libertarian – defending writers, artists, and creators of popular culture from politically motivated attacks – he has employed the platforms available to him to savage the reputations of left-wing opponents. Culture warriors such as Yiannopoulos have, unfortunately, done much to assist what became known as the alt-right: a messy ferment of right-wing iconoclasm (the 'alt-light', which includes Yiannopoulos himself) surrounding a core of unambiguous bigotry. The alt-right proper includes a variety of white segregationist, anti-Semitic, and outright fascist ideologies.

Yiannopoulos suffered a severe – possibly temporary, but possibly lasting – career setback in February 2017. His support base crashed after it was revealed that he'd made interview comments in which he'd defended pederasty: consensual sex involving post-pubescent boys and grown men. He has since stood by these comments, while clarifying that he had in mind sexual relationships between, say, a 17-year-old and a man in his late twenties. To be clear about this, Yiannopoulos has never explicitly defended paedophilia: pathological sexual attraction to pre-pubescent children. On the contrary, he has shown a consistent, almost obsessive, and apparently sincere hatred of paedophiles. He has, however, joked about his own experience with a predatory priest when he was only 13.

It's worth pausing to note that his downfall, temporary or otherwise, came from iconoclastic remarks and jokes relating to adolescent sexuality. These were unacceptable to influential figures on the political Right. Generally speaking – there were some honourable exceptions – the Right had shown no concern about his highly personal attacks on individuals whom it regarded as enemies.

While Milo Yiannopoulos received a sort of comeuppance, comparable, I think, to Al Capone's eventual prosecution for tax evasion, the online Right as a whole continues to thrive. Nagle observes that it has become even nastier than the Left's online call-out culture. Certainly, it promotes far uglier ideologies. Nagle concludes her book in what seems like despair:

> Now, one is almost more inclined to hope that the online world can contain rather than further enable the festering undergrowth of dehumanizing reactionary online politics now edging closer to the mainstream but unthinkable in the public arena just a few short years ago. (Nagle 2017: 120)

This entire situation is disheartening. One unsatisfactory consequence is a general chilling of online discussion – no one needs the kind of abuse that rival outrage warriors can unleash on anybody who tries to be objective and thoughtful. Another consequence is that it becomes easy to confuse the 'dissident or independent-minded leftists' that Nagle mentions with more disturbing far-right figures, some of whom may, among their bigotry, vitriol, and abuse, make accurate criticisms of the contemporary Left – indeed, some of the same criticisms as dissident leftists.

In a searching online review of *Kill All Normies*, the Irish political journalist Richard Seymour criticizes Nagle's research and some of her judgements. Seymour, who writes from a Marxist perspective, does, however, find merit in the idea that 'Tumblr liberalism' – the left-wing call-out culture that Nagle depicts throughout her book – and the alt-right 'are mutually co-constituting'. He doubts that Tumblr liberalism 'is a well and accurately defined object' for political theorizing and discussion, but he agrees that something matching Nagle's description 'exists in the real world' (Seymour 2017). In short, Seymour is sharply critical of Nagle but expresses his own displeasure with call-out culture:

> It would be absurd to pretend, however, that Nagle's distemper with 'Tumblr liberalism' is totally without foundation. That is, the idea that this formulation has incubated at times a self-regarding cult of suffering and victimhood, of which the obverse is a matchless viciousness, is patently obvious. (Seymour 2017)

There is more to say about Nagle's theses and her supporting arguments. I'll return to some aspects in Chapter 10. Meanwhile, the key point to emphasize is the remarkable cruelty that has become, to adopt Seymour's wording, patently obvious in online cultural conflict.

Cleaning house

We could take some practical steps to clean up the worst dirt in cyberspace. Leiter (2010) proposes a repeal or modification of section 230 of the Communications Decency Act, with its absolution of internet service providers (ISPs) and others from legal liability for actionable material. He suggests not so much placing responsibility for tortious material on ISPs, but at least placing it on intermediaries who spread the material. This would include, for example, blog owners who host defamatory comments. Compare Solove (2007: 152–4), who has similar concerns about section 230 and prefers to interpret it as not giving immunity once a provider is put on notice of harmful content. The section provides extraordinarily sweeping protections and should be reviewed by American lawmakers.

Leiter also sketches a scheme in which Google could arbitrate complaints about allegedly abusive material. For material found to be abusive, whether or not it is legally actionable, arbitrators could provide remedies such as delisting it from search results, demoting it from appearing in the first page of results, or labelling the search result with a star that links to the complainant's response (Solove makes somewhat similar proposals, 2007: 123–4). Though the details would need widespread discussion, such proposals seem generally reasonable and potentially practical. Any arbitration scheme would need to be implemented carefully, however, with neutral and expert arbitrators. It would be counterproductive if the scheme became politicized, with skewed outcomes in favour of certain kinds of complainants, and turned out to be just another weapon for culture warring.

In Europe, in particular, remedies for personally harmful (but not necessarily untrue) speech are emerging in the form of a 'right to be forgotten'. This development provokes large questions about how far we ought to go in protecting individuals if elimination of online references to them distorts the public record of events – and the potential complexities and dangers of a right to be forgotten could be the subject of a separate study. While the scope and operation of any such right will need to be monitored carefully, it at least responds to genuine social problems, and it should not be dismissed on simplistic grounds related to free speech absolutism.

Meanwhile, Solove (2007: 194–5) discusses media self-restraint as one response to privacy sensitivities, but as he points out this only ever works in a patchy way. For example, some restraint is shown by mainstream media outlets in revealing the identity of rape victims (even in jurisdictions where this is permitted), and restraint is usually shown in reporting on the children of political candidates. In the Wild West of the blogosphere, by contrast, there is no such culture of restrained reporting. Solove suggests the need for an ethical code to apply on the internet – such as deleting offending comments in a timely way when put on notice, taking steps to conceal the identities of people whose private lives have been revealed without consent, not posting photos of other people without obtaining their consent, and avoiding internet shaming. I don't like the odds of this 'code' gaining widespread acceptance, but it would be commendable. Nothing prevents us from adopting it as individuals and applying it as a standard when criticizing others.

Solove's suggestions have merit. They could make cyberspace a bit nicer. But in themselves, they won't stop cyber-witch hunts, public smearing and shaming, and other kinds of online abuse. The problems are too deep to be fixed by legal remedies.

Some final words on cybermobs

Why do cybermobs go after individuals in ways that are harmful out of proportion to anything they might have done wrong? Ronson quotes a 4chan user whom he interviewed, Mercedes Haefer, who justified the attacks on both Justine Sacco and Adria Richards. In the case of Sacco's tweet, Haefer's justification is based on a plainly warped conception of morality and social justice: 'And so the issue … is that she's a rich white person who made a joke about black sick people who will die soon. So for a few hours Justine Sacco got to find out what it feels like to be the little guy everyone makes fun of.' Haefer adds: 'Some sorts of crimes can only be handled by public consensus and shaming. It's a different kind of court. A different kind of jury' (Ronson 2015: 121).

Haefer justifies the cybermobbing of Adria Richards in a different way, but again the emphasis is on handing out punishment: 'Adria Richards got attacked because she got a guy fired for making a dongle joke that wasn't directed at anyone. He wasn't hurting anyone. She was impeding his freedom of speech and the Internet spanked her for it' (Ronson 2015: 120). Ronson also questioned Haefer about the misogynist nature – especially the calls for rape – of public shamings of women. Haefer replied that the usage often means 'destroy' rather than 'sexually assault', but also pointed out that with male victims of cybermobbing the talk is about getting them fired, whereas with women it's of their being raped. These are, in Haefer's perception, the established ways in Western culture of degrading someone's masculinity or their femininity. They are thus the worst things that 4chan users can imagine men and women going through (Ronson 2015: 121–2).

If this attitude is widely shared online, the result is that a sub-set (more likely a number of overlapping sub-sets) of the online population claims the authority to punish individuals who've committed no crimes. The self-appointed judges possess no relevant knowledge base, skills, self-awareness, or institutional legitimacy, and their victims may have done nothing wrong by ordinary moral standards. Even when their conduct is questionable, victims of cybermobbing experience punishment that is out of proportion to any wrongdoing. Thus, we see women degraded and terrified by threats of rape or calls for them to be raped. People of both sexes receive death threats; people of both sexes, as it turns out, lose their jobs. Some individuals have entire careers destroyed.

A seemingly well-meaning person such as Justine Sacco can have her life ruined over a single clumsy joke. Episodes such as those involving Sacco, Lindsey Stone, Tim Hunt, and Laura Moriarty show the dangers for any of us if we engage in all but the most uncreative and literal methods of communicating ideas in the current age of outrage, Twitter and cybermobs.

In his condemnation of cyber-cesspools, Brian Leiter is at pains to insist that we be permitted to engage in 'rough-and-tumble political debate and scathing social criticism', without 'faux civility'. It's okay, he suggests, to use 'scathing critique' of public figures who are 'charlatans and villains' (he mentions H.L. Mencken's writing as a good example of how this can be done) (Leiter 2010: 172). We can surely, he says, distinguish between this kind of satire and humiliating attacks on powerless individuals. I agree with this as far as it goes. But there is also a temptation – discernible in cyberspace – for talentless would-be Menckens to blur the distinction with their choices of targets to 'call out' and their attempts at scathing wit. In some contexts, even an eminent figure like Tim Hunt can prove to be powerless once a cybermob is unleashed.

Let's not adopt absurdly high standards of civility. Sometimes, as Leiter contends, we are faced by opponents who genuinely deserve little respect. But we can find ourselves vilifying good people who legitimately disagree with us – or who have merely made a point in an unusual and individual way – fooling ourselves that *these* particular people are charlatans or villains. United in our cybermob, we are petty little tyrants.

9 WHAT CAN YOU DO?

Reasons to be fearful – redux

Human beings are social animals, communicating animals, and conforming animals. In the gaps left by formal legal sanctions, we conform to the ways of the tribe more than is needed or socially healthy. Crucially, the government is not a unique enemy of freedom. Powerful though governments can be, pressures to conform in thought, speech, and action come from many other sources. They are all around us.

The results, can be unfortunate: harm to individuals who could have made social contributions; suppression of ideas worth consideration; impoverished public debate; misrepresentation of our real knowledge, opinions, and preferences; accumulating compromises with honesty and truth, until we live far from the land of reality; and, in many situations, a culture of wariness, or outright fear, as we walk on eggshells in all our dealings except with intimate friends. Very often, we believe (and then irresponsibly pass on) items of propaganda. We reach for off-the-shelf ideologies – systematic schemes of ideas about politics, economics, or society – and we insist on them inflexibly, even though they're inevitably contentious. In an atmosphere of permanent crisis, we refuse to countenance disagreement, and we respond with outrage not only to opponents but also to moderates on our own side of an argument, or to anyone who thinks independently.

It's a dismal picture, but it's pretty much the human condition and it's not helped by the growing Manichaeism in Western politics. For all its benefits in other ways, the internet makes the situation worse: spreading propaganda, intensifying ideological commitments, encouraging group polarization, and promoting witch hunts and outrage. If you're afraid, I don't blame you. So am I.

In a conformist world, we might well wonder 'What can you do?' meant in a literal way: 'How much room is left for personal choice?' or 'What can we do, these days, without attracting trouble?' This chapter, however, is more about what we can do to push back. I don't have all the answers, but I have a few thoughts.

Most fundamentally, we should recall the core principles and values found in traditional liberal thought. We should examine and clarify them – as I've attempted in the preceding chapters – and then recommit ourselves. We should act upon them consistently in the debates and struggles that lie ahead. Unfortunately, traditional liberal principles and values no longer capture the imaginations of many soi-disant liberals. How, then, are they supposed to capture hearts and minds in the wider community?

This is a challenge that we can meet. If we stand in the tradition of Enlightenment liberalism, it means standing for secular government, individual liberty, free inquiry and discussion, due process for people accused of wrongdoing, and more generally the rule of law. It means that we value reason, individuality, originality, creativity, spontaneity, and the search for truth. To protect these, we value privacy. We value equality, rather than hierarchies and subordination. We defend people who live, think, and speak in uniquely individual ways, rather than as representatives of communities, cultures, religions, political tribes, or demographic groups. We tolerate all ways of living and speaking that are freely chosen by those involved and not straightforwardly harmful to others.

As Enlightenment liberals, we won't insist on a single, valorized template for the good life, or even offer a small group of templates to choose from. We'll accept that even wrong ideas – and even ways of life that prove untenable or unattractive – have a part to play in the advance of knowledge, understanding, conduct, creativity, and taste. As far as possible, we'll favour tolerance and social pluralism.

Church and state (and mosque)

Liberal thinkers usually see the threats to liberty as coming from outside their own tribe – and historically that is mostly true. In the past centuries of European Christendom and its successor kingdoms and colonies, church and state demanded conformity. The power of the medieval church, with its specific code of moral requirements and its own comprehensive politico-socioeconomic ideology, reached into all corners of European society. Liberalism reacted *against* the demands of church and state.

The modern Catholic Church still has a full-scale blueprint for societies, and it still demands that the state enforce what churchmen see as the moral law, but there's an obvious difference. Far fewer people, nowadays, take the church's teachings and demands very seriously. Christianity's authority and power have weakened as an outcome of the Protestant Reformation, set in train just on five hundred years ago when Luther defied the church and issued his ninety-five theses.

(Of course, Luther never sought anything like modern forms of secularism and liberalism. Those grand ideas arose in the seventeenth, eighteenth, and nineteenth centuries, largely in reaction to religious persecutions and wars.)

Today, many people still reject a secular understanding of government and the apparatus of the state. They want to impose traditional religious morals – as interpreted by *them* – using public opinion, certainly, but also via state power. It was people like this, not liberals of any kind, who sought to ban much of the great literary fiction of the twentieth century. Today, it is mainly religious conservatives, not liberals of any kind, who oppose abortion, stem-cell research, and physician-assisted suicide. Over the last half-century, religious conservatives have resisted gender equality and gay rights, even as these have been endorsed by liberal-minded people and gradually gained acceptance in the West.

The most hard-line theocrats among today's religious conservatives have not absorbed the lessons from past wars of religion. They may not *want* to stop religious warfare, whether it is merely cultural warfare or something more like the real thing. They aim to prevail, and to push back the tide of secularization. Some theocrats have apocalyptic fantasies about their role in a cosmic struggle with an imminent End of Days, so for them social compromise and mutual toleration mean little. Worse, they cannot easily be talked out of their positions, since any argument brought against them will involve assumptions that they are (probably) willing to reject. Some are beyond persuasion, or at least the kind of persuasion that can be offered in books. In the last resort, secular, liberal-minded people may find it too futile to engage with them except as intractable opponents.

Christianity aside, many adherents of other religions take anti-liberal views of morality and politics. A separate book could be written on right-wing Hindu groups, among others. Many Muslims show highly conservative attitudes to a raft of moral and political issues. More often than not in the course of history, Islam has been interpreted by its scholars and authority figures as far more than a guide to personal spirituality. Like the medieval Catholic Church, Islam has offered a complete politico-socioeconomic blueprint. The Millian style of liberalism, with its repudiation of totalizing systems of control, is deeply alien to this tradition. So far, moreover, Islam is significantly less tamed than the Catholic Church. Islam, recall, has experienced the grand historical processes of the past five centuries very differently from Christianity.

There are strong tensions between Islam and Enlightenment liberal thought, much as there are strong tensions between many forms of Christianity and Enlightenment liberal thought. In those countries where it has political power, Islam encroaches deeply on areas that Westerners would now reserve to personal choice. But does this make Muslims our enemies?

No. First, Islam is not monolithic. Its texts and traditions are open to interpretation, and it has taken many forms. Most religious believers living within Western liberal democracies – Christians, Muslims, or otherwise – are not, when push comes to shove, zealots. They have little interest in detailed blueprints for earthly societies, and they see, however unclearly, the benefit of a strictly secular state: one that protects its citizens' earthly interests but not their salvation or their moral goodness. Most Western religious believers have embraced a fair bit in the way of secularism and liberalism. Their acceptance of secular/liberal principles and values may be confused, inconsistent, tentative, or half-hearted, but they are open to dialogue and somewhat tolerant of disagreement. In practice, we can usually muddle through living and talking with them. We shouldn't automatically stereotype pious religious people as theocrats or treat them as foes.

Contrary to the dogmas of contemporary revisionist liberalism, nothing about the liberal tradition requires that we hold particular religions, cultures, or cultural practices in any high regard – or that public resources should be expended upon supporting religions and cultures, or ensuring their survival if they no longer attract adherents. In a functioning liberal democracy, religions, cultures, and their associated practices must be tolerated as far as practicable, but they have no special right to be protected from criticism or satire. If they try to impose their doctrines or sectarian moralities through the law, we should oppose them. This has often been my theme in the past (e.g. Blackford 2012).

But at the same time, the civil rights of religious adherents must be protected. This is increasingly important, since political developments in

Europe and North America have made Muslims an especially vulnerable group. They are often subjected to unjustified hostility, and they're regarded by far-right demagogues as a civilizational threat. This view has influenced many elections in Europe, and in the United States it clearly influences the Trump administration. In many situations we must place a high priority on defending the rights of Muslims. Islam is not beyond criticism and satire, as I emphasized in Chapter 7, but Muslims in the West often need protection from nativism, xenophobia, and bigotry.

Liberal democracies flourish on an assumption that social harmony is more effectively produced through mutual toleration than through persecutions. Liberal toleration accords a basic legitimacy to all viewpoints, in the sense that their advocacy is permitted. This applies even to viewpoints that are critical of liberal toleration itself. There might be an outer limit to tolerable speech – reached, I've suggested in Chapter 4, with the worst kinds of dehumanizing propaganda. But the more views and expressions of them that we categorize as beyond the pale of toleration, the more illiberal we thereby become.

In her 2007 book, *Kingdom Coming*, journalist and author Michelle Goldberg examines America's difficulties with Christian nationalists: far-right Christian theocrats. She emphasizes, however, that we should defend the free speech of our opponents, partly for the sake of our own credibility. In particular, we can take 'a much more vocal stand in defense of evangelical rights when they *are* unfairly curtailed' (Goldberg 2007: 205 [italics in original]). Goldberg discusses the occasional situations when officials in the United States have gone overboard and silenced religious speech that is protected by the First Amendment, such as cases where children in public schools have been forbidden to hold their own Bible study groups outside of class, or to distribute candy canes with Christian messages. In the latter case the American Civil Liberties Union submitted a brief defending the students concerned.

As Goldberg states, this was clearly the correct approach (2007: 206). As an ideal, we should go on opposing our opponents but we must also defend their right to oppose us.

Self-policing and blanding down

As I emphasized throughout Chapter 7, threats to liberty now come from all sides. Very often, they come from authoritarians supported by the power of church or state. But sometimes they come from self-described liberals – in the contemporary American sense that does not necessarily involve commitment to Enlightenment liberal ideas. These threats to liberty, with associated demands for conformity, require new and specific responses.

In *Galileo's Middle Finger*, Alice Dreger suggests tactics for scientists wishing to avoid the ordeals suffered by Napoleon Chagnon, J. Michael Bailey, and others. One such tactic is avoiding language that can attract trouble. For example, biologists could be 'offensive' (by which Dreger seems to mean something like proactive) in avoiding the expression *good genes* as short for 'genes that make one more reproductively fit' (2015: 181). This advice – the proactive avoidance of certain kinds of troublesome language – could have come straight from Glenn Loury's 1994 article on political conformity, with its careful explanations of strategic communication and writing between the lines (see Chapter 5). Amusingly enough, though to Dreger's exasperation, Bailey, for one, evidently misunderstood the advice when she offered it in a conference speech in 2009:

> Mike Bailey got up and said that he agreed with me that scientists should be offensive – and he clarified that to mean that offending people was a sign of doing important work. (I groaned; exactly *not* what I meant, but there was that Galilean personality.) (Dreger 2015: 182)

Dreger's suggestion seems plain enough, but perhaps not everyone gets it. And yet … Bailey himself engages in a certain amount of defensive writing in *The Man Who Would Be Queen*. For example, he is careful at one point to explain that the term *evolutionarily maladaptive* is not a hostile or derogatory one:

> Homosexuality is evolutionarily maladaptive. I think this is an undeniable fact, although gay-positive people (and I am one) tend to cringe when they hear words like these. 'Evolutionarily maladaptive' sounds like an insult, but it isn't one. Lot of traits and behaviours that are evolutionarily adaptive are less than admirable: jealousy, selfishness, dishonesty, infidelity, greed, and nepotism are all easy to explain evolutionarily. In contrast, extreme altruism is evolutionarily puzzling. However admirable they are, people who sacrifice their lives

for the good of genetically unrelated others do not pass their genes to future generations. (Bailey 2003: 116)

This is an interesting passage, because it shows Bailey taking care to explain himself in something like the way that Dreger recommends (note that the passage appeared in print several years before Dreger's conference speech). It seems, therefore, that Bailey gets the general point, even if he misunderstood Dreger on a particular occasion. On the other hand, he does not actually avoid using the cringeworthy term *evolutionarily maladaptive*, and he'd likely rebel at any suggestion that he go further in softening his language or obfuscating about his ideas. (And in defence of the 'tone–dumb' individuals like Bailey, there is plenty of tone deafness around from the people who are likely to persecute them. Such people often seem oblivious to framing and irony – and to even the most basic ideas of charity when reading or hearing others' words.)

Dreger's advice – and Loury's – is smart. Yes, it's worthwhile taking some care before we act on it. We can all learn more about writing, and speaking, between the lines, even if we're frank about the substance of what we think. Even if they feel good, rhetorical zingers may not be the best idea when discussing hot-button topics. They can distract as much as illuminate. But writing and speaking between the lines – tip-toeing through minefields, walking on eggshells, incessantly worrying about committing micro-aggressions – involves a risk of its own. How far do we go with it? Must we become blander people, suppressing our personalities? Must we give up all the rhetorical ground to our opponents whenever we speak in public? Beyond a certain point, one that each of us needs to judge (as I've been doing while writing and revising this book, and as you will need to do), that is something to resist.

Tips and traps for players

Dreger has some other tips for scientists working in sensitive areas, among them that scientists should engage affected audiences early, support each other against baseless accusations, and not 'assume that just because a colleague is engulfed in smoke, that he or she has actually set a fire' (Dreger 2015: 181). These are crucial points, and they apply beyond the practice of science. We can all support each other against a range of unfair attacks, and we can avoid rushing to judgement. Rather than piling on when we see colleagues accused of perfidy, we can have each other's backs. Dreger herself is a good role model: she has shown her willingness to invest time (and risk her own reputation) defending individuals who've been unjustly accused and hounded.

There are many specific points that could be made about how we can help create a more liberal cultural and intellectual environment, and ultimately a more liberal society. Each one could be developed (and doubtless hedged and qualified) at length, but the following suggestions are a start:

1 Remember, liberalism and (especially) freedom of speech are about social power in general, not just governmental power. In some cases – as with defamation and privacy law – there can even be a role for the government in protecting individuals from private attacks. This may seem paradoxical, but the paradox is easily explained (see Chapter 4).

2 The news outlets that regard themselves as the institutionalized press are not sacrosanct. The press means all printed material – and beyond that, at least all publicly available written material – not a set of specially privileged institutions. Large media corporations, right up to major newspapers and television networks, often enforce conformity rather than challenging government power and standing for liberal values. Regard them with a critical eye.

3 Employers, with their Big Brother tendencies, are not sacrosanct either. In some cases, it's okay to restrict their prerogatives. We can criticize, and perhaps regulate, their surveillance of employees and job applicants. In particular, we can demand that employers stand their ground against pressure to fire people merely for disliked speech.

4 The same applies to all organizations, associations, and institutions that try to control speech and private conduct, and generally try to enforce conformity. We can criticize them, expose them, and challenge them.

5 Religious, cultural, and ethnic communities are not sacrosanct, though their members' civil rights should be. Don't side with communities against their own dissidents. Remember, these communities have downsides for many individuals – especially for many women who may find them stifling and oppressive.

6 We should apply the same rules to friends and foes. Is it good enough for a foe to be fired for conduct that offends a friend? Fine, then it's good enough for a friend to be fired for conduct that offends a foe. (It's better to have a rule that people don't get fired at all for offensive conduct or speech only remotely connected with the workplace.)

7 Be alert for propaganda. Study its techniques. Teach them to others – not to help them become propagandists, but to help them become better propaganda detectors.

8 Atrocities do happen. But stories featuring bizarre, extreme conduct that sounds too bad to be true (or too good to be true from the viewpoint of a propagandist) are often fabricated. Don't rush to judgement.

9 It is always in order to question the magnitude of a problem, testing the available evidence, and querying bizarre or extreme examples. A problem can be significant without rising to the level of an emergency demanding urgent, draconian remedies and suppression of dissent.

10 Trial by media (including trial by social media) is usually a bad idea. Much gets said that is highly prejudicial to people who may be innocent of wrongdoing. The criminal and civil courts are the right places to deal with serious allegations against individuals. If you really must get involved in trial by media, demand specifics and evidence.

11 We should help people who are persecuted or suffer discrimination because of group characteristics. For example, Muslims, people from disadvantaged racial groups, gay men, lesbians, and trans women and men should all be free to flourish in their own ways. If they're held back by prejudice, we should come to their defence. This follows straightforwardly from liberal values.

12 This does not mean that Muslims, or the members of any other group organized around traditional beliefs and practices, are beyond criticism. We don't need to fetishize religious and cultural groups, as revisionist liberals do, according them moral irreproachability. The tradition of Enlightenment liberalism has its own principles and values. They should be enough to motivate us.

13 We should treasure the Galilean personalities – incautious 'tone-dumb' people – in our midst. These individuals are easily caricatured and demonized, and their speech is easily cherrypicked for offensive words. But their outspokenness and frequent bluntness are socially valuable. Cherish them, and cherish anyone who takes the trouble to defend them.

14 We can think of ourselves as open, curious, honest people – people with expressive needs that cannot be taken lightly. That may not be more important than ensuring our own safety in an ideologically policed environment. But it is still important. We can look at ourselves in the mirror and remember who and what we are. We can strive for a certain kind of fearlessness, even if it's difficult to achieve.

15 We should never retract our ideas and words, or apologize for them, merely because this is demanded by a cybermob. That is how mobs enforce conformity. The more individuals and organizations are willing to face down mobs in cyberspace or elsewhere, the more those mobs lose their power.

In creating a more liberal society, the idea is not to seek absolute restrictions on certain exercises of governmental power. Constitutionally entrenched rights and freedoms can be helpful, but they can never be absolute when a multitude of situations arises with many values at stake. Conversely, much conformity is produced by non-government pressures. Opposing this is hard work involving complications, ambiguities, and tricky matters of judgement. It means examining and questioning exercises of power in every area of society and at every level: whether it's the demands of employers, the rules of clubs, or the endless unspoken conventions of what can and what can't be said and done in an equally endless array of situations. It means unremitting resistance to non-government as well as governmental censorship efforts.

One line of defence against conformity is simple fairness and charity: attempt to say whatever can reasonably be said for others' views and the means and circumstances of their expression. In some cases, not much can be said that's favourable – we might, for example, encounter genuine bigots, fanatics, charlatans, venal cynics, and the like – but even then we can try to be accurate rather than reaching for hyperbole, misrepresentation, and other tools of the propagandist's trade.

Mill asked us to adopt an approach to public discussion of condemning unfair styles of advocacy on all sides. According to Mill, we should especially refrain from denouncing individuals with ideas opposed to our own as thereby bad and immoral people. Instead, we should show charity to our opponents and their ideas, not overlooking whatever might seem compelling or attractive about whatever arguments they advance. We should honour those who are candid and honest – individuals who acknowledge whatever seems to favour their opponents' positions. Mill does not, interestingly enough, expect us to achieve perfect candour and honesty:

> This is the real morality of public discussion; and if often violated, I am happy to think that there are many controversialists who to a great extent observe it, and a still greater number who conscientiously strive towards it. ([1859] 1974: 118)

That's good advice. We should strive to do our best, knowing that it goes against our common human urges and that we'll sometimes or often fail. But if we don't try we'll never succeed.

As a final tip for players: one counter to conformity and its pressures might be greater understanding of them. We can study and teach not only the methods of propaganda but also what is known about motivated reasoning, group polarization, informational cascades (and how to shatter them), pluralistic ignorance, preference falsification, false enforcement and generally all the factors that produce compliance and zealotry at the possible expense of integrity and truth. As a priority, colleges and universities should develop relevant programmes of study. The idea, of course, is not to indoctrinate students with inherently controversial theories, but to teach them enough of what is reasonably well established to help them defend themselves against pressures to conform. More generally and pervasively, institutions of higher education should encourage a degree of epistemic humility, some scepticism about tribalism and groupthink, and more openness to views from outside the group.

'Defend the text'

In *Testaments Betrayed*, Milan Kundera gives high praise to erudite and serious literary critics – a breed whose meditations have sustained the traditions of narrative art, keeping alive the work of great creative authors

(Kundera mentions Joyce, Proust, and Dostoyevsky). But, Kundera laments, such meditation has been extinguished, at least in the popular press, giving way to 'a mere (often intelligent, always hasty) *literary news bulletin*' (1995: 24 [italics in original]).

In *Joseph Anton*, Salman Rushdie reflects after two decades upon the early attacks on *The Satanic Verses*. He says, 'The most powerful way to attack a book is to demonise its author, to turn him into a creature of base motives and evil intentions' (Rushdie 2012: 112). He mentions how, when asked by friends what they could do to help, he often pleaded with them: 'Defend the text' (2012: 115). That is, he asked for a more specific defence of the literary seriousness of his novel, and the integrity of its author, than could be found in a generic defence of freedom of speech. In the heat of cultural warfare – or worse than that, as with Rushdie's predicament after the fatwa – much will be said that is not true to the cultural products under attack or to the motives, abilities, and finished achievements of their creators. We might be legitimately critical of artistic flaws or failures, but we can do our best to give these cultural products and their creators a fair chance to succeed.

If nothing else, my research for this volume led to me to read many books that I would normally have overlooked (not all of which I've ended up citing). They included Wendy Doniger's *The Hindus*, Thornhill and Palmer's *The Natural History of Rape*, J. Michael Bailey's *The Man Who Would Be Queen*, and Laura Moriarty's novel *American Heart* – each of which has come under fierce attack from one quarter or another. On examination, each contains much that is worthy of consideration with an open mind. In particular, *The Natural History of Rape* is nothing like the crude caricature that I'd read about from its detractors.

That's not to say that I consider any of these books to be perfect: in addition to the 'good stuff', they may contain much that's mistaken or even (if not given responsible scrutiny) socially dangerous. *The Natural History of Rape*, for example, may be open to criticisms from a variety of perspectives. It floats some policy ideas that worry me, since they'd entail restrictions on the freedom of young people, particularly freedom from surveillance and control by their elders. This is a possible concern that the authors candidly acknowledge: 'Although it might be argued that reinstating structural barriers entails losses in personal freedom, the consequences of the absence of such barriers should also be considered' (Thornhill and Palmer 2000: 186). To my ears, at least, these words are not sweet music. We can discuss and consider all the issues, but I'd want to see far more research and policy consideration before we start Big Brothering teenagers with chaperones or with more sex segregation in schools and camps.

I don't seek to elevate some, or any, of the books that I've discussed or referred to in this volume to a canon of forbidden knowledge. I merely wish to emphasize that their authors have something worthwhile to say, and they ought to be given a fair hearing rather than dismissed or punished for nonconformity.

When it comes to novels, such as *The Satanic Verses* and *American Heart*, or various other cultural products with their own traditions, such as the cartoons published in *Charlie Hebdo*, there is room for astute, careful, honest, well-informed interpretation and discussion. But there's also room for penetrating critique of much that currently passes for literary and cultural criticism. Too often, this amounts to literal-minded and superficial scouring of whatever is under discussion – looking for ideological transgressions or offensive content. This is frequently coupled with weak understanding of context, framing, irony, technique, and traditions of art and expression. The result is dumbed-down, insensitive, ungenerous cultural discussion such as recently endured by Laura Moriarty.

We can do better than this. Part of the responsibility falls on schools, colleges, and universities. Part of it, though, falls on all of us to take part in good faith in serious cultural conversations. The Rushdie affair highlights how rare this can be: the public discussion of *The Satanic Verses* was often cynical, tribal, politicized, and self-serving. Too few of those involved showed the skill, courage, and motivation simply to defend the text.

Liberalism in a time of populism

There are difficult years ahead for Enlightenment liberalism. Many voters in the United Kingdom, the United States, and elsewhere are now sufficiently gripped by a sense of their own marginalization, during what they perceive as a time of political, economic, and moral emergency, that they're prepared to think what seemed unthinkable. They have turned to fearmongering leaders and desperate proposals.

In *Kill All Normies*, Angela Nagle observes that one type of analysis, in the immediate wake of Donald Trump's presidential victory, was to see the outcome as reflecting the frustrations of working-class or 'ordinary' people who felt left behind by neoliberal policies and economic change (Nagle 2017: 101). Nagle specifically refers to an article by American historian and journalist Thomas Frank, who wrote presciently – well before the election – about working-class anxieties (Frank 2016). As Nagle observes that there was a 'quite remarkable shift' on the Right to endorse this argument after the election 'as though the right had been making Thomas Frank's argument all along'. She quickly adds: 'In reality they had been making pro-inequality, misanthropic, economically elitist arguments for natural hierarchy all along' (Nagle 2017: 101).

Whether or not this description of social and economic elitism on the Right is completely accurate and fair, Nagle is correct that arguments relating to working-class distrust of economic change have a good pedigree on the Left. They should not be dismissed merely because they have lately grown in popularity with right-wing pundits. Many working-class and rural voters do, it seems, feel alienated and left behind by policies of globalization and free trade, whatever the merits of those policies might be in the abstract. This sense of alienation and abandonment provides openings for extraordinary political outcomes, such as the 'Brexit' vote in June 2016 for the UK to leave the European Union. It has assisted extraordinary political candidates, such as Donald Trump, Marine Le Pen, and Germany's Alice Weidel who advocate forms of right-wing populism.

In such a political environment, there can be many surprises. One was the election of a newcomer to politics, the charismatic centrist Emmanuel Macron, as France's president in May 2017. Another was the unexpectedly strong showing of the Labour Party under Jeremy Corbyn in the UK's general election in June of the same year – although the Conservative Party was returned to power as the largest party in a hung parliament. Right-wing populists are not prevailing uniformly, but they are attracting very large numbers of voters with rhetoric and policy that veer towards a political extreme. Their campaigns have been marked by anti-immigrant sentiment, and by isolationist and xenophobic ideas.

Like many others with a rational vantage on politics, I am gravely concerned at the current level of support for populist figures such as Trump and at the increasing visibility of hard-core white nationalists and segregationists. These developments are unhealthy, but liberals of all kinds need to show some self-awareness as we reflect on them.

We often speak of our right-wing and conservative opponents as authoritarians – and yes, many of them are – but what about the behaviour of too many self-styled liberals? Displays of cybermobbing, no-platforming, disruptive heckling, public shaming, smear campaigning, filing spurious allegations against dissenters, and all the rest, are not a good look. What on earth do we think we're doing if we expend energy on harming the careers of liberal-minded people – the likes of Erika Christakis, Bret Weinstein, Maajid Nawaz, or Laura Moriarty – forcing *them*, in turn, to waste energy defending themselves in public?

As it turns out, the campaign against Moriarty's *American Heart* has probably backfired: as a result of the publicity, Moriarty may end up selling more copies of her anti-facist novel than she otherwise would have. But the next person who might have made a valuable contribution through literature to the struggle against nativist and fascist tendencies in America will surely hesitate.

Even if we haven't, as individuals, taken part in the excesses of revisionist liberalism (or identity liberalism as Mark Lilla [2016, 2017] calls it), we've been collectively passive in response to them. Meanwhile, our real enemies prosper with a cumulative effect that could be disastrous on a global scale.

So, what can we do?

If we want to create a more liberal society – one based on freedom, with everyone encouraged and helped to flourish by their own individual lights – we need to take a long, hard look at ourselves. Are we thinking honestly? Are we thinking strategically? (These needn't be in conflict.) Are we alienating people with legitimate economic and social concerns, dismissing them as simpletons and bigots? It would be great – wouldn't it? – if we could persuade rural and working-class voters that right-wing populist strategies are unlikely to solve their problems, but first those voters need to listen to us, and that can't be taken for granted. Their attention has to be earned.

Rural and working-class voters are not highly trained policy wonks. It is not their task to devise policies and laws, and they can often be fooled by demagogues selling economic snake oil. But before we condescend to them, we'd do well to spend time genuinely listening to their grievances. Let's try to get an understanding of *the detail* of what is gnawing at voters in, say, Ohio, or the West Midlands of England, before we assume we know it all.

At the same time, I suggest some earnest self-interrogation. Among ourselves, within our own forums, we need to debate political, economic, and social problems from a wide range of viewpoints and with the barest minimum of taboos on ideas. We need to hear a variety of proposed solutions to the current, very complex challenges for Western democracies and the human future more generally. All of this will require commitment and energy.

Armed with core liberal principles and values, we can persuade many people to join the common effort to oppose right-wing populism and work for a better society. Given a chance, Enlightenment liberal ideas can still capture imaginations; they can attract endorsement in Western electorates. But viewed as an electoral strategy, this means compromise. It means embracing candidates, thinkers, and voters who are ideologically impure by the standards of left-wing identity politics and its associated call-out culture. Mark Lilla and I may show a subtle difference in our thinking – our readers can sift and compare – but I support the warnings against purism throughout his valuable little book on the state of American politics, *The Once and Future Liberal* (2017). This is a lesson we should take to heart, and it applies beyond the United States.

Without betraying liberal principles and values, we can form alliances – at least local and temporary ones – with many socially and politically concerned people who do not identify as liberals. On particular issues, we can stand alongside individuals and groups with a wide range of world views, ideologies, and self-descriptions. Socialists are committed to the emancipation and flourishing of workers, even if they propose solutions that are not always viable. On many issues, their views will be consistent with liberal principles and values. We don't have to adopt specifically socialist proposals as solutions to every social problem, but some might be worth considering. At any rate, more consciousness of class issues and material inequalities would help our understanding of the world and our current political predicament.

Political libertarians have far more trust in market solutions to social problems than I do, and we don't have to adopt political libertarian proposals as solutions to every social problem – though, again, some might be worth considering. Political libertarians do have a fundamental commitment to individual liberty, which makes them natural allies for Enlightenment liberals on many issues, especially when threats to liberty come from the government and its agencies. Even social conservatives – who may, admittedly, have principles and values of their own that override their limited commitment to individual liberty – can be our allies on particular issues. Moderate conservatives sometimes show an excellent understanding of free discussion and its importance.

We should engage in dialogue with all of these people, and with anyone else who will discuss serious issues in good faith. It's an exaggeration to say that *all* ideas should be on the table for discussion: I see no place on the table for Nazism, for example. But the more ideas we claim are off the table and beyond the pale of liberal toleration, the more authoritarian we look (and are). When that happens, it is noticed, to our detriment, in the wider world.

Above all, we need to return to our core ideas. Within the tribe of people who identify as liberals, actual liberalism has become passé. Yet, liberal principles and values – principles such as secular government, free inquiry and discussion, and the rule of law; values such as individuality, spontaneity, and original thinking – have wider cultural resonance if we only take the trouble to explain and advocate them. When we override these principles and values with supercharged anxieties about identity and offence, we throw away what made liberalism attractive in the first place.

10 CALL-OUT CULTURE, CONFORMITY, AND THE FUTURE OF LIBERALISM

Enlightenment liberalism revisited

In Chapter 8, I briefly discussed Angela Nagle's *Kill All Normies*, a book that I recommended for its insights into online cultural warfare. Nagle writes convincingly about the call-out culture on the Left, with its preferred tactics that include smearing, public shaming, no-platforming, and disruptive heckling. *Kill All Normies* offers some fresh ideas, and it was published after I'd completed the first full draft of *The Tyranny of Opinion*. In this final chapter, I'll engage more deeply with Nagle's approach.

First, however, allow me to sum up and clarify what I see as my own central themes. One anonymous reviewer for Bloomsbury (fortunately not the only one) suggested that the manuscript of *The Tyranny of Opinion* merely repackages an existing social consensus. That is, it defends freedom of speech – already a popular idea in liberal democracies such as the United States and the UK. I found this response frustrating, since it overlooks much of the detail of my arguments, especially those in the first five chapters, but it suggests a need for clarification.

I have not defended a vague, untethered concept of freedom of speech. I've defended the Millian harm principle, though with some modifications and reservations, and I've defended a particular conception of what is central to freedom of speech. More specifically, I've defended the liberty of thought and discussion described by Mill in Chapter II of *On Liberty*. The views I've elaborated and sought to justify throughout this work are far from being the current social consensus, though we often hear the broad, undefined idea of free speech being given lip service. There has never been a universal acceptance of the harm principle – witness the many paternalistic and moralistic laws enacted by liberal democracies since Mill's time and up to the present day – and whatever support it once had on the political Left, perhaps in the 1960s, has significantly eroded. The time is therefore more than ripe for a restatement and defence of the classic Millian view of liberty, adjusting it where needed to accommodate more recent historical developments, and showing how it is closely tied to liberal principles and values that themselves deserve explicit restatement.

Most people in liberal democracies do claim to support freedom of speech – that much is probably true. It is not true, however, that they agree on the point or purpose of this freedom, what it really amounts to, or where its boundaries lie. Many participants in democratic politics would be willing to forbid large swaths of speech that they view as culturally offensive. Some politicians, commentators, and other members of the political classes mouth slogans that distinguish free speech from what they consider hate speech, which they sometimes define to include wide categories of speech indeed (Malik 2010). Others, especially in the United States, insist on an absolute, unqualified right to say whatever we want about others. They oppose restrictions on even the most dehumanizing and incendiary hate propaganda. As a further twist, many approaches to free speech depart from Mill's conception of free thought and discussion in that they justify only a protection against government censors. This is, for example, the very influential view of Frederick Schauer (1982).

Mill, by contrast, was anxious to avoid informal social restrictions on our ability to think, speak, and live as we wish. He feared a tyranny of prevailing opinion even more than he feared oppressive legal restrictions. In the twenty-first century, this tyranny of opinion is not necessarily exercised by society as a whole insisting upon a consensus morality. Today, the pressures to conform are likely to come from employers, professional bodies, community groups, and intrusive news media, and from the politicized moral tribes that compete for authority in polarized societies.

The law can provide some protection of our freedom from the tyranny of opinion. It can, for example, offer remedies for violent retaliations, credible threats, humiliating invasions of privacy, unlawful terminations of employment, and wrongful attacks on our reputations. But the formal law can do only so much without making situations worse. Defamation law, for example, has an honourable role to play in current societies: it gives some needed protection. It can, however, also chill public discussion of important issues.

To fill in the gaps where the law cannot or should not assert its authority, we need a morality of public discussion, such as what Mill proposed in *On Liberty*, in which we avoid denouncing individuals with whom we disagree as bad and immoral people. We should show charity to our opponents and their ideas, acknowledge whatever is compelling in their arguments, and honour allies and opponents alike when they show candour and intellectual honesty. This approach to public discussion cannot be imposed by the formal law, with its relatively blunt tools, but we can each endorse it voluntarily, follow it as best we can, and recommend it to others.

The idea of a liberty of thought and discussion is not that we should say whatever we like about each other – however harmful or irresponsible it might be – with no legal or social consequences. The idea, rather, is that no opinions on general topics should be declared heretical and so excluded from the public square. Any exceptions should be defined and interpreted very narrowly, and not used as precedents.

None of this is the existing social consensus. On the contrary, it's a position with surprisingly few contemporary defenders. It is, however, an intellectually coherent and attractive approach once it is set out explicitly and in sufficient detail.

If I've accomplished nothing else in the preceding chapters, I've at least described – and attempted to defend – a Millian viewpoint on liberty of thought and discussion that is currently almost forgotten and merits a full restatement. This Millian viewpoint connects with Enlightenment liberal ideas of liberty, individuality, spontaneity, originality, and intellectual and social progress that have never been much favoured by the political Right and have largely been abandoned by the Left (which is increasingly focused on avoiding offence to members of historically oppressed groups).

The Millian viewpoint on liberty and free discussion is not just intellectually pleasing. It offers the best future for liberal democracies and liberalism itself.

Nagle on iconoclastic values

I find myself in some disagreement with Angela Nagle when I ponder her concerns about the aesthetic values of 'transgression, subversion and counterculture' (Nagle 2017: 115), values that have become de rigueur in some artistic milieux. Nagle traces these values back to the Marquis de Sade's libertine writings of the late eighteenth and early nineteenth centuries. These perhaps influenced Friedrich Nietzsche, directly or otherwise, and on Nagle's account both de Sade and Nietzsche influenced the urge to transgress accepted boundaries that was such a hallmark of the 1960s and 1970s social revolutions. For Nagle, this urge to transgress currently dominates popular culture in the West, and it particularly infects – she does appear to perceive it as a kind of infection – online cultural debates.

If, as Nagle argues plausibly, the values of transgression, subversion, and counterculture have lately been adopted by the alt-light and the hard-core alt-right, we might conclude that such iconoclastic values are of little practical benefit. We might even suspect that they've proven counterproductive to achieving fairer, kinder, less oppressive societies. If I'm reading Nagle correctly, she thinks these values encourage callous attitudes and cruelty. She urges us to reject them.

This is a deep issue. I'm not sure exactly how far Nagle and I disagree about it, and I'd like to see her explain her position in more detail. How much, exactly, of our cultural legacy does she suggest we abandon? Unfortunately, *Kill All Normies* ends in apparent despair rather than with a positive vision of the future for liberal or left-wing thought. Nagle is correct that values such as transgression, subversion, and counterculture obtained great emphasis and prestige in twentieth-century and current art, popular culture, and cultural theory. What is not so clear is how far we should blame them for contemporary social problems.

I have not, in the previous chapters, lauded transgression, subversion, and counterculture for their own sake. Liberal values tend to be milder-mannered: they are values such as individuality, spontaneity, and original thinking. These imply a certain resistance to the pressures to conform, but they don't imply a willingness to smash the whole social system. In *On Liberty*, it's true, Mill went so far as to say 'it is desirable ... that people should be eccentric' ([1859] 1974: 132). But he was referring to a kind of eccentricity that involves no harm to others or dereliction of our duties to society. In any event, an insistence upon art – and perhaps ways of life – designed to violate taboos and shock the bourgeoisie would create a new pressure to conform, not an acknowledgement of individuality. I'm inclined to conclude that Nagle's views and Mill's are reconcilable, but this is not a topic that Nagle addresses.

But even if her rejection of iconoclastic aesthetic values can be reconciled with Enlightenment liberalism, I remain slightly uneasy. In many circumstances, large-scale transgression of existing norms and public discourses might be necessary to bring about valuable social change. It might at least be *locally* and *instrumentally* valuable. It need not involve any kind of violent insurrection, but it might include shocking the old regime's adherents. Second-wave feminism – the women's movement that emerged in the 1960s and early 1970s – provides a good example. In substance and style it was scandalously transgressive of 1950s and early 1960s norms.

During the early decades of the twentieth century, women had been assigned a social role as enforcers of religion and conventional morality; they were expected to tame the men in their lives and to rein in male vices, desires, and rebellious impulses. By the 1950s, men arguably experienced less moral policing of this kind – from women and from each other – but there was a long way to go, as the 1960s demonstrated. Meanwhile, women were still expected to display piety and traditional virtues. The post-war laws, *mores*, and public discourses surrounding femininity emphasized domestic bliss, marital chastity, and women's absence from public life and most workplaces. This trapped many women in monotonous, unadventurous, severely restricted lives.

In the circumstances, the women's movement was not only justified but desperately necessary. For middle-class women, at least, it was a genuine liberation movement. Its basic assumptions about gender equality were simple but radical. Its goals included women's sexual liberation, and it both responded and contributed to women's growing dissatisfaction with what the social historian Callum Brown calls 'the traditional Christian ideal of marriage, motherhood and domesticity' (2017: 6). While feminist movements have always included varied – even warring – elements, and although organized feminism has taken many twists and turns in its emphases since the mid-1970s, the transgressive aspect of second-wave feminism was socially imperative.

I would need to write a very different book to examine the complexities of modern feminisms and their various alleged 'waves', and this would take me away from my point. I am using second-wave feminism as just one example of a broader idea. If we seek large-scale peaceful change, the values of transgression, subversion, and counterculture can be indispensable. Countercultural visions and experiments in living may be vital ingredients for social reform. None of this should be condemned in a broad way. Rather, let's ask in each case exactly which boundaries are being transgressed and subverted, and why. Perhaps Nagle would agree with this much, and she is correct that transgression, subversion, and counterculture can be used to advance undesirable causes as well as desirable ones. For all that, *Kill All Normies* suggests an underlying conservative sensibility, almost as if Nagle would like to return to the 1950s.

Be that as it may, she is correct to deplore the cruelty of many online cultures. I doubt, though, that this cruelty is best seen as growing from a Sadean or Nietzschean rejection of Christian moral restraints. Those restraints have done little in the past to prevent cruelty and oppression. Oppression has often been given moralistic and theological justifications, as with the persecutions by ardent Christians of pagans, Jews, heretics, homosexuals, and alleged witches. History suggests that large-scale episodes of cruelty to others arise more often from misguided moralism, often associated with religion or political ideology, than from nihilism, Sadean libertinism, or a Nietzschean transvaluation of values. When morally decent people engage in cruel mob behaviour, they typically do so to punish what they regard as misconduct or to destroy opponents whom they no longer view as tolerable human beings. This is especially so for mobs that emerge in cyberspace.

Consider again Jon Ronson's interview with Mercedes Haefer, which I summarized in Chapter 8. It suggests that participants in cybermobs view themselves as forming 'a different kind of court. A different kind of jury' (Ronson 2015: 121). The problem is not a rejection of Christian, or any other, moral restraints. Rather, the individuals who join in a cybermob understand themselves as morally virtuous. Instead of rejecting all morality, they are punishing what they perceive as heresy and sin.

Part of the problem is a rejection of something much more specific than morality itself. Online mobs reject principles such as the rule of law and due process for people accused of wrongdoing. More generally, they reject ordinary (though perhaps very modern and unintuitive) ideas of tolerance and proportion. The idea that not all bad behaviour must be punished – let alone punished disproportionately to the wrongdoing – seems to cut no ice in the online world. The problem is thus not a lack of morality; if anything, the problem is too much moralistic thinking that has not been transformed and tamed by liberal ideas.

One other aspect of online punitiveness and cruelty should be fairly obvious by now. Extreme views, including extreme views about who should be punished and how, are fed by ideology, propaganda, and outrage. They are amplified by tribalism and group polarization, and by a sense (found on many sides of politics) of living through a time of social emergency. Punitiveness and cruelty are enabled by anonymity and spurred by the thrill of mob participation. If there's a solution to this cluster of problems, it won't lie in abandoning, as Nagle puts it, 'the entire paradigm' (2017: 116) of countercultural rebellion. A more promising solution – though admittedly not much easier to implement – would be a return to traditional liberal ideas. These can find a place for iconoclastic values even while keeping them in their proper place.

Feeding a cycle of outrage?

In his detailed review of *Kill All Normies*, Richard Seymour expresses a concern that I've tried to take to heart while preparing the final drafts of this book. The concern is that books like Nagle's – or, by extension, this one – will feed an existing cycle of outrage, not persuading anybody but merely provoking anger from those who are criticized for their tactics. Seymour asks that this criticism at least demonstrate an understanding and evaluation of why people acted as they did – what it was that motivated them in their circumstances.

Seymour does not object to Nagle's harsh treatment of the online Right, and if anything he seems to believe she is too soft on participants in alt-light shenanigans. He does, however, view *Kill All Normies* as too harsh towards left-wing activists and too derisory or impatient in conveying what motivates them. He refers specifically to Nagle's accounts of three cases from the UK: attempts to prevent public appearances by Germaine Greer in 2015 and gay rights activist Peter Tatchell in early 2016, and the disruptive, physically intimidating, heckling of Maryam Namazie when she spoke at Goldsmiths University, London, in 2015.

Nagle is, indeed, forthright in her disapproval of the tactics used against Greer, Tatchell, and Namazie. Seymour does not necessarily approve of these tactics, either, but he protests that Nagle simplifies the grievances of the activists who used them. As he explains the point, it's important to identify and evaluate the specific criticisms that were made of Greer, Tatchell, and Namazie:

That makes all the difference between, say, a tactical misfire in dealing with individuals whose behaviour and statements have been genuinely invidious, and an outright malicious and slanderous attack on people with whom one differs. (Seymour 2017)

Seymour is correct in principle: we should indeed try to understand the motivations of opponents, especially if we hope to persuade them. I've given this some weight when pondering particular cases such as the campaign against Erika and Nicholas Christakis. One problem is that there are simply limits to how much detail can be covered in any one book – and we should not forget that *Kill All Normies* is a slim volume. It is more a manifesto than an academic tome. When we can, however, we ought to extend charity even to people whom we're criticizing, inquiring into how they think rather than writing them off as foolish or morally corrupted. In evaluating attacks on a range of people, it is also worth distinguishing between victims who have done little or nothing wrong and others who might deserve severe criticism for their views and conduct, even if they should have been allowed to speak on a particular occasion. There's a huge difference between, say, Erika Christakis, or Laura Moriarty, and someone whom I'd never want to stand beside such as Troy Newman.

What, then, of Seymour's three examples? Germaine Greer has made an enormous cultural contribution as a feminist author and thinker. Nonetheless, Seymour is right about an important issue. Greer does seem to be genuinely hostile to trans women in a way that J. Michael Bailey and Rebecca Tuvel are not. It is, as Seymour emphasizes, worthwhile making such distinctions. That said, Nagle's descriptions of the situations involving Greer, Tatchell, and Namazie in 2015/2016 do not seem to me to be notably unfair as a matter of overall balance. Yes, it might have been better to point out Greer's genuine hostility to trans women. Greer was, however, assigned to speak at Cardiff University on a topic unrelated to transgender issues, and she'd had little to say about those issues for many years. Moreover, her hostility does not translate into political opposition to people transitioning and obtaining medical assistance.

Seymour alleges, in effect, that Tatchell is hostile to Islam, but even if that is true it was not a good reason to request his removal from a panel entitled 'Re-radicalising Queers: Should we toe the line or cause a stir?' Tatchell is entitled to criticize Islam, and in particular its attitudes to homosexuality, though in doing so he runs the risk of making factual mistakes over particular issues. Seymour may be correct that Tatchell has made mistakes in the past about the extent of homophobic violence inspired by Islamic teachings, but nothing like this was the topic of the panel.

Furthermore, irrespective of Tatchell's views about Islam as a belief system, the accusations against him in 2016 were based primarily on his recently expressed support for the right of Greer and others to express their views. This was what motivated the accusation that Tatchell was transphobic. Spurious accusations like these are often used to punish and intimidate people with disliked views. In all, there would have been no point in Nagle's attempting to sort out all the rights and wrongs of Tatchell's past remarks on Islam and homosexuality.

As for Namazie, she is an outspoken ex-Muslim and a revolutionary communist. It is not surprising if she is highly critical of Islamism and jihadism – and also of Islamic doctrine itself. As Seymour points out, she has, on occasion, expressed herself in ways that many Muslims find offensive. He does *not* point out, however, that Namazie has, for many years, spoken up strongly and consistently against anything she regards as anti-Muslim bigotry, especially from far-right groups, and against anything that she regards as enabling or normalizing anti-Muslim bigotry. In late 2015 and early 2016, this led her into a public dispute with Sam Harris over issues related to Muslim profiling (in the context of airport security) and Muslim immigration into Europe.

This culminated in Namazie's appearance on Harris's 'Waking Up' podcast. Here, in the midst of a frustrating argument for both participants, Namazie spoke against any security profiling of Muslims (as opposed to profiling restricted to politically engaged Islamists) and in favour of open European borders for Muslim refugees – though she clarified that this would not mean allowing individual people into Europe without vetting their backgrounds. Namazie later published a transcript of her dialogue with Harris (Namazie 2017). In this case, it is Seymour who is being unfair, offering an impression of Namazie that does not do justice to her actual views.

In would be difficult to untangle all this, presenting a more detailed, though even-handed, account of the views and conduct of Greer, Tatchell, and Namazie, based upon their careers as a whole. This could get out of control and distort a short book like *Kill All Normies*. I doubt that any good-faith effort to provide more detail would have had an impact greatly different from Nagle's published text. A particular difficulty here is that every author and reader will have different views about what incidents are most significant in a long-established activist's history. No account will please everybody. No account is impervious to being attacked from one viewpoint or another.

Nonetheless, might Seymour be correct that a book such as *Kill All Normies* will feed a new cycle of outrage? He suggests that the people whom Nagle criticizes strongly, such as the students at Goldsmiths University who heckled Namazie, are unlikely to 'respond well to such a one-sided scolding'. He claims, indeed, that *Kill All Normies* is 'punitively moralistic' towards various people who mistreated Greer, Tatchell, and Namazie. But this overreaches.

Though Nagle is forthright in her criticisms, the first point to note is that she goes no further than *criticizing* people for their words or actions. Even if she makes some mistakes and misjudgements, she does not attempt to destroy anyone's livelihood, make anyone's life miserable, or intimidate anyone into silence. She names some individuals whose actions were already on the public record, but she does not shame opponents over obscure, trivial, or dubious wrongdoings. In short, she criticizes where she thinks it is due, but she doesn't otherwise punish people for their actions and words.

Overall, Nagle seems to me a pretty good role model for others who engage in public discussion. She does not write like an outrage warrior, and if no one were more punitive than her, the quality of debate over political and cultural issues would improve. Seymour is probably correct that those whom she criticizes will not respond with contrition. If, however, we want to encourage a better ethic of public discussion, we have no choice but to criticize those who violate it. This might not win over individuals who engage in smearing, shaming, propaganda, and outrage, or who employ the tactics of no-platforming and disruptive heckling. Some of them might even redirect their outrage at us, making wild accusations such as Peter Tatchell received in 2016. In writing and publishing *Kill All Normies*, Nagle thus runs a risk of being smeared, heckled, no-platformed, and so on, in her turn. So do I in writing and publishing this book. None of that would be productive.

But some people might change their minds about using these tactics. Nagle has much to say about why they've been counterproductive. I've tried to explain why they fit badly with liberty of thought and discussion, and why that liberty is worth protecting. Neither of us is scolding for the sake of scolding. Even if we can't persuade the individuals whose actions have merited our criticisms, we can draw the wider public's attention to the issues, explain why they're important, and work towards a better environment for exchange of ideas.

Nagle on New Atheism and Elevatorgate

Seymour would have been on stronger ground if he'd criticized Nagle for her comments on so-called New Atheism and her description of a sequence of events in 2011 that was labelled at the time as Elevatorgate. Here, Nagle does provide considerable detail. However, she sheds no light on the motivations, in the situations that confronted them, of the people whom she criticizes – notably Richard Dawkins, whom she portrays as something of a villain. Almost all of her account of this topic is misleading, as if she researched it solely by reading one side's propaganda. Even her understanding of what is meant by *New Atheism* appears shaky.

As a disclaimer, I have a personal connection to the dispute that Nagle describes. I know many of the people involved in what happened in mid-2011, I had some (minor) involvement myself, and I have some connections with authors who've been described as New Atheists. This gives me a bias of my own – hereby noted – but it also gives me a depth of knowledge that Nagle evidently lacks.

The terms *New Atheists* and *New Atheism* were coined by Gary Wolf, a contributing editor to *Wired* magazine, in his article 'The Church of the Non-Believers' (2006). Wolf profiled Richard Dawkins, Daniel Dennett, and Sam Harris, referring to them and those endorsing their work as the New Atheists, and criticizing them for what he viewed as an overly dogmatic and militant rejection of theistic religion.

These three authors had all recently published books that were critical of religious belief: *The End of Faith* (Harris 2004), *Breaking the Spell* (Dennett 2006), and *The God Delusion* (Dawkins 2006). They'd adopted strikingly different, but perhaps complementary, approaches: Harris argued that beliefs form part of the motivation for action, and so the most dangerous beliefs can lead to persecutions and atrocities; Dennett's theme was that religion can and should be studied as a natural phenomenon with its own causes in the empirical world; while Dawkins compared persistent belief in God to beliefs that we would ordinarily consider delusions. These were, of course, controversial claims, and they were advanced with varying degrees of mockery and denunciation of religious belief. Nonetheless, the writings and speeches of all three authors were mild compared with most public debate over hot-button topics. Dennett, in particular, went out of his way to express himself as inoffensively as his subject matter permitted.

Dawkins, Dennett, and Harris were soon joined by the late Christopher Hitchens, who published his own anti-theistic book, *God Is Not Great!*, in 2007 and promoted it through a series of formal debates against theologians and religious apologists. Though Hitchens proved to be a fierce debater with a gift for clever comebacks and put-downs, his performances (and those of his various opponents) were temperate by most standards.

What was new about the New Atheism – a term, note, that Dawkins, Dennett, Harris, and Hitchens did not choose for themselves? Perhaps not much, though the late Victor Stenger produced an admirable attempt at synthesis in his book *The New Atheism: Taking a Stance for Science and Reason* (2009). Most of the arguments employed by Dawkins and the other New Atheists had predecessors in earlier critiques of religion. There was, however, suddenly a market for books with anti-religious themes after America's lurch towards more theocratic policy-making under George W. Bush – and then the events of 11 September 2001, which provoked much scrutiny of Islam. As a result, books that would once have reached relatively small audiences were picked up by large trade imprints and became best sellers.

The publication of the early New Atheist books – reinforced by Hitchens' debates against the likes of Dinesh D'Souza – encouraged online activism against creationism, religious apologetics, and religious intrusion into politics. A strong atheist blogosphere developed during the Bush administration, spearheaded by the popular 'Pharyngula' blog, the brainchild of P.Z. Myers, a Minnesota-based biologist and relentless critic of creationism. However, there was also much New Atheist activism and counter-activism in the traditional media and more generally in the offline world. Mainstream news outlets promoted vigorous discussion of atheism. Large conventions were held in cities across the world to spread the ideas of Dawkins, Dennett, Harris, and Hitchens, and many books were written either in support or in criticism of their ideas.

Nagle shows no real understanding of the New Atheism and its varied expressions, and I find her description of Elevatorgate almost unrecognizable. Since I was caught up in those events, more or less on the side that Nagle castigates, I won't offer any detailed account of my own. However, the Ugandan blogger and broadcaster James Onen, who played no part that I know of in the initial dispute, produced a thorough blow-by-blow description a few months later (Onen 2011). Anyone who finds all this interesting, and who might be tempted to accept Nagle's version of events uncritically, should at least read Onen's version for some balance.

Much of what happened during the Elevatorgate debacle was a protest, by Dawkins and others, against the left-wing call-out culture that Nagle criticizes throughout *Kill All Normies*. By 2011, this culture had become dominant in the atheist blogosphere – contrary to the intentions of the original New Atheists such as Dawkins. It included the usual kinds of purity policing, shaming, dogpiling, and generally abusing dissidents. Just as Nagle states with respect to call-out culture more generally, the attacks within the atheist blogosphere 'increasingly focused on other liberals and leftists often with seemingly pristine progressive credentials, instead of those engaged in any actual racism, sexism or homophobia' (Nagle 2017: 77).

However, the situation quickly degenerated to a point where some participants on both (or all) sides of the dispute were engaging in cruel, indefensible tactics. In this case, there was also enough clumsiness, even from the best-intentioned people, to feed a cycle of outrage of the kind feared by Richard Seymour. In a case such as Elevatorgate, there is plenty of blame to spread around for anyone who likes that sort of thing. It's better, though, not to heap it all in the wrong direction.

As a postscript, further disputes took place within the atheist blogosphere during the years that immediately followed Elevatorgate. Predictably, some high-profile participants in the atheist blogosphere's call-out culture were themselves eventually subjected to what Nagle calls 'the dreaded call-out' (2017: 8) for ideological impurity over specific issues. Nagle does not mention this, and she probably was not aware of it when she wrote *Kill All Normies*, but it wouldn't surprise her since it follows a familiar historical pattern.

Concluding remarks

In 'Self-Censorship in Public Discourse', Glenn Loury raises some serious, important questions. Among them, he asks: 'What are the responsibilities of individuals within a community whose public discourse on important matters lacks candor?' and 'Is there a role for courage and heroism?' (Loury 1994: 453).

I certainly don't feel heroic. But as I've worked on this book and talked about it with numerous friends and colleagues, they've often told me that that they are afraid to discuss these issues in public. They're afraid, indeed, to say what they think about *many* issues where they'd find themselves isolated and vulnerable. The problem isn't the reactions of tribal opponents. They're afraid, instead, of their friends and colleagues and allies. They're afraid of being shamed, smeared, dogpiled, ostracized, harassed, devastatingly labelled, falsely accused, and perhaps harmed in their careers, by the very people who ought to have their backs.

It is, of course, difficult to substantiate my claims about private conversations. By its very nature, the evidence can't be revealed. But that's the situation whenever the distribution of private opinion differs from that of publicly expressed opinion. If your experience does not resonate with this, test it a bit further. Even if – lucky you! – you have no opinions that you're afraid to reveal in public, have a private word about this book with others in your closest circles. You'll likely find, as I have, that many people – good, decent, thoughtful, humane, socially concerned people – are living in what they experience as an environment of fear.

Furthermore, they have good reason. The dramatic events at Yale in 2015, involving Erika and Nicholas Christakis, nicely illustrate why. Erika Christakis has since (2016) written of her experience of being told by many colleagues that they privately supported her but were frightened to speak up. Likewise, she says, many students met with her and Nicholas confidentially to discuss intimidation that they'd received from their peers. In such an environment, few of us would dare to dissent.

Put bluntly – with a touch of Galilean personality – this is unacceptable. We shouldn't have to live and work in a culture where we must hide our true opinions. It's oppressive to individuals; it undermines valuable kinds of originality and diversity; it distorts public and expert opinion; and it plays into the hands of our real enemies.

In introducing his magisterial *Private Truths, Public Lies*, Timur Kuran states that, as he studied the phenomenon of preference falsification, he became more aware of the hypocrisies and insincerities of himself and others. But he also became more aware of resistance to this, and he developed a respect for nonconformity: 'I gained more respect for the nonconformist, the pioneer, the innovator, the dissident, even the misfit. It is my hope that the reader will come to share in this appreciation' (Kuran 1995: viii). Those words have helped inspire this book.

I won't exhort others to levels of courage that I realize I don't meet, and I am well aware (see Chapter 1) that I'm more buffered than most. We all have different skills, resources, support systems, and vulnerabilities. We all have demands on our time and energy. We all need to choose our battles wisely. I am asking you, nonetheless, to think about this carefully – and to take a stand, as loudly as you dare, for liberal values and for freedom

REFERENCES

Asch, Solomon E. (1952), *Social Psychology*, Englewood Cliffs, NJ: Prentice-Hall.

Bailey, J. Michael (2003), *The Man Who Would Be Queen: The Psychology of Gender-Bending and Transsexualism*, Washington, DC: Joseph Henry Press.

Barry, Bruce (2007), *Speechless: The Erosion of Free Expression in the American Workplace*, San Francisco: Berrett-Koehler Publishers.

Baumeister, Roy F., and Mark R. Leary (1995), 'The Need to Belong: Desire for Interpersonal Attachments as a Fundamental Human Motivation', *Psychological Bulletin*, 117: 497–529.

BBC Trending (2016), 'The Saga of "Pizzagate": The Fake Story that Shows How Conspiracy Theories Spread', BBC News site, 2 December. Available online: http://www.bbc.com/news/blogs-trending-38156985 (accessed 21 March 2018).

Berg, Chris (2016), *The Libertarian Alternative*, Melbourne: Melbourne University Press.

Berry, Jeffrey M., and Sarah Sobieraj (2014), *The Outrage Industry: Political Opinion Media and the New Incivility*, Oxford and New York: Oxford University Press.

Bikhchandani, Sushil, David Hirshleifer, and Ivo Welch (1992), 'A Theory of Fads, Fashion, Custom, and Cultural Change as Informational Cascades', *Journal of Political Economy*, 100: 992–1026.

Blackford, Russell (2002), 'The Supposed Rights of the Fetus', *Quadrant*, 389 (September): 11–17.

Blackford, Russell (2007), 'Slippery Slopes to Slippery Slopes: Therapeutic Cloning and the Criminal Law', *American Journal of Bioethics*, 7 (2): 63–4.

Blackford, Russell (2012), *Freedom of Religion and the Secular State*, Chichester, West Sussex: Wiley-Blackwell, 2012.

Blackford, Russell (2015a), 'An Odor of Sanctimony: Responses to the *Charlie Hebdo* Murders', *Free Inquiry*, 35 (3): 8, 40–41.

Blackford, Russell (2015b), 'The people we don't want to stand with: Free speech – again – and the troubling case of Troy Newman', Cogito blog (The Conversation), 1 October. Available online: https://theconversation.com/the-people-we-dont-want-to-stand-with-free-speech-again-and-the-troubling-case-of-troy-newman-48412 (accessed 21 March 2018).

Blackford, Russell (2016), *The Mystery of Moral Authority*, Basingstoke, Hampshire: Palgrave Macmillan.

Blackford, Russell (2017), *Science Fiction and the Moral Imagination: Visions, Minds, Ethics*, New York: Springer.

Blackford, Russell, and Udo Schüklenk (2013), *50 Great Myths About Atheism*, Chichester, West Sussex: Wiley-Blackwell.

Board of Hypatia (2017), 'Statement by the Non-Profit Board of *Hypatia*', 18 May. Available online: http://hypatiaphilosophy.org/np-board/non-profit-board-statement-may-18-2017 (accessed 21 March 2018).

Borovoy, A. Alan (1988), *When Freedoms Collide: The Case for Our Civil Liberties*, second ed., Toronto: Lester & Orpen Dennys.

Brogaard, Berit (2015), 'Berit Brogaard: Group Polarization and the Internet', guest blog post at Leiter Reports: A Philosophy Blog, 13 March. Available online: http://leiterreports.typepad.com/blog/2015/03/berit-brogaard-group-polarization-and-the-internet.html (accessed 21 March 2018).

Brown, Callum G. (2017), *Becoming Atheist: Humanism and the Secular West*, London and New York: Bloomsbury.

Catanese, Kathleen R., and Dianne M. Tice (2005), 'The Effect of Rejection on Anti-Social Behaviors: Social Exclusion Produces Aggressive Behaviors', in Kipling D. Williams, Joseph P. Forgas and William von Hippel (eds), *The Social Outcast: Ostracism, Social Exclusion, Rejection, and Bullying*, 297–306, New York and Hove, East Sussex: Psychology Press.

Chagnon, Napoleon (2013), *Noble Savages: My Life Among Two Dangerous Tribes—The Yanomamö and the Anthropologists*, New York: Simon & Schuster.

Christakis, Erika (2015), 'Email From Erika Christakis: "Dressing Yourselves," email to Silliman College (Yale) Students on Halloween Costumes', Foundation for Individual Rights in Higher Education (website), 30 October. Available online: https://www.thefire.org/email-from-erika-christakis-dressing-yourselves-email-to-silliman-college-yale-students-on-halloween-costumes/ (accessed 21 March 2018).

Christakis, Erika (2016), 'My Halloween Email Led to a Campus Firestorm—and a Troubling Lesson about Self-Censorship', *Washington Post*, 28 October. Available online: https://www.washingtonpost.com/opinions/my-halloween-email-led-to-a-campus-firestorm--and-a-troubling-lesson-about-self-censorship/2016/10/28/70e55732-9b97-11e6-a0ed-ab0774c1eaa5_story.html?utm_term=.b52fec5fbef7 (accessed 21 March 2018).

Christakis, Nicholas A. (2016), 'Teaching Inclusion in a Divided World', *New York Times*, 22 June. Available online: https://www.nytimes.com/2016/06/23/education/teaching-inclusion-in-a-divided-world.html?_r=0 (accessed 21 March 2018).

Citron, Danielle Keats (2014), *Hate Crimes in Cyberspace*, Cambridge, MA, and London: Harvard University Press.

Cliteur, Paul (2016), 'Taylor and Dummett on the Rushdie Affair', *Journal of Religion and Society* 18: 1–25. Available online: https://dspace2.creighton.edu/xmlui/bitstream/handle/10504/74592/2016-1.pdf?sequence=1 (accessed 21 March 2018).

Cohen, Nick (2016), 'The White Left has Issued its First Fatwa', *The Spectator*, 31 October. Available online: https://blogs.spectator.co.uk/2016/10/white-left-issued-first-fatwa/ (accessed 21 March 2018).

Conly, Sarah (2013), *Against Autonomy: Justifying Coercive Paternalism*, Cambridge and New York: Cambridge University Press.

Coronel, Sheila, Steve Coll, and Derek Kravitz (2015), 'Rolling Stone and UVA: The Columbia University Graduate School Journalism Report', *Rolling Stone*, 5 April. Available online: http://www.rollingstone.com/culture/features/a-rape-on-campus-what-went-wrong-20150405 (accessed 21 March 2018).

Dawkins, Richard (2006), *The God Delusion*, London: Bantam.

de Grazia, Edward (1992), *Girls Lean Back Everywhere: The Law of Obscenity and the Assault on Genius*, New York: Random House.

Dennett, Daniel C. (2006), *Breaking the Spell: Religion as a Natural Phenomenon*, New York: Viking.

Devlin, [Lord] Patrick (1965), *The Enforcement of Morals*, London: Oxford University Press.

Doniger, Wendy (2008), *The Hindus: An Alternative History*, New York: Penguin.

Dreger, Alice (2008), 'The Controversy Surrounding *The Man Who Would Be Queen*: A Case History of the Politics of Science, Identity, and Sex in the Internet Age', *Archives of Sexual Behavior* 37: 366–421.

Dreger, Alice (2014), 'What if we admitted to children that sex is primarily about pleasure?', *Pacific Standard*, 16 May. Available online: https://psmag.com/what-if-we-admitted-to-children-that-sex-is-primarily-about-pleasure-9d3956c38ff5#.gzvzr3x62 (accessed 21 March 2018).

Dreger, Alice (2015), *Galileo's Middle Finger: Heretics, Activists, and the Search for Justice in Science*, New York: Penguin.

Dreger, Alice (2016), 'Zero Tolerance: Censored by the Left', Alice Domurat Dreger Blog, 1 June. Available online: http://alicedreger.com/zero (accessed 21 March 2018).

Feinberg, Joel (1985), *Offense to Others*, New York and Oxford: Oxford University Press.

Fisher, Mark (2013), 'Exiting the Vampire Castle', *The North Star*, 22 November. Available online: http://www.thenorthstar.info/?p=11299 (accessed 21 March 2018).

Frank, Thomas (2016), 'Millions of ordinary Americans support Donald Trump. Here's why', *The Guardian*, 8 March. Available online: https://www.theguardian.com/commentisfree/2016/mar/07/donald-trump-why-americans-support (accessed 21 March 2018).

Friedersdorf, Conor (2016), 'The Perils of Writing a Provocative Email at Yale', *The Atlantic*, 26 May. Available online: https://www.theatlantic.com/politics/archive/2016/05/the-peril-of-writing-a-provocative-email-at-yale/484418/ (accessed 21 March 2018).

Gates, Gary J. (2011), 'How Many People are Lesbian, Gay, Bisexual, and Transgender?', Williams Institute, April. Available online: http://williamsinstitute.law.ucla.edu/wp-content/uploads/Gates-How-Many-People-LGBT-Apr-2011.pdf (accessed 21 March 2018).

Goldberg, Michelle (2007), *Kingdom Coming: The Rise of Christian Nationalism*, paperback ed., New York and London: W. W. Norton.

Graham, Ruth (2017), 'YA Novel About "Mob Mentalities" Punished after Online Backlash', *Slate*, 16 October. Available online: http://www.slate. com/blogs/browbeat/2017/10/16/kirkus_withdraws_starred_review_after_ criticism.html (accessed 21 March 2018).

Greene, Joshua (2013), *Moral Tribes: Emotion, Reason, and the Gap between Us and Them*, New York: Penguin.

Grewal, Zareena (2015), 'Here's What my Yale Students Get: Free Expression and Anti-racism are not Mutally Exclusive', *Washington Post*, 12 November. Available online: https://www.washingtonpost.com/posteverything/ wp/2015/11/12/heres-what-my-yale-students-get-free-expression-and-anti-racism-arent-mutually-exclusive/?utm_term=.695d89d47594 (accessed 21 March 2018).

Grossmann, Matt, and David A. Hopkins (2016), *Asymmetric Politics: Ideological Republicans and Group Interest Democrats*, New York: Oxford University Press.

Hacker News (2013), Comments by 'mr-hank' and others on Hacker News Discussion Board, March. Available online: https://news.ycombinator.com/ item?id=5398681 (accessed 21 March 2018).

Haidt, Jonathan (2012), *The Righteous Mind: Why Good People Are Divided by Politics and Religion*, New York: Random House.

Harris, Sam (2004), *The End of Faith: Religion, Terror, and the Future of Reason*, New York: W. W. Norton.

Harris, Sam, and Maajid Nawaz (2015), *Islam and the Future of Tolerance: A Dialogue*, Cambridge, MA: Harvard University Press.

Hitchens, Christopher (2007), *God Is Not Great! How Religion Poisons Everything*, New York: Twelve Books.

Hogg, Michael A. (2005), 'All Animals Are Equal but Some Animals Are More Equal than Others: Social Identity and Marginal Membership', in Kipling D. Williams, Joseph P. Forgas, and William von Hippel (eds), *The Social Outcast: Ostracism, Social Exclusion, Rejection, and Bullying*, 243–61, New York and Hove, East Sussex: Psychology Press.

Hypatia Board of Associate Editors (2017), Statement. Formerly available online: https://www.facebook.com/hypatia.editorialoffice/posts/1852550825032876 (originally accessed 3 July 2017; unavailable to the public as of 21 March 2018).

Intercultural Affairs Committee (2015), 'Email From The Intercultural Affairs Committee', Foundation for Individual Rights in Higher Education (website), 27 October. Available online: https://www.thefire.org/email-from-intercultural-affairs/ (accessed 21 March 2018).

Jaigirdar, Adiba (2017), 'Books by Muslims to Support Instead of Reading *American Heart*', BookRiot, 12 October. Available online: https://bookriot. com/2017/10/12/books-by-muslims-instead-of-american-heart/ (accessed 21 March 2018).

Jesus and Mo (n.d.) Website. Available online: http://www.jesusandmo.net/ (accessed 21 March 2018).

Kekes, John (2008), *The Art of Politics: The New Betrayal of America and How to Resist It*, New York and London: Encounter Books.

King, Richard (2013), *On Offence: The Politics of Indignation*, Melbourne and London: Scribe.

Kirchick, James (2016), 'New Videos Show How Yale Betrayed Itself By Favoring Cry-Bullies', *Tablet* (Campus Week), 12 September. Available online: http://www.tabletmag.com/jewish-news-and-politics/213212/yale-favoring-cry-bullies (accessed 21 March 2018).

Kirchick, James (2017), 'Yale Cements its Line in the Academic Sand by Awarding the Student "Truthtellers" Who Bullied Faculty', *Tablet* (The Scroll), 26 May. Available online: http://www.tabletmag.com/scroll/235844/yale-cements-its-line-in-the-academic-sand-by-awarding-the-student-truthtellers-who-bullied-faculty (accessed 21 March 2018).

Kirkus (2017), Anonymous review of *American Heart* by Laura Moriarty, *Kirkus Reviews*, 16 October. Available online: https://www.kirkusreviews.com/book-reviews/laura-moriarty/american-heart/ (accessed 21 March 2018).

Kitcher, Philip (1993), *The Advancement of Science: Science without Legend, Objectivity without Illusions*, New York and Oxford: Oxford University Press.

Kundera, Milan (1995), *Testaments Betrayed: An Essay in Nine Parts*, trans. Linda Asher, New York: HarperCollins.

Kuran, Timur (1995), *Private Truths, Public Lies: The Social Consequences of Preference Falsification*, Cambridge, MA, and London: Harvard University Press.

Lantos Foundation (2016), Letter from the Lantos Foundation for Human Rights and Justice to Southern Poverty Law Center, signed by Katrina Lantos Swett, dated 7 November 2016. Available online: https://static1.squarespace.com/static/55a82f98e4b04c71cd94927d/t/58220bd9ff7c50bcb91562 5a/1478626266272/Letter+to+SPLC.pdf (accessed 21 March 2018).

Leiter, Brian (2010), 'Cleaning Cyber-Cesspools: Google and Free Speech', in Saul Levmore and Martha C. Nussbaum (eds), *The Offensive Internet: Speech, Privacy, and Reputation*, 155–73, Cambridge, MA, and London: Harvard University Press.

Leiter, Brian (2013), *Why Tolerate Religion?* Princeton, NJ: Princeton University Press.

Letter of Support (2015), 'Letter of Support For Erika and Nicholas Christakis'. Available online: https://docs.google.com/document/d/16Fa8lyQ17utjiw1L NkCoE22pvq2uRk_SVHHPmRgvpIA/edit?pli=1#heading=h.53s9msgj6b7 (accessed 21 March 2018).

Levy, Neil (2002), *Moral Relativism: A Short Introduction*, Oxford: Oneworld.

Lewis, Anthony (2007), *Freedom for the Thought That We Hate: A Biography of the First Amendment*, New York: Basic Books.

Lilla, Mark (2016), 'The End of Identity Liberalism', *New York Times*, Sunday Review section, 18 November. Available online: http://www.nytimes.com/2016/11/20/opinion/sunday/the-end-of-identity-liberalism.html?src=me&_r=1 (accessed 21 March 2018).

Lilla, Mark (2017), *The Once and Future Liberal: After Identity Politics*, New York: HarperCollins.

Loury, Glenn C. (1994), 'Self-Censorship in Public Discourse: A Theory of "Political Correctness" and Related Phenomena', *Rationality and Society* 6: 428–61.

Locke, John ([1689] 1983), *A Letter Concerning Toleration*, Indianapolis: Hackett.

Lukianoff, Greg (2014), *Freedom from Speech*, New York: Encounter Books.

McCallum, Ronald (2000), *Employer Controls over Private Life*, Sydney: University of NSW Press.

McKie, Robin (2015), 'Tim Hunt and Mary Collins: "We're not Being Chased Out of the Country. Our New Life's an Adventure"', *The Guardian*, 20 December. Available online: https://www.theguardian.com/uk-news/2015/dec/19/tim-hunt-mary-collins-weve-not-been-chased-out-of-the-country (accessed 21 March 2018).

Malik, Kenan (2010), *From Fatwa to Jihad: The Rushdie Affair and its Legacy*, paperback ed., London: Atlantic Books.

Manne, Kate, and Jason Stanley (2015), 'When Free Speech Becomes A Political Weapon', *Chronicle of Higher Education*, 13 November. Available online: http://www.chronicle.com/article/When-Free-Speech-Becomes-a/234207 (accessed 21 March 2018).

Marche, Stephen (2016), 'Gawker Smeared Me, and Yet I Stand With It', *New York Times*, 31 May. Available online: http://www.nytimes.com/2016/05/31/opinion/i-stand-with-gawker.html?_r=1 (accessed 21 March 2018; print version published as 'I Stand With Gawker').

Marcuse, Herbert (1969), 'Repressive Tolerance', in Robert Paul Wolff, Barrington Moore, Jr., and Herbert Marcuse, *A Critique of Pure Tolerance*, 93–137, London: Jonathan Cape.

Marlin, Randal (2002), *Propaganda and the Ethics of Persuasion*, Peterborough, ON: Broadview Press.

Mensch, Louise (2015), 'The Tim Hunt Debacle: Why Feminists Cleared a Nobel Prizewinner', Medium (website), 15 December. Available online: https://medium.com/@LouiseMensch/the-tim-hunt-debacle-c914395d5e01#.t4j9wd6xt (accessed 21 March 2018).

Mill, J. S. ([1859] 1974), *On Liberty*, ed. and introd. Gertrude Himmelfarb, London: Penguin.

Moodie, Clemmie, and Rory Tingle (2017), 'L'Oreal's first transgender model is SACKED by the cosmetics giant after claiming "ALL white people" are racist in extraordinary Facebook rant', *The Daily Mail*, 1 September. Available online: http://www.dailymail.co.uk/news/article-4842092/L-Oreal-transgender-model-says-white-people-racist.html (accessed 21 March 2018).

Nagle, Angela (2017), *Kill All Normies: The Online Culture Wars from Tumblr and 4Chan to the Alt-Right and Trump*, Winchester, UK, and Washington, DC: Zero Books.

Namazie, Maryam (2017), 'Transcript of Sam Harris–Maryam Namazie Podcast on Immigration and Muslim Profiling', Maryam Namazie website (transcribing an interview with Sam Harris on the latter's 'Waking Up' podcast), 1 February. Available online: http://maryamnamazie.com/harris-namazie/ (accessed 21 March 2018).

Neier, Aryeh (1979), *Defending My Enemy: American Nazis, the Skokie Case, and the Risks of Freedom*, Boston: Dutton.

Nozick, Robert (1974), *Anarchy, State, and Utopia*, New York: Basic Books.

O'Gorman, Hubert J. (1975), 'Pluralistic Ignorance and White Estimates of White Support for Racial Segregation', *Public Opinion Quarterly* 39(3): 313–30.

Onen, James (2011), 'Elevatorgate', Freethought Kampala (blog), 11 September. Available online: https://freethoughtkampala.wordpress.com/2011/09/11/elevatorgate/ (accessed 21 March 2018).

Open Letter (2017). Open letter to Hypatia, addressed 'To Hypatia Editor, Sally Scholz, and the broader Hypatia community', undated. Available online: https://docs.google.com/forms/d/1efp9C0MHch_6Kfgtlm0PZ76nirWtcEsqWHcvgidl2mU/viewform?ts=59066d20&edit_requested=true (accessed 21 March 2018).

Orenstein, Walker (2017), 'Read the Email Exchange that Sparked Protests Against an Evergreen Professor', *The News Tribune* (Tacoma), 1 June. Available online: http://www.thenewstribune.com/news/politics-government/article153826039.html (accessed 21 March 2018).

O'Rourke, K. C. (2001), *John Stuart Mill and Freedom of Expression: The Genesis of a Theory*, London and New York: Routledge.

Owen, J. Judd (2001), *Religion and the Demise of Liberal Rationalism: The Foundational Crisis of the Separation of Church and State*, Chicago and London: University of Chicago Press.

Oxford English Dictionary, third edition (online version).

Perry, Keith (2014), 'Lib Dem Candidate Receives Death Threats for Tweeting Prophet Mohammed cartoon', *The Telegraph*, 21 January. Available online: http://www.telegraph.co.uk/news/politics/liberaldemocrats/10588267/Lib-Dem-candidate-receives-death-threats-for-tweeting-Prophet-Mohammed-cartoon.html (accessed 21 March 2018).

Pew Research Center (2017), 'Public Opinion on Abortion: Views on Abortion 1995–2017', Pew Research Center website, 7 July. Available online: http://www.pewforum.org/fact-sheet/public-opinion-on-abortion/ (accessed 21 March 2018).

Prentice, D.A., and D. T. Miller (1993), 'Pluralistic Ignorance and Alcohol Use on Campus: Some Consequences of Misperceiving the Social Norm', *Journal of Personality and Social Psychology* 64(2): 243–56.

Ronson, Jon (2015), *So You've Been Publicly Shamed*, London: Picador.

Rosenbaum, Ron (2010), 'Cyber-Anonymity', in Adam Bellow (ed.), *New Threats to Freedom*, 240–7, West Conshohocken, PA: Templeton Press.

Rosenfield, Kat (2017a), 'The Toxic Drama on YA Twitter', *New York Magazine* (Vulture), 7 August. Available online: http://www.vulture.com/2017/08/the-toxic-drama-of-ya-twitter.html (accessed 21 March 2018).

Rosenfield, Kat (2017b), '*Kirkus* Editor-in-Chief Explains Why They Altered That *American Heart* Review', *New York Magazine* (Vulture), 19 October. Available online: http://www.vulture.com/2017/10/american-heart-review-kirkus-editor-on-why-they-changed-it.html (accessed 21 March 2018).

Rushdie, Salman (1988), *The Satanic Verses*, London: Penguin.

Rushdie, Salman (2012), *Joseph Anton: A Memoir*, London: Jonathan Cape.

Salovey, Peter, and Jonathan Holloway (2015), 'Email From Peter Salovey and Jonathan Holloway to Silliman Community [Moving Forward Together]', Foundation for Individual Rights in Higher Education (website), 17 November. Available online: https://www.thefire.org/email-from-peter-salovey-and-jonathan-holloway-to-silliman-community/ (accessed 21 March 2018).

Schauer, Frederick (1982), *Free Speech: A Philosophical Inquiry*, Cambridge: Cambridge University Press.

Searle, John R. (2010), *Making the Social World: The Structure of Human Civilization*, Oxford and New York: Oxford University Press.

Seymour, Richard (2017), 'The Negative Dialectics of Moralism' (review of *Kill All Normies: The Online Culture Wars from Tumblr and 4Chan to the Alt-Right and Trump* by Angela Nagle), Patreon (blog post), 4 August. Available online: https://www.patreon.com/posts/negative-of-13632021 (accessed 21 March 2018).

Sharlet, Jeff (2000), 'Prognosis: Death', *Chicago Reader*, 24 February. Available online: https://www.chicagoreader.com/chicago/prognosis-death/Content?oid=901522 (accessed 21 March 2018).

Singal, Jesse (2017), 'This Is What A Modern-Day Witch Hunt Looks Like', *New York Magazine*, 2 May. Available online: http://nymag.com/daily/intelligencer/2017/05/transracialism-article-controversy.html (accessed 21 March 2018).

Singh, Simon (2008), 'Beware the Spinal Trap', *The Guardian*, 19 April. Available online: https://www.theguardian.com/commentisfree/2008/apr/19/controversiesinscience-health (accessed 21 March 2018).

Smith, David Livingstone(2011), *Less Than Human: Why We Demean, Enslave, and Exterminate Others*, New York: St. Martins Press.

Solove, Daniel J. (2007), *The Future of Reputation: Gossip, Rumor, and Privacy on the Internet*, New Haven, NJ, and London: Yale University Press.

Spegman, Abby (2017), 'Evergreen Settles with Weinstein, Professor at the Center of Campus Protests', *The Olympian*, 16 September (updated 18 September). Available online: http://www.theolympian.com/news/local/article173710596.html (accessed 21 March 2018).

Stanley, Jason (2015), *How Propaganda Works*, Princeton and Oxford: Princeton University Press.

Stenger, Victor J. (2000), *The New Atheism: Taking a Stand for Science and Reason*, Amherst, NY: Prometheus Books.

Sunstein, Cass R. (2009a), *Going to Extremes: How Like Minds Unite and Divide*, New York: Oxford University Press.

Sunstein, Cass R. (2009b), *On Rumours: How Falsehoods Spread, Why We Believe Them, What Can Be Done*, London: Allen Lane.

Taylor, Charles (1989), 'The Rushdie Controversy', *Public Culture*, 2(1): 118–22.

Thaler, Richard H., and Cass R. Sunstein (2009), *Nudge: Improving Decisions About Health, Wealth, and Happiness*, paperback ed., New York: Penguin.

Thornhill, Randy, and Craig T. Palmer (2000), *A Natural History of Rape: Biological Bases of Sexual Coercion*, Cambridge, MA, and London: MIT Press.

Tierney, Patrick (2000), *Darkness in El Dorado: How Scientists and Journalists Devastated the Amazon*, New York and London: W. W. Norton.

Tuvel, Rebecca (2017), 'In Defense of Transracialism', *Hypatia: A Journal of Feminist Philosophy* 32(2): 263–78.

Willer, Robb, Ko Kuwabara, and Michael W. Macy (2009), 'The False Enforcement of Unpopular Norms', *American Journal of Sociology* 115(2): 451–90.

Wolf, Gary (2006), 'The Church of the Non-Believers', *Wired*, 1 November. Available online: https://www.wired.com/2006/11/atheism/ (accessed 21 March 2018).

Wolff, Robert Paul(1968), *The Poverty of Liberalism*, Boston: Beacon Press.

Zimmerman, Michael (2017), 'The Evergreen State College Implosion: Are There Lessons to be Learned?', *Huffington Post*, 2 July. Available online: http://www.huffingtonpost.com/entry/the-evergreen-state-college-implosion-are-there-lessons_us_5959507ee4b0f078efd98b0e?ncid=engmodushpmg00000004 (accessed 21 March 2018).

INDEX